Religion and Nationalism i

An incisive, original and richly detailed account of Sikh ethno-nationalism in the Punjab. Impressive in its breadth and historical sweep, Harnik Deol's thought-provoking book offers a valuable corrective to Western theories of nationalism. Her clear and penetrating analysis of Punjabi society and politics reveals the continuing power and vitality of religion in the subcontinent, and the dangers it poses to the fabric of modern India.

> Anthony D. Smith, Professor of Ethnicity and Nationalism,
> London School of Economics

Dr Deol advances a very persuasive argument to explain the recent troubles in the Punjab, an argument based on caste, the Sikh religion, and the modern Punjab economy. Personally I find it convincing.

> Professor Hew McLeod,
> University of Otago, New Zealand

Deol's work locates the Khalistan struggle within the wider interplay of nationalism, ethnicity and religion in the Indian subcontinent, providing an important historical dimension to the study of contemporary South Asia.'

> Dr Ian Talbot,
> University of Bristol

Religion and Nationalism in India examines the growth of a nationalist sentiment among the Sikh community in the Punjab. This timely and significant study expolres the reasons behind the rise in Sikh militancy over the 1970s and 1980s. It also evaluates the violent response of the Indian state in fuelling and suppressing the Sihk separatist movement, resulting in a tragic sequence of events which has included the raiding of the Golden Temple at Amritsar and the assassination of Prime Minister Indira Gandhi. The book reveals the role in this movement of a section of young, semiliterate Sikh peasantry who were disaffected by the Green Revolution and the commercialization of agriculture in Punjab. Drawing on a wide range of sources, Deol examines the role of popular mass media in the revitalization of religion during this period, and the subsequent emergence of sharper religious boundaries.

Deol controversially challenges the relevance of classical, Eurocentric theories of nationalism in analysing its powerful influence in South Asia. Her unique combination of Indian politics and history with a theoretical approach makes this fluent and incisive book essential reading for students and scholars interested in ethno-nationalism in the modern world.

Harnik Deol obtained her PhD at the London School of Economics and she is currently working on trade and investment-related issues in the developing world for the Commonwealth Business Council/Worldaware.

Routledge Studies in the Modern History of Asia

Religion and Nationalism in India

The case of the Punjab

Harnik Deol

London and New York

First published 2000
by Routledge
11 New Fetter Lane, London EC4P 4EE

Simultaneously published in the USA and Canada
by Routledge
29 West 35th Street, New York, NY 10001

Routledge is an imprint of the Taylor & Francis Group

© 2000 Harnik Deol

Typeset in Baskerville by
Prepress Projects, Perth, Scotland
Printed and bound in India by
Thomson Press (India) Ltd.

British Library Cataloguing in Publication Data
A catalogue record for this book is available
from the British Library

Library of Congress Cataloging in Publication Data
Deol, Harnik, 1966–
    Religion and nationalism in India : the case of the Punjab /
Harnik Deol.
        p. cm. – (Routledge studies in the modern history of Asia)
    Includes bibliographical references and index.
    1. Nationalism – India – Punjab.   2. Religion and politics – India
– Punjab.   I. Title.   II. Series.
    DS485.P87 D44   2000
    954'.5–dc21   99-058052
    CIP

ISBN 0–415–20108–x (hbk)

430367 70

To the memory of
my father

Sardar M. S. Deol (1931–94)

Contents

Illustrations

Maps

Tables

Preface and acknowledgements

India is a subcontinent, with a population of over 900 million, covering a wide range of ecological zones. The countless linguistic and religious groupings if not engaged in open conflict are on the verge of it. The many ethno-nationalist movements there have generated a growing concern among social scientists in recent years. The aim of this book is to ascertain the vital conditions and processes that give rise to ethnic conflict in contemporary India, and to place these developments in a broader historical context. The research is also an attempt to recast the theory of nationalism and purge it of its Eurocentric and élitist bias. In my view, an adequate theoretical comprehension of nationalism outside Europe has to come to terms with Asian institutions and history.

Any attempt to encompass so vast a theme is bound to be selective. This book, which is a substantially revised version of my PhD thesis presented at the London School of Economics in 1996, therefore concentrates on the Punjab and gives a detailed account of the development of the Sikh movement for an independent state in India. My choice of the Sikh case has been influenced by the fact that I belong to the Punjab and am most familiar with its history and events. My interest in the subject was stimulated by the turmoil in the Punjab in the 1980s. This involvement may help to explain some of the biases and the choice of this specific case.

As will be apparent to the reader, two books have deeply influenced my comprehension of nationalism. The first book is Benedict Anderson's *Imagined Communities*, and the other book is the classic work by Barrington Moore Jr, *The Social Origins of Dictatorship and Democracy*.

I am grateful to Oxford University Press, New Delhi, for permission to reproduce Map 1.1.

I have benefited enormously from the guidance and support of my supervisors, Anthony D. Smith and the late Alfred Gell. The examiners of the original thesis – James Mayall and Dennis Austin – helped me clarify some of the shortcomings. This research would not have been possible without the help and encouragement of my family in India and my friends in London. Finally, my mother, Ravinder, is always a source of inspiration and strength, which has made this book possible.

Harnik Deol
March 2000

Introduction

South Asia today presents a mosaic of artificial administrative entities left behind by the British imperial power. In the half-century since independence, the stability of the post-colonial state in South Asia has been threatened by recurrent and violent conflict between the central authorities and a variety of ethnic minorities. The Muhajir uprising in Pakistan, Tamil separatism in Sri Lanka, tribal insurgency in Bangladesh's Chittagong Hill Tracts, montagnard irredentism in Indian Kashmir and Sikh separatism in India present a congeries of contemporary breakaway movements in the Indian subcontinent.

India's complex social structure presents a kaleidoscopic cultural universe, a plethora of regional distinctions, a motley complex of traditions, and nearly 500 languages and dialects are spoken by nearly 900 million people (Van der Veer 1994: 165). It is indeed remarkable that this broad cultural ensemble is subsumed under a central political authority, which is itself an artificial administrative entity. It is natural for these diverse ethnic groups to assert their cultural identity. The principal bases of identity assertion perceived as threats to the national state in India are religion, language and tribe. Soon after India's independence in 1947, the foremost controversy to push India to the brink of civil disorder was the linguistic issue. However, the carving of territorial units based on language resolved the language issue in the 1950s and 1960s. Since the 1980s, it is assertions of religious identity, particularly in conjunction with territorial bases, that have afflicted the Indian national state. The Sikh demand for an independent state and the Muslim claims for autonomy in Kashmir are the two foremost movements for political secession in contemporary India that possess both religious and territorial bases. According to one survey, the destruction, in terms of the number of people who have lost their lives and the damage caused to public property, wrought by these conflicts is far worse than the destruction caused by the three Indo-Pakistan wars (*The Tribune*, 15 November 1995). These internal wars for political secession are the subject of this study, and the Sikh movement for sovereignty in India is the central example.

When considering the Sikh unrest, two important facts must be borne in mind. First, Punjab has progressively shrunk in size over the last half-century.

The Punjab province today occupies only a fraction of the area it occupied in the first half of the twentieth century. Secondly, since 1966 the cultural distinctiveness of Punjab is provided by the fact that a majority of its population is Sikh. This fact acquires a particular significance when it is remembered that the Sikhs are a national minority, at the same time enjoying a distinctive history and cultural identity, and consistently claiming a heritage entirely different from that of either Hindus, with whom they have no history of antagonism, or from Muslims, with whom they have a history of powerful antagonistic struggles. The Sikhs are a people objectively distinct in religion, though not in language, from other ethnic groups in the north, who have succeeded in acquiring a high degree of internal social and political cohesion and subjective self-awareness, and who have achieved political significance as a group within the Indian Union (Brass 1974: 277). The Punjabi-speaking Sikhs seemingly possess the classic ingredients of nationality formation: a geographical region, an arena of history and language linked to culture, and a religious ideology. Moreover, Punjab is the granary of India and is the richest state in India, with an average income of £220 per year. Punjab has borders with Pakistan and the Kashmir region; therefore, it is a region of strategic importance. Events that take place within its borders constitute another perspective on the future of Indian polity and society. Most importantly, a land of remarkable cultural diversity, Punjab, as is well known, is an example of change and transformation. Examples of new forms of collective consciousness, social movements and intellectual ferment abound and enable the social scientist to explore these societal tensions.

Located at the north-eastern margins of India, the region of Punjab has been the gateway into the Indo-Gangetic plains for invaders over the last three millennia. The northern boundary of Punjab was marked by the vast Himalayan mountains, while the river Indus in the west demarcated the western border of the province, and the river Yamuna marked the eastern boundary separating Punjab from the Gangetic plains. Extending from the foothills of the Himalayas, the Punjab is an extensive plain sloping gently down from the snow-clad mountains in the north and the west towards the scorching deserts in the south.

The name Punjab, meaning 'the land of five rivers', is based on the five feeder rivers – Jhelum, Chenab, Ravi, Beas and Sutlej – which once flowed through Punjab. At present, the topography of Punjab is etched by only three of the major five rivers, which have created three intrafluvial tracts. These internal physiographic zones have influenced many of the internal cultural and regional cleavages among the Sikhs. The region enclosed between the river Ravi and the river Sutlej is the Majha region. The Majha is often considered to be the 'cradle of Sikhism' because of the presence of major Sikh shrines and pilgrimage centres associated with the Sikh gurus. Vigorous campaigns associated with the Sikhs have often proliferated in this territory. Between the river Beas and the river Sutlej lies the narrow fertile tract of Doaba, also known as the garden of Punjab. The territory enclosed between the river Sutlej and the river Chenab is the Malwa region. This territory never became part of Lahore state under Maharaja Ranjit Singh. Under British suzerainty, several Sikh chiefs of Malwa had to cede their dominions to the imperial rulers. Here it is useful to note that in its initial phase the Sikh unrest was confined to the Majha area. However, as the Sikh movement gained momentum, the Majha and the Malwa regions became the main areas of resistance. Some attribute this to the proximity of these areas to the border with Pakistan, which allows an easy escape route, whereas others have emphasized the history and tradition associated with each socio-geographic region.

This fertile region, roughly triangular in shape, had formed part of the ancient Indus Valley civilization in the third millennium before Christ, when Dravidian city-states had dotted the Indus Valley. Scholars cannot agree whether the Aryan invaders swept the region in the second millennium before Christ or whether they established small republics all over Punjab. It was in Punjab that Vedic Hinduism flourished and many classic Sanskrit works written. Not only did the Vedic Aryans evolve a new system of religious belief and practice, but they also established the social system based on caste. The dark-skinned Dravidians were relegated to the unprivileged status of *dasas*, 'or slaves'. The Sikhs of Punjab are believed to have descended from the Aryan settlers. Indologists widely agree that Indian civilization was among the oldest in the world and its cradle was in Punjab. During the fourth century before Christ, Greek armies under Alexander swept across Punjab and imprinted an unmatched artistic pattern on the land. Soon after Alexander's departure, the Punjab was brought under the rule of the powerful Mauryan empire. During this period, Buddhism came to dominate the religious life of the people of Punjab. In the second century before Christ, the Greek king Menander established his power in Punjab; Greek coins bear testimony to the Hellenic influence in Punjab.

A series of invasions by Arab, Afghan, Turkish and Persian conquerors from the seventh century was to leave an Islamic imprint on the land and its people. In the mid-eighteenth century the Afghan invaders successfully separated the province of Punjab from the remainder of India. This conquest was followed by the establishment of the vast Sikh empire under Maharaja Ranjit Singh during the eighteenth century. Sikh political power collapsed on 29 March 1849 with the British conquest of Punjab after two Anglo-Sikh wars. The independence of India in 1947 and the sanguinary partition of British Punjab between India and Pakistan, on the basis of Hindu and Muslim majority areas, resulted in the massive reorganization of the territorial boundaries of Punjab. In September 1966, the Punjab province was further trifurcated under the Punjab State Reorganization Bill. The southern, Hindi-speaking, plain districts were formed into a new state of Haryana, the other Hindi-speaking hill districts to the north of Punjab were merged with neighbouring Himachal Pradesh, and the remaining Punjabi-speaking areas formed the new state of Punjab. At present, the geographical area of Punjab is 5,033,000 hectares and the population is 20,190,795, of which 70.28 per cent is rural and 29.72 is urban. Further, 36.93 per cent of the population is Hindu and 60.75 per cent is Sikh according to the figures provided in the Statistical Abstract of Punjab for 1991–2.

Aims and methods

The book traces the transition of the Sikhs from a religious congregation in the sixteenth century into an ethnic community in the eighteenth century, and from an ethnic community into a nation in the late twentieth century. The aim of the book is to analyse some of the historic conditions and processes that gave rise to ethno-nationalist movements in late-industrializing societies such as India. The method used here is largely historical. I have presented a general historical account of the evolution of the Sikh community using secondary sources for the earlier period (1469–1947) and a mixture of primary and secondary sources for the later period (1947–95). Among the primary sources consulted are important resolutions and minutes of meetings of the major political party in Punjab, the Akali Dal. In addition, speeches and letters written by Akali Dal leaders have been examined. I have found newspaper reports and editorials on significant events in Punjab since the 1970s particularly useful. These data are augmented by empirical research involving in-depth interviews with representatives of three sections of the Punjabi population, namely the politicians, newspaper editors and the Sikh activists involved in the movement for secession. These interviews were conducted during fieldwork in Punjab between October 1992 and April 1993. I am indebted to Mr S. S. Bal for providing me with valuable information and data on the Sikh guerrillas. These sources are supplemented by statistical data from government sources concerning the socio-economic development of Punjab. The research also explores statistical data on circulation figures and the readership profiles of major newspapers in Punjab. Among the secondary data I have found historical accounts, tracts and books written on the Sikhs during the pre-colonial and colonial period particularly useful.

Historical analysis, however, takes us only some of the way towards an understanding of Sikh nation formation. It needs to be supplemented by a sociological analysis of the social base of separatist movements in contemporary India. Here, I focus on two key aspects of the social base: the agricultural revolution and the revolution in communications, both of which occurred from the 1960s onwards. Together these help to explain the timing of the transition to the later phase of Sikh nationalism with its central demand for an independent Sikh state.

This book is not about class structure or economic variables, except where they impinge on the transition to Sikh nationhood. The hypothesis is that three hitherto unrelated sets of factors account for the evolution of the Sikh community. The first is economic, notably the green revolution; the second is social communications, notably the vernacular press; and the third is the religious ideals of the Sikh community, notably the emphasis on the community of warriors and martyrs. My argument is that the conjunction of these sets of factors helps us to understand the nature and timing of the evolution of the Sikh nation formation.

The questions that my research raises include, first, some specific questions relating to the contemporary Sikh unrest. If the demand for a separate Sikh state is a recent phenomenon, then the obvious question is why have the Sikhs articulated this demand only recently? What were the conditions and processes that gave rise to Sikh ethno-nationalism? What is the nature of this ethno-nationalism? Second, at a more general level, the questions that are relevant for this purpose include: How do objectively distinct ethnic groups become subjectively conscious political communities? Why do people feel loyalty to their nation as well as their family, region, class and religion? What are the historical roots of Sikh ethnic nationalism? What is the social base of ethno-nationalist movements? How does the transformation in communication facilitate ethnic consciousness?

Here I attempt to develop a conceptual framework within which to seek an understanding of Sikh ethno-nationalism, and therefore I first consider the classic modernization theories of nationalism (Chapter 1). By linking the emergence of nationalism to the industrial transformation in Western Europe, classic theories of nationalism formulate a universal model of nationalism. This model overlooks the specific impact of colonialism and the cultural and historical specificities of non-Western state formation. In the effort to identify the specific historical conditions, the deeper social processes by which nations came to be imagined in the colonial context, the first chapter will explore the distinctive nature, growth and scope of the anti-colonial nationalist struggle in India.

Several questions underpin this endeavour to explain Sikh ethno-nationalism by drawing on the pattern of India's distinctive historical, religious and social experience. In particular, how does religion continue to be the dominant social bond that defines the characteristics of the Indian nation? How do religious identity assertions pose a grave threat to the Indian national state? What factors account for the emergence of religion as a crucial element in the politics of contemporary India? If the much noted religious renaissance in India is not merely a reassertion of religious piety, is it possibly what scholars refer to as a reassertion of nationalism rather than religion? What are the key features of religious nationalist movements? What are the factors that account for the resurgence of religious nationalism at this moment in India's history? Systems of life and thought have critical implications for modern politics because they regulate social life and predispose a society towards a distinctive pattern of state formation. Chapter 2 first presents a discussion of the central cultural beliefs of Indian civilization. This is followed by a consideration of the historical context in which religion and modern democratic institutions have colluded in India. Finally, the emerging pattern of religion and politics in India and the resurgence of religious nationalism will be considered. Given the vast territorial, cultural and historical complexity of India, it would be misleading to examine the emergence of Hindu religious nationalism as a single phenomenon. The discussion will hinge on those themes that are relevant to the understanding of the emergence of ethnic nationalism among Sikhs.

The Sikh movement for sovereignty during the 1980s was not a sudden development. The two subsequent chapters look at the deep social and historical roots linked to the growth of contemporary Sikh self-consciousness. In Chapter 3 the early evolution of the Sikhs will be looked at, starting with the inception of the Sikh religious congregation during the period of the Sikh Gurus[1] and ending with a clearly defined, fully formed ethnic community during the period of British colonial rule. Particular attention will be devoted to the induction of a distinct set of symbols, a sacred scripture, a sacred city, a community name to the Sikh separatist armoury. The focus is on the institution of the Khalsa order by the last Sikh Guru, Guru Gobind Singh, and the religious reform movements in the nineteenth century that sought to renew the Sikh ethnic community in the face of Hindu attacks.

In Chapter 4 the account of the three-stage evolution of the Sikhs until the present post-revolutionary situation and the growth of a specific Sikh nation aiming to create a Sikh state of Khalistan in Punjab will be examined. Here special attention will be paid to the post-independence reorganization of Punjab and how the changing territorial boundaries of Punjab have woven an expression of a homeland into the self-definition of the Sikhs. Besides possessing an already powerful set of religious symbols, a new symbol, that of language, was added to the separatist armoury. The focus is on the nature of the demand for a Punjabi *suba* or 'a Punjabi-speaking state' and the tactics and strategies used by the Hindu and Sikh élites. In this context, the role and the attitude of the central government, the attitude of the minority Hindu community in Punjab and the nature of Sikh politics are examined. The processes that gave rise to the Sikh armed resistance for the formation of a separate Sikh state of Khalistan and the impact of charismatic leaders like Sant Jarnail Singh Bhindranwale will also be considered. The impact of Operation Bluestar[2] in the radicalization of the Sikh diaspora will also be considered. Finally, the conditions that led to the disintegration of the Sikh guerrilla movement will be examined.

This study seeks to explain the nature and timing of breakaway movements in the Indian subcontinent. In Chapter 5, an attempt will be made to locate the social base of the Sikh movement for secession. My attempt to discern a pattern of mobilization takes issue with the influential study by Miroslav Hroch (1985) based on the East European situation. Hroch argues that the nationalist movement begins with an élite of intellectuals and subsequently fans out to include the professional classes and finally reaches out to other sections of society – the masses of clerks and peasants. In this context, data were collected to establish the socio-economic background of nearly 100 activists in the Sikh ethno-nationalist movement. Its central task was to bring into focus the nexus between the dislocation and alienation experienced by a section of the Sikh peasantry as a consequence of the transition to commercial agriculture, which made sections of the Sikh peasantry available for mobilization. Situations that favour a peasant-led ethno-regional struggle as a consequence of the transition to commercial agriculture will also be looked at.

Finally, this study looks at the social and cultural sphere beyond the English-speaking élite in India. The religious polemics expressed in South Asian dialects have been closed to many students of the subcontinent. Consequently, the role of the vernacular press in socio-political movements in India has been virtually overlooked. Chapter 6 examines the extent to which widely available and influential media such as the vernacular press and cassettes produce inclusive and exclusive forms of nationalist identities that recharge nationalism with varying degrees of symbolic significance. The vast expansion in readers of newspapers and listeners of radio cassettes justifies the selection of this aspect as central to the process of identity formation.

I will end with a brief conclusion summarizing the argument and underlining some implications, theoretical and empirical, of this study.

1 The trouble with classic theories of nationalism

In this chapter an attempt will be made to explain the distinctive nature, growth and scope of the anti-colonial nationalist struggle in India. This concern has emerged from an attempt to develop a conceptual framework within which to seek an understanding of Sikh ethno-nationalism. Broadly speaking, an attempt will be made to identify the deeper social processes by which nations came to be envisaged in the colonial context. Emphasis will be on the specific historical conditions that gave rise to nationalism in India. This chapter comprises three sections. In the first section the key concepts used in this study of 'nations' and 'nationalism' will be defined. The beginning of the second section describes the classic modernization theories of nationalism. This is followed by a discussion on the Eurocentric limitations of the modernization theories of nationalism. In the third section, the processes that gave rise to the socio-religious reform movements during the nineteenth century under British suzerainty will be identified. The socio-religious reform movements preceded the anti-colonial nationalist struggle. Then the social base and nature of Indian nationalism will be considered.

Concepts and definitions

The field of enquiry is bedevilled by attempts to define the terms 'nations' and 'nationalism'. Despite the profound influence of nationalism in the modern world, both the terms have proved notoriously difficult to define. Despite several attempts by various scholars to define the term 'nationalism', the term remains conceptually evasive. The protean nature of nationalism is perhaps responsible for this conceptual confusion. The presence of many variants of nationalism makes it difficult to define the term by any one criterion. Although scholars are far from being agreed on the meaning of the terms 'nation' and 'nationalism', I have adopted a more inclusive representation of the term 'nationalism'. In this book, nationalism represents an ideology and movement on behalf of the nation and incorporates both political and cultural dimensions.

If nationalism is viewed as an ideological movement, appropriating European classic doctrinal formulations, such as the concepts of popular freedom and sovereignty, then undoubtedly nationalism arose in Europe in the eighteenth century. Further, the rise of nationalism in the West was a predominantly mass democratic political occurrence. As the scientific state emerged as an engine for social progress, European society broke out of the conceptual mould of a religio-ethnic community so as to develop parliamentary democracy. Nevertheless, this view of nationalism is derived from a historical transformation that was unique to Europe and is not rooted in the social and political realities of non-European societies. This exclusive concern with European modernity underpins the major historical and sociological approaches to nationalism, and from this springs the conceptual muddle that mires nationalism.

What is unique about modern nationality?

For some scholars, the doctrine of nationalism is based on the twin ideals of autonomy and self-government. The desire to liberate territories subjugated by alien conquest is not new, but the impulse to transform society into a people's state and to redraw the political boundaries in conformity with ethnographic demands is unique to the modern world. The nationalist movement in India wanted to liberate the people from the constraints of British imperial rule. Nationalism is a revolutionary force that aims at transferring sovereignty from an external ruler, or a monarch, to the collectivity of people. This is made possible through the institution of the modern national state, the highest political form in which the citizens are the ultimate locus of sovereignty. The sovereign state makes possible the political and cultural integration of the masses through organized activity, such as the promotion of popular education, universal suffrage, and so on. But, whether the rationalism and the scientific temper embodied in the modern state have the potential to destroy the hold of faith on public life depends on the specific historical circumstances under which nationalism emerges. In the Indian subcontinent, religion remained the dominant social bond that defined the characteristics of the nation, despite the development of modern parliamentary democracy. It is for this reason that the Hindi term *'hindutva'* signified the equation between Hindu cultural identity and the Indian nation, whereas the Urdu term *'qaum'* designated the ideal of a religio-political community of Muslims and the Punjabi term *'panth'* was emblematic of a moral and political collectivity of believers in the Sikh faith.

Despite its wide intellectual currency, the term 'nation' is not easy to define. Once again, there are important differences in ways of defining the term 'nation'. Some emphasize objective elements, whereas others give significance to subjective factors. It is possible to incorporate both these approaches and avoid single-factor characterization of nations. I have adopted the following working definition of the nation: a nation is an imagined political community seeking a historic homeland for its own people, whose solidarity is sustained by the presence of cultural channels of communication, notably ethnicity

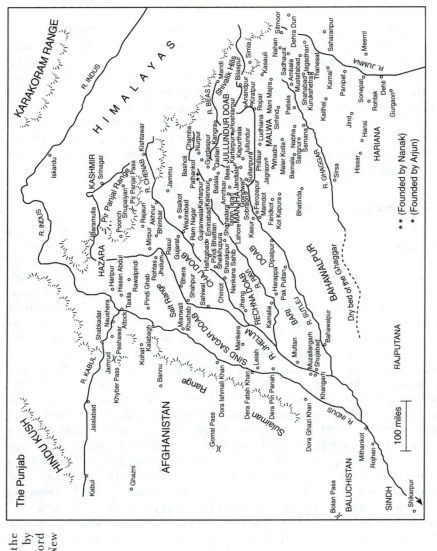

Map 1.1 General map of the Punjab. Reprinted by permission of Oxford University Press, New Delhi

and language and whose boundaries are in continual flux. In the modern world, any body of people who consider themselves to be a nation can claim the right to self-determination, or the right to a separate sovereign independent state for their territory. The nation is a modern construct that became salient in the Indian subcontinent in the second part of the nineteenth century. Can this definition describe the Sikh nation?

Many scholars argue that the Sikhs constituted a nation even in pre-modern times. The noted historian Joseph D. Cunningham has placed emphasis on the consolidation of power by the Sikh kingdoms and has argued that the Sikhs developed from 'a sect into a people' under Guru Gobind, and from a people to a 'nation' under Ranjit Singh (Cunningham 1966: 92). The theme of the development of Sikh self-consciousness is emphasized in a classic account by the Sikh historian Khushwant Singh. He views the struggle of Sikh forces against the British in the second Anglo-Sikh War in 1848 as 'a national war of independence' (K. Singh 1962: 147). However, this book proposes that, at present, the objective criteria that define membership in the Sikh nation are those of the *kes-dhari*[1] Sikhs who speak Punjabi and write it in the Gurmukhi script and those *kes-dhari* Sikhs who identify with the distinctive historical consciousness and behaviour of the Sikh people.[2] The Sikh nation is in the imagination because the members do not know most of their fellow members, yet in their minds they constitute a homogeneous community. The Sikh nation is envisaged as a community, because it disregards the inequality and heterogeneity that actually exists among the Sikhs. It was the development of social mobilization and political organization during the past century that played a decisive role in the development of the modern Sikh nation, as defined above. The passage of the Gurudwara Reform Act of 1925 provided the Sikhs with a solid institutional framework in the form of the SGPC and its political arm, the Akali Dal.[3] Both these institutions have successfully articulated Sikh political aspirations since India gained independence. Paul Brass has argued that 'The Akali Dal has not been simply a political expression of pre-existing Sikh aspirations, but it has played a critical role in creating a modern Sikh nation' (Brass 1974: 433).

Two other terms need preliminary definition. First, the term 'secessionism' refers to 'a demand for formal withdrawal from a central political authority by a member unit or units on the basis of a claim to independent sovereign status' (Hechter 1992: 267). The persisting secessionist movements in India are the Sikh demands for sovereignty and the Muslim claims for autonomy in Kashmir. Secessionism is different from separatism, which does not aim at such withdrawal. Second, an 'ethno-regional movement' is distinguished from other regional movements by the emphasis on ethnic distinctiveness, on ethnic markers such as language or religion, in a bid to seek a separate region within an existing state, as well as seek an independent sovereign state. So, the term 'ethnic nationalism' refers to minority or majority nationalism that emphasizes ethnic distinctiveness.

The origins of nationalism in Europe

Modernization theories of nationalism

To appreciate the nature of nationalism among the Sikhs, it must be differentiated from its counterparts in Europe. To understand these European counterparts, two influential accounts of nationalism, both inside and outside Europe, that stress the role of modernization must be considered. The leading exponents of modernization theories of nationalism are Elie Kedourie, whose classic works include *Nationalism* (1960) and *Nationalism in Asia and Africa* (1971), and Benedict Anderson, whose work *Imagined Communities* (1991) is perhaps the most cited and original text in the field.[4] These influential theorists explain the genesis of nationalism through the industrial transformation of European society and its spread throughout the rest of the world through colonialism. Although their approach differs over the emphasis on different processes of modernity, both their theories have stimulated lively debates on the question of the European origins of nationalism and its global osmosis.

One of the most original theories of nationalism put forth by the distinguished political philosopher Elie Kedourie is first considered. Elie Kedourie's book is an interesting starting-point because it raises several critical issues that infuse mainstream writing about the national question and will require more detailed explanation later. Kedourie's approach is that of a historian of nationalist ideas and accords a pivotal role to the disaffected intellectuals who invented the doctrine of nationalism at the beginning of the nineteenth century in Europe. This period of European history, argues Kedourie, was characterized by profound social and political upheaval. The revolutionary philosophies of Enlightenment and classical humanism challenged the existing belief systems and social practices, which had been venerated for centuries. This revolt in European systems of life and thought was accompanied by a breakdown in the transmission of religious beliefs and political experience from one generation to the next. This created powerful social strains and eighteenth-century Europe seemed devoid of spiritual comfort. As Kedourie notes,

> Put at its simplest, the need is to belong together in a coherent and stable community. Such a need is normally satisfied by the family, the neighbourhood, the religious community. In the last century and a half such institutions all over the world have had to bear the brunt of violent social and intellectual change, and it is no accident that nationalism was at its most intense where and when such institutions had little resilience and were ill-prepared to withstand the powerful attacks to which they became exposed.
>
> (Kedourie 1960: 101)

The nationalist principle was an attempt by European intellectuals to restore the sinews of 'lost community' in the modern world. Thus, nationalism was a conspicuous outgrowth of the personal discontent of European intellectuals who sought millennial solutions to this violent change.

But why did European domination evoke nationalism in Asia and Africa? Kedourie's classic work *Nationalism in Asia and Africa* (1971) is centred around this pertinent question. In cognizance with his general theory, Kedourie explains the diffusion of the doctrine of nationalism through the Western-educated élite in Asia and Africa. In other words, the osmosis of European manners and ideas through the indigenous professional classes was decisive in the proliferation of nationalism in Asia and Africa. The indigenous élite imbibed current European political thought and were deeply stirred by the dominant strands in the modes of modern European thought. Moreover, the prestige of European prosperity, its military might and the success of its administrative methods generated a desire to emulate and adapt the European belief system. By contrast, 'the traditional societies showed up so lamentably in comparison' (Kedourie 1970: 27). This generated discontent with the existing traditional societies and an impulse to adopt European doctrines. Moreover, the planetary spread of European power from the sixteenth century onwards was accompanied by the growth of conceptions of biological contamination. The racial discrimination that these marginal men were subjected to, coupled with the oppressive sense of inferiority, erupted in the twentieth century anti-colonial movements that sought to oust imperial rulers and establish new states in the ex-colonial territories. Kedourie emphasizes that nationalism was an ideal wholly conceived and elaborated in Europe and a completely alien concept in Asia and Africa. He notes,

> Almost any Asian or African nationalism, considered as a scheme of thought or a programme of action, suffers from artificiality, from seeming a laborious attempt to introduce outlandish standards and out-of-place categories, and nowhere do they seem more out-of-place than in trying to adopt the European category of the nation-state.
>
> (Kedourie 1970: 30)

In a 'traditional' hierarchical society, an individual occupies a well-defined space in a meaningful and coherent cosmic order. This fulfils the basic need of an individual and is a source of immense security. But the process of 'Europeanization of government and economy', the transformation from a self-sufficient subsistence economy into the increasing involvement with the world economy, pulverized the social fabric of these societies (Kedourie 1970: 27). The psychological strain experienced by the masses as the processes of modernity impinged upon them was successfully articulated by the indigenous élite through the 'European' doctrine of nationalism. Thus, the disaffected Western-educated élite constituted the vanguard of anti-colonial nationalism in Asia and Africa.

Finally, Kedourie has emphasized key aspects that endow the nationalist principle with a European outlook. The key feature of the nationalist doctrine is the historicist conception of the nation. According to Kedourie, the doctrine of nationalism rests on the European intellectual tradition of secular millenarianism. To define a nation, it is necessary to evoke the nation's past. This attempt to resurrect a past is linked to the tendency to enforce uniformity of belief, particularly religious homogeneity, among members of a body politic. The nationalist doctrine is based on those premises that were unique to European politics in medieval and modern times. Thus, according to Kedourie, nationalism as a doctrine holds that the only legitimate political association is one that binds together people speaking the same language, sharing the same culture and cherishing the same heroes and ancestors. Therefore, nationalism expresses a preoccupation with history that has come to be a dominant theme of the modern European outlook and which has also been taken up wherever European culture has penetrated (Kedourie 1970: 35).

Benedict Anderson's widely acclaimed book *Imagined Communities* (1991) is a powerful attempt to formulate a theory of nationalism from a Marxian historian's perspective. Anderson regards nationalism as a 'cultural artifact' and examines the discrete historical forces that gave birth to an originary nationalism in America towards the end of the eighteenth century. He then goes on to explain the global spread and adoption of the idea of the nation, first by popular movements in Europe and later by the anti-imperialist movements in Asia and Africa.

The depth of Anderson's work lies in his presentation of the conditions and processes that gave rise to nationalism in Western Europe. The nation, he argues, is a modern construct. It became possible to 'think' the nation only after the erosion of three fundamental cultural conceptions, first in Western minds and later elsewhere. These systems of life and thought were, first, the concept of a cosmically central classical community, linked by a distinct sacred script. Second was the idea of sacral monarchy, which gave legitimacy to the dynastic states that formed the world political system. Third was the belief that cosmology and history were identical; the origins of the world were indistinguishable from the origins of humankind. These world-views imparted meaning to the uncertainties and the fatalities of human existence. However, the development of a capitalist economy, social and scientific discoveries and the rapid expansion of communication brought about a profound transformation in modes of apprehending the world. The gradual demotion of these interlinked certainties was in Anderson's words,

> No surprise then that the search was on, so to speak, for a new way of linking fraternity, power and time meaningfully together. Nothing perhaps more precipitated this search, nor made it fruitful, than print capitalism, which made it possible for rapidly growing numbers of people to think about themselves, and to relate themselves to others, in profoundly new ways.

> (Anderson 1991: 36)

Anderson further goes on to establish the link between the origins of national consciousness and the introduction of print capitalism.[5] But how did the fixing of print languages give birth to a new national consciousness? First of all, print languages enabled communication across diverse local and social groups. The printed word made it possible for a vast number of unrelated and anonymous fellow readers to imagine themselves as a self-conscious community. This profound historic development was accompanied by the creation of vernacular languages for administrative purposes. However, only print languages could possibly be elevated to this new politico-cultural eminence. In this way, print capitalism facilitated the development of national state languages. Anderson argues that it was neither the requirements of a capitalist economy nor the impact of Enlightenment that provided the framework for the rise of new national consciousness. But it was, in fact, the printmen who made it possible to conceive of a nationally imagined community.

By the second decade of the nineteenth century, the conceptual model of a sovereign national state was available for pirating. The composite of American and French elements provided the blueprint of an independent national state. This model was adapted by the anti-imperialist movements in Asia and Africa in the twentieth century. Global imperialism necessitated the rapid expansion of the bureaucratic apparatus. This impelled a need for an educated, indigenous population to fill the subordinate positions in the administrative hierarchy. The colonial school system churned out a literate native population. However, the emerging bilingual intelligentsia were to confront the racist character of nineteenth-century imperialism, pushed through the colonial school system, as well as the state machinery. These disaffected, literate men promoted anti-colonial nationalism as a response to the shared experience of racism and became central to the rise of anti-colonial nationalism. Finally, since these marginalized men had access to the models of the nation-state, the Western civic concept of the nation was applied to set up new states in the ex-colonial territories.

Critique of modernization theories

These modernization theories have not gone unchallenged. Anthony D. Smith's well-known book *The Ethnic Origins of Nations* (1986) challenges the modernist view that nations and nationalism are purely modern phenomena. Against this, Smith maintains that the modernization theories are based on an ahistorical and essentializing conception of society as either 'traditional' or 'modern'. By focusing on the historical and social origins of nations, Anthony D. Smith reveals the striking resemblance to the 'modern' idea of a nation of the ethnie or ethnic community: notably, a desire to liberate territories conquered by alien invasions, even in pre-modern eras. Hence the persistence of myths and memories, symbols and values, rituals and recitations, language and scripts, which define and differentiate human population everywhere in the world and at all times. Smith argues that ethnicity provides one of the most pivotal and durable models for human association, and this ethnic model has been adopted in the formation of modern nations. In other words, historically, the formation of modern nations was made possible because of the presence of a relatively homogeneous ethnic core. Thus, Smith expounds an entirely convincing case that the nature of modern nations is best understood by examining their antecedent cultural attributes of memory, myth and symbol embodied in customs and traditions. Later I shall show how these ideas apply in the Punjab case.

The master narrative of European modernity posits a similar dichotomy between 'modern' European and 'traditional' non-European societies. It has become standard practice in scholarly narratives to portray the 'traditional', non-European societies as economically and political backward and dominated by religious assumptions and traditions. By contrast, 'modern', European societies are characterized by the proliferation of industrial capitalism and the concomitant erosion of a religious world-view. Likewise, Hans Kohn, the pioneering historian of nationalist ideologies, had put forth an influential distinction between the rational, civic nationalism of the 'West' and the authoritarian, organic, mystical nationalism of the 'East' (Kohn 1945: 18–20, 329–31). He argued that the type of nationalism that emerges in a society depended on the stage of social and political development. Outside the Western world, in Central and Eastern Europe and in Asia, nationalism not only arose later, but was a defensive, imitative response by the educated élite. The disaffected intelligentsia from backward societies promoted nationalism to compensate for their feelings of inferiority when threatened by the superior industrially advanced Western culture. Thus, nationalism in Asia and Africa is believed to be a regressive phenomenon, a nostalgic retreat into history to claim descent from a once grand civilization.

To digress for a moment, a classic example of this binary opposition is the portrayal of the system of a 'traditional moral economy', as opposed to the 'modern rational capitalist economy'. A few empirical details concerning the idea of Asiatic stagnation and the notion of an autarkic village community in 'traditional' India, marked by hierarchical, ritual and non-ritual forms of exchange, will help shed light on the import of this dichotomy. There is widespread agreement among a variety of scholars that traditional cultural conceptions determined India's jajmani system and that religious traditions encompassed the politico-economic domain.[6] Nevertheless, there is abundant empirical evidence of the existence of powerful centralizing institutions as well as the expansion of economic networks in pre-colonial India. The significance of private landed property in pre-colonial India was a body of fact that the colonial regime deliberately suppressed, so that non-private land could be aggregated by the Crown to produce revenue.[7] Similarly, there is considerable awkward evidence of market towns, or *'qasbas'*, flourishing cities, trading centres and regional markets, the development of banking and the use of money, all interlinked through the network of commerce and migration. These are just a few features which suggest that the notion of the custom-bound, autarkic village community in pre-colonial India is merely a product of a romantic imagination. In the light of the discussion presented above, there is some ground for suggesting that pre-colonial India had its own pattern of change. Therefore, the notion of a pristine 'traditional' Indian society, untouched by any processes of change until the pervasive incursion of capitalism under the British colonial rule, is a misconception.[8] Just because the transition from feudalism to capitalism completed itself in Europe, must a standpoint be adopted that rejects outright any historical facts and causally efficacious processes outside the non-European world? This digression is sufficient, I hope, to highlight some of the misconceptions germane to the theme of explaining nationalism outside Europe, to which I shall now return.

The master narrative on nationalism posits the anti-colonial struggles for political sovereignty as a simple product of the diffusion of 'civilized' European ideas as part of the process of modernity to the backward colonial world. Kedourie's study of nationalism is replete with this broadly diffusionist outlook, which in one breath castigates nationalism – 'the drug may also excite its addicts to a frenzy of destruction' and proclaims with a hint of irony that nationalism is 'Europe's latest gift to the world' (Kedourie 1971: 147). This perspective is self-contradictory. On the one hand, nationalism is regarded as a destructive phenomenon; on the other hand, the transmission and spread of nationalism outside Europe is considered progressive. Similarly, the position of the marginal intellectual depicted in Asia and Africa is somewhat ambiguous. On the one hand, these élites are purported to be the carriers of 'modern' European ideas; on the other hand, they are believed to fashion 'traditional' ideologies of religious activism.

There are a number of pitfalls in this approach that call for a critical revaluation of the existing corpus of writing on the national question. First of all, the availability of the conceptual model of a sovereign national state alone does not motivate anyone to adopt a foreign model, however successful. The processes by which it became possible to adopt and adapt the model of the national state are generally not seriously addressed. For instance, why did the 'marginal man' in Asia and Africa choose this particular European idea and not any other ideas? Is he completely alienated from his society? How does he spread the new ideas that he has imbibed to the rest of the society? Second is the failure to consider the specific impact of colonialism. This factor by itself may be judged a decisive contribution towards the eventual establishment of a sovereign state in the ex-colonial territories. This objection is based on the ubiquitous presupposition that 'modern' Europe is the result of a historical transition, whereas the social and political transformation in the countries of Asia and Africa is simply a by-product of revolutionary convulsions centred around Europe. Modernization theories of nationalism are a very good example of the geographical diffusionism that lies at the root of modern European thought. By presenting a Eurocentric, universalistic model of modernization, European history is held to provide the blueprint for the category of world history. On the one hand, the significant differences between 'Western' and 'Eastern' nationalisms are widely acknowledged. On the other hand, most of the historical and sociological approaches to nationalism hold that since nationalism as an ideological movement first arose in the West, we must therefore judge and explain non-Western nationalism by reference to this Western criterion. Third, the historical agency of the people involved in the anti-colonial nationalist struggles is denied. After all, the anti-colonial struggle to seize state power was also a product of economic exploitation and oppression. Thus, current writing on the national question grossly oversimplifies the nature of anti-colonial struggles.

This study is an attempt to break out of the existing conceptual mould by identifying the specific historical conditions and processes that gave rise to nationalism in India. Undoubtedly, the rise of Western domination ensured the importation of European ideas and concepts. Nevertheless, the emerging ideological formations were a glorious synthesis of the European and the indigenous elements, as will be revealed later. Colonialism and the expansion òf the world system impinged on the existing structures and processes, but they did not determine them. Therefore, it is of critical importance to view the anti-colonial national liberation struggle against a historical backdrop of the antecedent state and ideological systems.

Now compare and contrast the features that Indian nationalism shared with the West, as well as those which differentiated Indian nationalism from the bourgeois nationalism of Western Europe. Describing the conditions that gave rise to nationalism in Western Europe, Benedict Anderson observes, '...in Western Europe the eighteenth century marks not only the dawn of the age of nationalism but the dusk of religious mode of thought' (Kedourie 1971: 11). In other words, economic change and the development of rapid communications disintegrated the existing cultural systems in Western Europe, thereby impelling a need to bind the population together in new ways. Likewise, Elie Kedourie attributes the birth of nationalism to the profound social and political upheaval that shook Western Europe in the eighteenth century. He argues that nationalism was an explosive psychological reaction to the revolt in European systems of life and thought.

By contrast, the appearance of nationalism in India was not marked by the ebbing of religious belief, rather nationalism in India fermented in an age of intense religious awakening. More importantly, enhanced communication facilitated the reformulation and rapid transmission of religious discourses. This observation poses a challenge to the ubiquitous traditional–modern dichotomy, which posits that the introduction of modern communications marked a transition from religious culture to secular culture; this transformation contributed directly to the rise of national consciousness. This idea is based on an uncritical generalization from the Western European case. Socio-religious reform movements were forerunners of the anti-colonial nationalist struggle. This indicates that nationalism in India arose under very different historic circumstances. Since modernization theorists impute the arrival of national consciousness to the gradual demotion of the religious world-view, does this mean that the historic need to conceive of a national community should not have arisen in India? But the need did arise, and nationalism did arrive in India. Partha Chatterjee (1986) has rightly observed that Indian nationalist discourse is derived from the European type, but it is different because of the colonial context within which it arose. As a political movement, nationalism arose in India towards the end of the nineteenth century. It grew in protest against and in conflict with the existing state pattern. I bring up these simple-minded observations primarily because nationalism in India did not find its justification in a rational societal conception, as may have been the dominant trend in Western Europe. To sum up, at least provisionally and very tentatively, I would like to suggest that every nationalism is, in some way, an indigenous development. Nationalism in India is radically different from its European counterparts because of the religious framework through which it operates.

I now consider the specific historic circumstances under which nationalism arose in India. In doing so, some of the deeper social processes by which nations came to be imagined in the colonial context will be identified.

The genesis of nationalism in India

Pax Britannica 1857–1947: the proliferation of socio-religious reform movements[9]

Mainstream writing on the genesis of nationalism in Asia and Africa has generally overlooked the pivotal role of Christian missionaries. To write about this theme in this chapter is to question this omission and engage in conceptual debates on the nature of nationalism in India. At the heart of the first ideological battle in colonial India was the Christian church. The vast majority of the British Protestant missionaries were evangelicals. To effectively propagate evangelical Christianity, the Christian missionaries introduced new institutional forms during the late eighteenth century. The founding of printing presses by the Christian missionaries was a pre-condition of the philological–lexicographic revolution during nineteenth-century British colonial rule. The print medium was established in order to generate a steady stream of tracts, pamphlets and religious texts. Since public discourses on the life of Christ were accompanied by the free distribution and circulation of evangelical literature, the bulk of the printed communication was in regional languages. The outstanding communication skills of missionaries played a creative role in the development of the indigenous press and publishing. Further, the printing process standardized scripts, lexicons and grammatical rules and fostered the standardization of vernacular languages in India.

Another powerful channel for catechizing was the establishment of a network of church-sponsored schools. Bible classes were included in the school curriculum. For decades mission schools were the only schools to provide anglo-vernacular education. The term 'anglo-vernacular' education is emblematic of a syncretic education process, combining knowledge of vernacular languages with an English education. Although school textbooks were considered to be surrogates for the Bible and the threat of conversions loomed large, the appeal of the mission schools for the native population was an English language education. The rapid expansion of imperial bureaucracy in the nineteenth century had fuelled the need for English-educated Indians to fill the subordinate echelons of administration. Moreover, the colonial administrators relentlessly pursued a policy that undermined the indigenous educational system and projected the superior educational standards of the mission and state-run schools. By the 1880s, India was rife with mission establishments.[10]

The well-organized Church was a powerful institution of European power. The nineteenth-century British colonial state was informed and moulded by British Protestant and Irish Catholic doctrines. In the eyes of the imperial administration, both British rule and evangelism stood for Christian civilization. This view is aptly demonstrated by a leading administrator in Punjab, Donald McLeod, who declared, 'If the Bible be the word of God and the books revered by the Hindus and the Mohammedan contain mere fables, then it must be intended that the Christian rule prepare the way for the spread of the gospel'.[11] To the native population, the imperial alliance between the civil administrators and the missionaries was formidable. The overall impact of this process is summed up by C. A. Bayly; he observes, 'the impact of the intense missionary propaganda, the dominance by European and Indian Christians of the new print media, and the simultaneous appearance of government school masters in town and country, were profoundly unsettling for the established Indian order' (Bayly 1994: 7). Moreover, the susceptibility of the upper class of society to the proselytizing activities of the evangelicals enraged the local community.

The cultural forces unleashed by the British Raj sparked a series of religious reform movements among all the major religious communities in colonial India. These reform movements set the stage for the political battle with the imperial state that arose in 1885 with the formation of the Indian National Congress. Socio-religious reform made certain components of religious discursive tradition available for the development of a nationalist ideology. The historic role of these socio-religious reform movements in British India must be understood within the context of three interacting civilizations. To the indigenous Hindu–Buddhist civilization was introduced the Perso-Arabic civilization of the Muslim conquerors who had gained political control of nearly two-thirds of the subcontinent in the fourteenth century. The decay of the Mogul system gave the British the chance to establish a territorial foothold and interject the British version of Western civilization during the eighteenth century. Thus, three layers of civilization interacted and moulded the nineteenth century socio-religious reform movements.

Let us try to perceive this transformation in its major contours. Conventional approaches to the study of religious reform movements in colonial India seek to explain how the rising middle class, empowered by its position in modern capitalism, attempted to gain hegemony by enunciating a standard cultural idiom through the religious reform movements. After the penetration of the capitalist world economy under the aegis of the British Raj and the expansion of imperial bureaucracy, an influential class of bilingual, professional men emerged. These men were primarily based in urban areas where they acquired new skills in the mechanics of print culture. In order to come to terms with the profound social transformation under colonial rule, these men set up socio-religious associations and voluntary bodies; they established schools and published tracts and vernacular newspapers to uphold the interests of their respective religious communities. In *Imagined Communities*, Benedict Anderson develops a persuasive thesis on the relationship between the creation of print languages and national consciousness. He notes, 'the convergence of capitalism and print technology on the fatal diversity of human language created the possibility of a new form of imagined community, which in its basic morphology set the stage for the modern nation' (Anderson 1983: 46). It is this connection between print languages and national consciousness that will now be examined.

Although in Western Europe print technology was received within the wider context of the impact of the Reformation, the emergence of Protestantism and its attendant rationality, in India, by contrast, the impetus for print capitalism was provided by a significantly different set of historical conditions. The evangelical wave permeating in the early nineteenth century encouraged a derogatory view of Hinduism and Islam. Unitarian Christianity soaked with rational ethics attributed the present decadence of the native society to the existing belief system and social practices. Imbibing the spirit of the time, the exponents of the socio-religious reform movements set about re-evaluating their cultural traditions. The reformatory zeal impelled the reformers to call for the creation of a more just society, free from polytheism, idolatry and caste prejudices; promote the concept of monotheism; attempt to redefine the status of women by granting them the right to education; promote the remarriage of widows; and condemn practices such as female infanticide. This pitted the reformers against orthodox members of their own religious community as well as against their opponents, who derided their theological precepts. This process of recasting and revitalizing group identities, energized and hardened pre-existing religious affiliations. Thus, far from eroding the sacred community through the dethronement of sacred languages, as Anderson has argued, print capitalism in fact reinforced the significance of language as the basis of religious identity.

Further, the historic process of the creation of print languages and the development of vernacular languages of state reinforced the fusion of linguistic and religious identification. The overall impact of this historic process was the creation of areas of greater ideological uniformity within the broad boundaries of religion and the ascendancy of religion-based linguistic identity over all other competing identities such as class, gender and profession. This was evident as Urdu came to be identified with Islam, Hindi became a marker of Hindu identity, and Gurmukhi script and Punjabi language were turned exclusively into emblems of Sikh identity. Scriptures have served as the concrete and objective markers of religious identity even in pre-modern times. But a particular script embodying the religious identity of a people was a new development. The perfect isomorphism between religion and language that we find in contemporary South Asia has its historical antecedents in this social upheaval that shook the Indian subcontinent in the nineteenth century. Remarkably, neither is the Qur'an written in Urdu language, nor are the Hindu scriptures written in Hindi, whereas the compositions in the Sikh holy scripture, Adi Granth, are a melange of various dialects, often coalesced under the generic title of Sant Bhasha. This perhaps gives credence to Hobsbawm's well-known thesis (see Hobsbawm and Ranger 1983) that some traditions are 'invented' and formally instituted by political élites. They represent a response to novel situations and an attempt to establish continuity with a historic past, although the continuity with the past is largely factitious. In the context of invention of tradition, language as a key symbol to promote social cohesion among a religious community seems to have been a major innovation by the élite of the Indian subcontinent. Nevertheless, this was not an entirely factitious invention. After all, the scriptural book was written in the script that came to embody the religious identity of a people. Hindu claims over Hindi rested on the fact that Hindi was a modern variant of Sanskrit, whereas Urdu was an Indo-Persian linguistic synthesis and written in the Arabic script. Likewise, Adi Granth was written in the Gurmukhi script.

An examination of the processes of construction and transformation of religious identities in colonial India during the eighteenth and nineteenth centuries has been the subject of considerable scholarly inquiry. The view that early Indic culture was inherently pluralistic and marked by the absence of concern for demarcating religious boundaries is well established among Indian scholars.[12] Only later, with the introduction of a new statistical ethnology and methods of surveying and mapping by the British was a standard, highly uniform religious tradition established in India. Partha Chatterjee (1993) takes the same argument a step further to argue that caste in India is a fabrication of the British Census and Population Survey. What is lost sight of in this kind of reading is the striking presence of indigenous forms of anthropological knowledge that provided the framework for the colonial knowledge of the district gazetteers. As C. A. Bayly correctly notes, 'the "Institutes of Akbar", a flexible mix of maxims for kingship, Islamic ethnology and revenue and military details, spawned a range of more local imitations in the eighteenth and early nineteenth century' (Bayly 1994: 20). Extensive comment is quite unnecessary. It should suffice to note that modern institutions such as the Census and Population Survey enhanced the pre-existing religious categories and were crucial in defining caste and religious communities. This issue has been further discussed in Chapter 4. In addition, there is a tendency to blame the 'divide and rule' policy of the British for nurturing and inciting religious conflict in order to neutralize the emerging Indian nationalism.[13] Once again, contempt for the British element oversimplifies and falsifies the nature of the interaction between religious communities in pre-colonial India.

So far attention has been focused on the process of recasting social identities in colonial India. The creation of print languages, the development of vernacular languages of state and the introduction of a new statistical ethnology enhanced pre-existing religious affiliations. Further, in response to the aggressive proselytism of the Christian missionaries, backed by the British colonial state, the ideologues of the socio-religious reform movements sought to revitalize their cultural traditions. They drew on religious authority in order to legitimize change. These new processes and ideological formations were interesting forerunners of the anti-colonial nationalist struggle and provided the framework for the development of a nationalist ideology. More importantly, these new developments seem to have been confined to the new, urban professional élite. But the intelligentsia were just minuscule literate reefs amidst enormous illiterate oceans. The vast mass of the population in British India was not literate and resided in rural areas. Moreover, the growing numbers of literates does not imply that everyone was reading books or newspapers. How then might the extraordinary success of the socio-religious reform movements be explained? In order to appreciate the response of the masses to the socio-religious reform movements it is crucial to examine the relationship between the ideologues of nationalism and their society.

The anti-colonial nationalist movement and the struggle for India's independence

The striking character of the Indian nationalist movement was to bring the masses into the struggle to expel the British. Broadly speaking, two key factors allowed this development. First, *pax Britannica* prevented the fateful coalition between India's landed élite, the main beneficiaries of the British Raj after 1857, and the rising commercial and manufacturing classes, who felt cramped by British policies that sought to exploit a protected Indian market. Second was the alliance between the powerful commercial classes and a weak peasantry, the tillers of the soil, which seems rather paradoxical because of their conflicting interests. However, it was the rise of Mahatma Gandhi as a dominant figure in the nationalist movement that enabled the successful alignment between the native bourgeoisie and the peasantry. It was under Gandhi's leadership that the Congress party emerged as a powerful mass organization. The main thrust of Gandhi's programme was to make villages more important. Central to this programme was the conception of *swadeshi*, or 'local autonomy'. Gandhi defined the term *swadeshi* as follows:

Swadeshi is that spirit in us which restricts us to use and service of our immediate surroundings to the exclusion of the remote. Thus, as for religion, in order to satisfy the requirements of the definition, I must restrict myself to my ancestral religion. That is the use of my immediate religious surrounding. If I find it defective, I should serve it by purging it of its defects. In the domain of politics I should make use of the indigenous institutions and serve them by curing them of their proved defects. In that of economics I should use only things that are produced by my immediate neighbours and serve those industries by making them efficient and complete where they might be found wanting...

(Gandhi 1933: 336–7, 341–2)

In this way, the Mahatma looked back at an idealized peasant life in order to salvage the true, pure religion of his people. Only the revival of traditional village India, purged of all meaningless accretions such as superstition and repressive features, such as untouchability, could provide a model of the good society. Nevertheless, quite a few critical scholars view Gandhi's notion of *swadeshi* as a backward-looking idealization of peasant life. As Barrington Moore points out, 'Never did it occur to Gandhi that to maintain village India would be to condemn the mass of India's population to a life of squalor, ignorance, and disease' (Moore 1981: 376).

Although there is no doubt that Gandhi was the spokesman of the Indian peasantry and the village artisan, his outlook was rooted in the Indian experience. It is well known that the import of British textiles, which began in 1814 and continued through the nineteenth century, almost destroyed the indigenous handicrafts. The weavers belonging to the artisan castes, who produced goods of high quality for the market, were effectively damaged by the import of British products. Further, during the late eighteenth century and the first part of the nineteenth century, the British imposed a new system of taxing farming and land tenure. Historically, the first main form of settlement was the permanent settlement (also known as the *zamindari system*). The British took over this arrangement from the Moguls, who had ruled and taxed through native authorities, especially the *zamindar*, who had been the intermediary between the ruler and the peasant. Under the *zamindari system*, the British took nine-tenths of the revenue that the *zamindar*, or 'the native tax-collecting official', collected from the peasant tenants. The other system for collecting revenue was the *ryotwari system*. This system was imposed in southern India, in the absence of the *zamindars*. Since revenues were collected directly from the cultivators, the term *ryot*, or 'cultivator', is used to describe this system of farm taxation. It is important to understand that under British administration large sections of the peasantry and the artisans bore the brunt of the intrusions of capitalism.

The doctrine of *swadeshi* affirmed native mercantile interests. Gandhi endorsed the slogan of 'buy Indian' and launched a peaceful mass non-cooperation movement to boycott British products. Further, Gandhi opposed political strikes, for they contradicted his doctrine of non-violence. As he remarked in 1921, 'It does not require much effort of the intellect to perceive that it is a most dangerous thing to make use of labour until labourers understand the political condition of the country and are prepared to work for the common good' (Gandhi 1933: 1049–1050). He hoped that as the workforce became better educated the principle of arbitration would replace strikes (Gandhi 1933: 1048).

Outside the arena of institutional modes, the reformers successfully intervened in everyday life. They objected to the British Raj undermining their existence in the economic domain and claimed that in the cultural domain their world-view was under siege. The peasantry fiercely resisted any efforts to surrender its cultural autonomy, particularly to those social groups who extracted revenues and services from it, since religion is part a system of cultural conceptions through which human beings interpret and conceptualize the social world around them. Also, the evocation of myths and mass ritual events are deeply ingrained in everyday life and are part of a more all-embracing cosmology. The common modes of apprehending the world bound together the entire society. The dynamic of Indian nationalism was to enable men and women to bury their insecurity in the face of natural forces by feeling themselves to be partaking in a historic collectivity. Sacred shrines, the symbolic embodiments that bind the community of believers through a shared cosmological understanding, became the foci of political campaigns to oust the British. Not only did saints and holy men, whose priestly privilege had been threatened by the whole edifice of Western scientific culture introduced by the British, play a significant role in the anti-colonial nationalist movement, but modern politicians, like Mahatma Gandhi, had an outlook more becoming of the traditional holy Hindu man. Thus we see that Indian nationalism, far from being an alien concept wholly conceived in Europe, as Kedourie and others have led us to believe, was firmly rooted in the political and social realities of India. This is precisely what makes Indian nationalism so different from its European variant. Although nationalism falls within the realm of statist politics, it is imbued with cultural elements that explain the logic of nationalism. That is why it is critical to examine the way in which the modern discourse on individualism, equality and secularism articulated by classical liberals in the West was engaged by the Indian élite.

Let us return for the moment to the collision between rationalism and the ecclesiastical authority. Anthony D. Smith in his influential book *The Ethnic Revival* (1981a) has accorded a pivotal role to the problem of legitimacy arising out of the institution of the 'scientific state'. He argues that the displacement of the religiously sanctioned dynastic state by the 'scientific' state leads to a moral crisis. Smith has coined the term 'dual legitimation' for this crisis. By 'dual legitimation' is meant the fundamental choice that societies have to make 'between a social structure dominated by religious authority or by 'rational-legal' authority of the scientific state'.[14] The spectacular success of a man-made 'scientific state' with its centralized administration challenged the efficacy of divine authority. There was a growing belief that injustice and suffering were not transcendental, cosmic problems, rather they were man-made problems. These essentially social and practical problems could be resolved through collective planning and action by means of the engine of the 'scientific' state. The response of the élites to this challenge varied, giving rise to different kinds of nationalism.

Smith would designate to the category of 'reformists' the major revivalist figure of late nineteenth-century Hindu nationalism, Swami Vivekananda, who sought to reconcile the religious tradition with his commitment to social welfare through the engine of the state. He envisioned a classic Aryan civilization that had played a seminal role in world progress. Swami Vivekananda pledged to restore this Hindu nation to the forefront of world progress. He rejected the passive isolationism prescribed by Brahmin priests through caste laws prohibiting contact with people from other countries. Rather, he presented the vision of a dynamic, mobile Hindu nation whose past glories sprang from an interchange with other cultures. He argued that social decay and inner degeneration sprang from the religious quietism of the traditionalists. The nationalist movement in India was an integrative movement, counterposed to the materialist atomist West as well as to the ossified social and cultural native traditions. These socio-religious movements were forms of protest and dissent. The key factor initially spurring the drive for socio-religious reform was the overall process of coming to terms with the profound changes generated by British colonial rule. A striking characteristic of the new élite, the exponents of social and cultural reform, was their propensity to identify with a religious community and to draw on religious authority for the legitimization of change.

Thus, the advancing armies of capitalism – commercialization and rapid communication – did not completely sweep away the established cultural episteme. In 1906, under the radical influence of B. G. Tilak, the Congress Party adopted the goal of self-government, or *swaraj*. This word is derived from classical Hindu philosophy and depicts the state of self-rule or a balanced state of self-control, the highest spiritual state through which a human being establishes perfect harmony with the rest of the world and escapes from the cycle of perpetual reincarnation. Moreover, Indian nationalism is suffused with images that glorify the Hindu Indian past. The period of the Gupta empire (320–540 AD) is epitomized as the golden age, before the Muslim invasions. In this way, the Indian nationalists struck a responsive chord in Hindu culture and successfully galvanized the country into opposing the British. The dominant version of Indian nationalism, articulated by leaders of the Indian National Congress, imagined an Indian nation cast in the idiom of the majority Hindu religious tradition. Thus, Hindu religion formed the basis of Indian national identity. However, this was to have fateful political consequences. First, the discourse of Indian nationalism subsumed minority religious traditions – Jains, Buddhists and Sikhs – under the rubric of majority Hindu nationalism. Consequently, momentous political issues concerning the rights of minorities were thereby obscured. Second, the Hindu coloration imparted to Indian nationalism alienated the Muslim population. This found expression in the elegant articulation by M. A. Jinnah that Muslims and Hindus were separate nations. This became the ideological basis for the creation of Pakistan as a homeland for Indian Muslims and led to the division of the imperial state of British India. Thus, since the beginning of modern politics in India in the nineteenth century, the narrative of the nation has been derived from religious identification.

The nature of nationalism in the post-colonial states has been examined by Clifford Geertz from an anthropological perspective. In his edited collection of essays, *Old Societies and New States* (1963), Geertz indicates that there are two competing yet complementary components in the nationalism of post-colonial states. The ethnic component is portrayed as a commitment to 'primordial ties' of religion, language, race and territory, which endow a distinctive identity to individuals, whereas the civic component is portrayed as a desire to build a dynamic modern state. Since state and ethnic boundaries rarely coincide, the result is endemic conflict. In the new states the people's sense of self remains rooted in cultural givens of blood, race, religion or language. But there is also a growing realization of the advantages of building a sovereign state as a powerful instrument of collective progress. Since allegiance to a civil state requires subordination of the natural 'primordial' ties in favour of an overarching, unfamiliar civil state, this threatens the loss of identity 'either through absorption into a culturally undifferentiated mass or, what is even worse, through domination by some other rival ethnic, racial or linguistic community that is able to imbue that order with the temper of its own personality' (Geertz 1963: 109). Political progress in the new states is centred around keeping these two interdependent, competing loyalties aligned.

The weight of the present evidence seems to indicate that the nationalist movement did not assume a revolutionary form, nor did it cause political or economic upheaval in India. Nevertheless, the outcome of these forces was the institution of the modern national state in India. In his pioneering essay on the advent of political democracy in India, Barrington Moore laments that there has not been in India up to the present time 'a revolutionary break with the past' (Moore 1981: 431). More importantly, he reasons that the British presence imposed a reactionary element, a negative critical reaction. 'In the Indian situation, around the middle of the nineteenth century, dissident aristocrats and peasants could work together only through a passionate hatred of modernization' (Moore 1981: 353). Thus, despite the development of formal structures of democracy since 1947, e.g. an independent judiciary and free general elections, there has been no substantial modernization of India's social structure. In fact, democracy provides a rationale for refusing to overhaul on any massive scale a social structure that maintains the privileges of the Indian élite.

To sum up, the process of developing an industrial society in India did not coincide with the emergence of a class of people with the capacity and the ruthlessness to force through these radical changes. The Hindu nationalists undertook the task of directing the path towards socio-political modernization through the recovery of national pride. Earlier it was noted that the reformers searched in the past to salvage the pure, genuine religion and revitalize its dignity in a rationalist world. The leading ideologues of nationalism in Asia and Africa reasoned that the material advancement of the West had effaced the spiritual life of those societies. They reasoned that industrialism only brought material anomic cosmopolitanism, and their endeavour was to retain faith in nature, family and religion in their society. They believed that it was possible to develop a modern national state and yet retain a vigorous private and public religious life. Clearly, nationalism in India did not emerge in the wake of religious decline, rather the nationalist movement was characterized by religious reform. Western liberals have condemned Indian nationalists for looking back at an idealized past, for glorifying the Indian village community, in order to provide the model of a good society. They argue that Gandhi, like many Western liberals, was too distressed by the horrors of modern industrial life. As Barrington Moore bitingly states, 'To me this sympathy merely seems to be evidence for the *malaise* in modern liberalism and its incapacity to solve the problems that confront Western society' (Moore 1981: 378).

Conclusion

An attempt to explain the origins of nationalism in India can serve as a check upon those theories which explain all nationalisms with reference to the bourgeois revolution that culminated in the Western form of democracy. India has not witnessed a bourgeois revolution, nor has there been an industrial or a peasant revolution in India. Remarkably though, there has been the establishment of a formal structure of democracy in India. Therefore, the historical preconditions that ushered nationalism in India differ sharply from those of Western Europe and the United States. If nationalism is an alien doctrine outside Europe, if empires and tribes are more 'natural' in the Asian and African context and if neither imperialism nor poverty can adequately explain the spread of nationalism, what can?

At the structural level, bureaucratic expansion in India permitted preferment to much greater numbers and gave rise to a commercial bourgeoisie that had far more varied social origins. Nevertheless, British occupation permitted collaboration between the commercial classes and the peasantry, who felt cramped by British policies. The vast masses of the Indian peasantry provided the backbone of the anti-colonial nationalist struggle in India. An important contributing cause of peasant insurrection was the deterioration in the peasants' situation under the British Raj.

At the ideological level, there has never been a historic shift, a revolutionary break with the past in India. Western cultural devaluation, the challenge of exogenous modernization and political subjection impelled a yearning for a return to an idealized ethno-religious past. Hindu revivalists operated within the parameters of their ethnic and religious traditions, and the Hindu nationalists imagined the classic Northern Aryan and Hindu version of Indian nationalism. The genius of the Indian nationalists lay in incorporating the vast multitude of unlettered peasantry, the motley complex of cultural traditions, the linguistic plethora into the imagined universe of the Indian nation. Nevertheless, this historicist conception of a Hindu nation denied the sectarian and caste differences among Hindus. It further excluded other minority religious and regional traditions. Even anti-Brahmanical religions such as Buddhism, Jainism and Sikhism were claimed to be part of the Hindu *rashtra*, or 'nation', on the grounds that they originated in India, whereas Islam and Christianity, which come from outside, were excluded. In the simplest terms, religion remained the dominant social bond that defined the characteristics of the nation. Nationalism in India did not find its justification in a rational societal conception, as was the case in Western Europe. Rather, the notion of *swaraj*, or political self-government, provided the legitimacy for the institution of the modern national state in India. By that time, the model of the sovereign national state had become an international norm.

Broadly speaking, the introduction of modern organizational structures and techniques, such as printing, the founding of a broad network of voluntary associations and the spread of modern-style education created a new public arena in Indian social life. The new institutional framework became an important resource for sustaining organized activity and promoting a new national consciousness. The Hindu reformers adopted modern organizational techniques that helped in creating a public arena for a Hindu nation. Further, the apotheosis of language, a socially standardized system of symbols, for administrative convenience or as a means of unifying state-wide communications generated religion-based linguistic nationalism. Print capitalism facilitated the historic formation of languages of everyday life based on the sacred languages of scriptures. Thus, Hindi, Urdu and Punjabi became the languages of sacred communication of Hinduism, Islam and Sikhism; this heightened communal consciousness. Finally, these religio-linguistic nationalisms laid the bases for national consciousness, which gave rise to the anti-imperialist national resistance. To sum up, the transformation in communication made possible a new phase in the development of nations. These developments in India provide a striking contrast to the universalist claim that the introduction of modern communications signifies the erosion of a religious world-view and societal transformation into secular culture.

2 The contradictory unity of the Indian state

India's complex and variegated social structure comprises large and distinctive religious, linguistic, regional, tribal and caste groups. It is natural for these diverse ethnic groups to assert their cultural identity. The three principal bases of identity assertions perceived as threats to the Indian nation are language, region and religion. Although the identities anchored to the first two are accepted as legitimate, as evidenced by the creation of administrative units based on them, religious identity assertions, particularly in conjunction with a geographical region, are regarded as posing a grave threat to India's political integrity. The Sikh demands for a separate state and the Muslim claims for autonomy in Kashmir are examples of two breakaway movements in India that have religious and territorial bases. However, current events in India reveal that the gravest threat to India's integrity is, in fact, posed by the extremist activities of the majority Hindu population.

As a prelude to the consideration of the emergence of the Sikh ethno-nationalist movement in the Indian Punjab, this chapter will examine the emergence of the radical Hindu political parties in the national politics of India. Close attention will be paid to the manner in which Hindu parties use religious symbolism in order to gain political power. The historical and sociological contexts of politics in India, and the political implications of Hinduism and the pattern of its interaction with politics will also be considered. Given the vast territorial, cultural and historical complexity of India, it would be misleading to examine the emergence of Hindu nationalism as a single phenomenon.

The aim is not to explain the phenomenon of religious nationalism in its full social and historical complexity. The discussion will hinge on those themes that are relevant to understanding the emergence of religious nationalism among the Sikhs of the Indian Punjab. In this manner, it is hoped to link the emergence of Sikh ethno-nationalism with the more general processes at work in Indian society. This chapter seeks to address the central question: why do religious identity assertions pose a grave threat to the Indian nation-state?

Religion remains deeply entrenched in the personal and social lives of all Indians. There is no indication of a decline in religion in everyday life. The performance and participation in rituals, religious festivals, religious observance, in fact, reflects a fresh religious fervour and vibrancy. Never before in Indian history have religious pilgrimages attracted such huge congregations as modern means of communication and transportation become widely available, new buildings for religious worship are appearing everywhere and religious books continue to outsell all others in India. The national television broadcast of seventy-eight serialized episodes of the Hindu epic *Ramayana*, between January 1987 and July 1988, marked a historical event in the history of Indian television. An estimated 80–100 million people watched the series (Lutgendorf 1990: 136), the largest audience ever. If the much-noted religious renaissance in India is not merely a reassertion of religious piety, is it possibly what scholars refer to as reassertion of nationalism rather than religion? What factors account for the emergence of religion as a crucial element in the politics of contemporary India? In what way is the nature of communities related to religion? What are the key features of religious nationalist movements?

This chapter is organized into five sections. The introductory section identifies the religious minorities in India. The second section examines the central cultural beliefs of Indian civilization. The third section provides an account of the distinctive nature and development of Indian nationalism, followed by an examination of the interplay between religion and modern democratic institutions in India. The fourth section considers the emerging patterns of religion and politics in India and the resurgence of religious nationalism. The last section looks into the question of what explains the resurgence of this form of religious nationalism at this historical moment.

Who are the religious minorities in India?

According to the 1981 census, Hindus made up 82.60 per cent (549.8 million), Muslims 11.4 per cent (75.5 million), Christians 2.4 per cent (16.2 million), Sikhs 2 per cent (13.1 million), and Buddhists and Jains 1.2 per cent (7.9 million) of the total population in India. However, none of the religious groups in India is cohesive. They are deeply divided into caste, regional, linguistic, urban–rural and socio-economic categories.

India is the third largest Muslim country in the world. The Muslims in India have historically been a minority, even at the height of Mogul rule. The Muslims in India are geographically dispersed and form a majority only in the state of Jammu and Kashmir, where they form 64.2 per cent and the Hindus 32.3 per cent of the total population. The picturesque Kashmir valley has been the centre of a violent irredentism movement since the early 1980s. The remaining bulk of the Muslim population is concentrated in selected urban centres in North India. The striking feature of the minority Muslim population in India is that they are mainly converts from the disadvantaged low Hindu castes. The Muslim masses are not legatees of centuries of political dominance exercised by a small Islamic élite whose culture was largely Persian.

As Hindu–Muslim rivalries across the borders of India and Pakistan remain unabated, Hindu radicals persistently impugn the loyalty of India's Muslim minorities.

India's 13.1 million Sikhs form a majority of 60.8 per cent in the state of Punjab. The Sikhs attained a majority as a result of massive reorganization of the territorial boundaries of Punjab, first in 1947 and again in 1966. The pre-partition Punjab was 51 per cent Muslim, 35 per cent Hindu and 12 per cent Sikh. The partition of the subcontinent into two sovereign states, India and Pakistan, led to the largest transfer of population in history. It resulted in the massacre of nearly a million people, and over 13 million crossed the borders of the newly formed states. The partition of 1947 witnessed the migration of Muslims out of the Indian side and the movement of Hindus and Sikhs out of the Pakistani side. In 1951, refugees from Pakistan made up one-fifth of the total population of Indian Punjab. The post-partition Punjab was 64 per cent Hindu, 33 per cent Sikh and 2 per cent Muslim (1961 Census). The 1971 census figures represented 60 per cent Sikhs, 38 per cent Hindu and only 1 per cent Muslim (Roach 1986: 107).

The Sikhs form a distinctive diaspora within India as well as abroad. In 1971, when the Sikhs constituted 1.9 per cent of the total population of India, more than 20 per cent of the Sikhs were living outside Punjab (Grewal 1990: 210). By 1981, 2.8 million Sikhs, more than one-fifth of the population, lived in other parts of India (Roach 1986: 108). The Sikh diaspora is scattered worldwide. At present, a third of the total Sikh population lives outside Punjab, and over a million live outside India. The overseas migration was largely impelled by British recruitment, which initially made migration to the British empire accessible. The relation between transnational migration and nationalism and the question why transnational migration reinforces religious and nationalist identities will be discussed in Chapter 5.

Christians form a majority in India's north-eastern states of Nagaland, Meghalya and Mizoram (Table 2.1). These three states are small, and India's Christians are less cohesive and are not so politically vocal. Indian Christians are mainly converts from low Hindu castes or tribes. They usually speak the language of the region in which they live. The tribal population in India is geographically concentrated, overwhelmingly rural, disadvantaged and impoverished. The scheduled castes or the untouchables form 15–25 per cent of the Indian population. The scheduled castes in India form a minority by virtue of their low social status, their economic situation and the discrimination to which they are subjected by the dominant castes. None of India's several thousand castes is in the majority in any region. Therefore, they do not identify themselves with any homeland.

Religion and culture in India

The framework for explaining the current phase of communal politics in India since the late 1970s, which is developed here, draws on the pattern of

Table 2.1 States where national religious minorities are a majority: classification of population by religion and as a percentage of total population of the state

	Hindus	*Muslims*	*Christians*	*Sikhs*
Jammu and Kashmir	32.3	64.2	0.1	2.2
Punjab	36.9	1.0	1.1	60.7
Nagaland	14.3	1.5	80.2	0.1
Meghalya	18.0	3.1	52.6	0.1
Mizoram	7.1	0.4	83.9	–
India	82.6	11.4	2.4	2.0

Source: Census of India, 1981

India's distinctive historical and social experience. The abstraction of religious experience from all other forms of experience, although recent, is particular to the history of the West. This profound transformation in the belief system is usually linked to industrialization, modern science and the growth of the nation-state; it is also linked to the distinct nature of the Christian belief system, and the distinct social origins and spread of Christianity. This constitutes a central theme of the Western intellectual tradition.

Systems of life and thought rooted in religious traditions predispose a society towards a certain pattern of relationship between religion and politics. These metaphysical positions have critical implications for modern politics because they regulate social life and patterns of behaviour. The following discussion examines the distinctive characteristics of the traditional belief system in India. Ainslie T. Embree, a distinguished historian from South Asia, in his book *Utopias in Conflict: Religion and Nationalism in Modern India* (1990) identifies five fundamental concepts and values that underlie classical Indian religious thought. These principles, or cosmological understandings, form the basis of the Indian belief system and social practices. They are (1) the concept of time, (2) karma, (3) rebirth, (4) dharma and (5) truth. Further, by tracing their relationship to the social and political sphere some general inferences may be drawn.

Before we begin an appraisal of these cosmological principles, it may be appropriate to emphasize the limited and specific scope of this discussion. These complex cosmological principles are derived from the great ancient Vedic epics, *Mahabharata* and *Ramayana*, written in the Sanskrit language. The limitations of conveying their meaning in non-Indian languages must not be underestimated. Moreover, there are critical modifications of a cosmological principle articulated in ancient epics and their interpretation and significance in actual social practices. The symbolic meaning as a cultural idiom varies significantly according to local, regional and cultural practices. These are to be regarded as generalizations that allow the possibility of exception to every generalization. Moreover, the religious world-view displays significant regional and cultural diversity and has been subjected to historical change and alteration. Even so, only a small section of the population may subscribe to this uniform religious experience. Contrary to Embree's claim that these principles are shared by all religious communities in the Indian subcontinent, I will adopt the view that these world-views are shared by those religious traditions whose ancestral roots are in the Indic philosophical tradition, such as the Buddhists, the Jains and the Sikhs, and do not incorporate Christians and Muslims as Embree seems to suggest. Bearing in mind the above qualifications, the following analysis is useful for identifying the core cosmological principles and values that provide meaning to human existence in India.

The concept of time

Indian civilization is characterized by the theory of cycles or recurring periods of creation and destruction. The following are the chief characteristics of the classical Indian cyclical conception of time. First, time moves in concentric cycles. Each world system makes one complete cycle, or a mythic era, or *'yuga'*, that is of immense duration spanning 300 million years. Humanity at present lives in the darkest of all eras, or *'Kaliyuga'*. The present world system was 'created out of the combination of matter and spirit by means of the action of *maya*, the illusory cosmic energy of Brahma the creator. The universal dissolution and destruction comes about when Brahma vanishes into himself' (Smith 1966: 5). Second, this process of cyclical regeneration is eternal. This notion of time as infinite is vitally different from the Hebraic concept of time as a linear progression that has a beginning and an end. It is characterized by incessant repetition of cycles, each of vast duration. The third characteristic is the all-embracing nature of Indian time. There is a lack of demarcation between humanity and nature, and between humanity and the Divine. In other words, Divine history and human history fall along the same continuum.

The conception of time taken by religion has vital implications for the view of history held by its constituents. The Indian conception of time has a tremendous, limitless quality that has enormous implications for understanding the place of humanity in the cosmos. The endless, cyclical movement of time signifies the process of perpetual renewal and decay of the universe. The vastness of the cosmic process makes valuation of the existence of the universe or of human involvement appear trifling. Furthermore, no event is unique, no moment is final.

Those in the conservative tradition interpret this notion of time to explain what they believe to be the lack of historical awareness among Indians. Ainslie T. Embree points out, 'nor is there likelihood of people taking too seriously their achievements in constructing political institutions. There is not likely to be, in short, the kind of attention to political history that has been common in the Western world and in China' (Embree 1990: 28). This view that Indians lack a sense of history is well established among Indological experts. This observation is derived from another aspect of Sanskrit literature that, although it includes historical writing *(itihasa)*, affirms the notion that all forms of knowledge are derived from the Vedas, which transcend time and history. Further, this perspective holds that human history is metaphysically regarded as a lower level of experience in the Indic tradition. This is based on the notion that the essential self of man is never involved in the affairs of this natural world of experience. Donald Smith (1966) once said, 'Hinduism's concern with political institutions and the course of human history is thus at most a secondary concern. The ultimate philosophical and religious values of Hinduism do not require a Hindu state, or any particular kind of political structure, for that matter' (Smith 1966: 5–6).

Peter van Veer in his book *Religion and Nationalism: Hindus and Muslims in India* (1994) has challenged the view that the propensity to avoid historical referentiality is an indication of the absence of historical awareness. Peter van der Veer contends that this conception of time, in fact, relegates history to a lower level of reality, such that history is ultimately not important. He points out, 'Religious discourse tends either to deny historical change or else to prove its ultimate irrelevance....Religious nationalism combines this antihistorical feature of religious discourse with an empiricist search for "facts" that has been highly influenced by orientalism' (Van der Veer 1994: xii). He contends that the Hindu nationalist interpretation of Indian history, deeply rooted in religious discourse on change and time, attempts to reconcile the position of Hindu religion on history with the modern need for historical facts. He argues that, on the one hand, Hindu nationalist discourse denies evidence of historical change in its paradoxical need to create an imagined, perennial nation, existing beyond time and history; on the other hand, Hindu nationalist narrative is characterized by a modern, empirical search for historical facts and selection of archaeological data that, in turn, are heavily influenced by orientalist historiography.

No other historical moment could be more appropriate for falsifying the conservative perspective discussed above. The current attempts of Hindu nationalists to reinterpret and reconcile the Hindu metaphysical position on time in order to reinterpret Indian history and impart real meaning to the world emphasize this point. Moreover, these attempts by the Hindu nationalists intensify religious strife in India. I propose to make two qualifications to van der Veer's persuasive explanation of the Indian view of history. First, other religious traditions in India, such as those of the Sikhs and the Buddhists, share with Hinduism a similar metaphysical position about time. But in practice, the Buddhists and the Sikhs show a remarkable concern for the course of human history. Moreover, in contrast to Hinduism, both these traditions have as their founders historical figures who are not shadowy mythological figures. The Sikhs regard these recent efforts by the Hindu extremists as an imitation and influence of the Sikh cultural conceptions about the Hindu faith. In India, the historical process of reformulating metaphysical conceptions has been influenced strongly by the historical experience of colonialism and by mainstream Western historiography

The European influence is evident in the use of calendars in India. Calendars perform significant social and ritual functions and define religious identities. The West-European calendar is recognized as the official calendar by the government of India. However, religious festivals and auspicious occasions are calculated from indigenous Indian religious calendars, both by the Hindus and by the Sikhs. The usage of dual calendars, both Indian and European, varies significantly from urban to rural areas and the subordinate sections of the population.

The discussion so far, along with the empirical analysis considered, contests Kedourie's claim that 'history as a distinct mode of thought arose in Europe in the seventeenth century out of the practical preoccupation's of religious and political polemic in which men appealed to the past in order to attack or defend an institution or a dogma' (Kedourie 1970: 35). Clearly, an attempt to resurrect a past in order to invoke collective identity is not entirely unique to European history, as evidence of religious discourse on history in the Indic tradition illustrates. Even so, the hallmark of the European seventeenth century history was that it drove a wedge between cosmology and history, a fundamental cultural conception that fused the origins of the world with that of mankind. From this sprang the modern requirement for the search for historical facts. The success of Hindu nationalists in combining the indigenous religious discourse on change and time with the Western empiricist search for facts was noted early in this account.

However, this does not necessarily mean that a religion which regards history as unreal, or if real ultimately unimportant, will be less concerned with securing or maintaining temporal power, and this undermines Donald Smith's (1966) theory of history that greater concern with the course of history tends to increase a religion's involvement in politics.

Karma

Karma is another key concept shared by Indic cultural traditions. Karma is the inexorable law of cause and effect. Karma literally means action; it implies the notion that human actions have inescapable consequences. Every action, be it mental or physical, good or bad, bears appropriate result. An individual's destiny in the succeeding life will be the moral consequence of deeds performed in this life. To go on a pilgrimage *(tirtha-yatra)* to important sacred centres, particularly on auspicious occasions, such as bathing festivals *(kumbh melas)*, is scripturally recommended karma. A *tirtha* is a crossing place on a river, a metaphor for a place to cross over to the other world of ancestors and gods. Sanskrit texts mention seven cities that grant release. These holy cities are Banaras, Kanti, Hardwar, Ayodhya, Dwarka, Mathura and Ujjain. In India the practice of pilgrimage is common among Jains, Buddhists, Sikhs, Muslims and Hindus. The important role of the sacred centres, as symbolic foci of religious identities and in the transmission of religious identities, reflects why control over sacred sites is so crucial in religious nationalism. The attempts made by the state to control Sikh religious centres, or *gurudwaras*, especially the Golden Temple at Amritsar, is the subject of Chapters 3 and 4.

Dharma

Dharma is a complex Sanskrit term implying diverse meanings. In essence, it refers to cosmological, ethical, social and legal principles that provide the basis of cosmic moral social order, which is believed to sustain the universe. The social significance of this fundamental concept is its manifestation in the structure of social relationships known as caste. In the social context, it refers to a set of obligations, an appropriate mode of conduct defined by birth – the fundamental fact of human existence. This set of duties is determined by the social status (*varna*), the stage of life (*ashrama*) and the qualities of inborn nature (*guna*). Furthermore, in classical Hindu social thought, the religio-political system is integrated; each of the economic and political roles in society has its set of moral responsibilities or dharma. For instance, the prime duty of the king is to uphold the dharma of the social whole. This was enunciated by the Hindu political theorist Kautilya in *Arthsastra* in the fourth century BC.

Other religious traditions in India interpret the Hindu concept of dharma differently. The Buddhists acknowledge dharma (*dhamma* in Pali) as the foundation of the universe; *dhamma* as a cosmic law is not linked with belief in the supernatural but affirms non-violence (*ahimsa*) and compassion as supreme values. In the Jain tradition, the core of dharma is formed by the notion of non-violence (*ahimsa*). It also connotes a spatial category – an eternal respect for the movement of life. This explains the belief that every care and precaution must be taken to preserve all forms of life substance – earth, water and wind. The Sikhs refer to the term *dharam* to describe their way of life, which is the same for all Sikhs, irrespective of differences in their social situation. Dharma, or moral duty, is the first of the five domains (*khanda*) that constitute life space. The others include the domains of spiritual knowledge, human effort, divine benevolence and truth. The Sikh faith sanctions sacrifice in defence of dharma. The small sword carried by some Sikhs symbolizes a form of defence of dharma.

Belief in rebirth or reincarnation

The concept of rebirth is associated with the cyclical conception of time and the belief in karma. Human deeds cannot find fruition in one life. Rebirth is part of an endless chain of existence, of transformation and continuity, determined by karma. It is a privilege to be born a human being because it is the only opportunity to attain liberation from the cycle of reincarnation. The essential self in man (*atman*, also referred to as soul) and the ultimate Reality are one. Liberation from the cycle of rebirths is attained through an individual's complete realization of the self with the Supreme Being. The highest spiritual goal is escape from the cycle of history. Spiritual liberation (*moksha*) pertains to man's essential self, the higher level of reality, whereas the three key ends of man – the expression of man's natural instincts (kama), material prosperity (artha) and the ethical life (dharma), pertain to the empirical, lower life. It is worth noting that a worldly concern such as politics pertains to lower life.

The concept of truth

Indian thought acknowledges the existence of many levels of truth, although all truth is one. This is based on the assumption that all human beings do not possess an equal moral, spiritual, mental or physical ability to perceive truth. Moreover, the availability of truth is determined by the social position of the individual. The concept of truth has frequently been fused with the notion of toleration, the supposedly unique characteristic of Indian civilization, just as the underlying conception of hierarchy marks the concept of truth. Similarly, all social practices are encapsulated within a Hindu cosmological realm, but in a hierarchical arrangement, some gaining a superior and others an inferior position.

Ainslie Embree (1990) maintains that these fundamental values interweave with each other producing an unchanging pattern of Indian life. This characterizes the unique, self-contained universe of Indian civilization. Embree describes three historical encounters of Indian civilization with alien values and institutions. These great historical moments in Indian history are, first, the coming of Islam to India throughout the eighth to twelfth centuries; second, the establishment of political power by the Portuguese in the sixteenth century; and, third, the eighteenth century, when the East India Company began to exercise rule. Embree concludes his examination by suggesting that despite these powerful foreign influences there is little evidence of absorption or synthesis of the central core of the indigenous religious and cultural tradition. Thus, Embree presents an argument on the unyielding response of Indian civilization and the inflexible, uniform nature of its systems of belief.

The discussion on the changing conception of time and history reveals the fluid nature of these cultural conceptions. In fact, these paradigms were formulated at a particular historical moment and the variations in these paradigms signify periods of historic and social change. The eminent Indian historian Romila Thapar suggested that there is no standard original version of the great Vedic epic *Ramayana* (Gopal 1991: 141–63).[1] It has an uncertain origin as an oral form of narrative. It was altered and refashioned several times. She maintains that the transformation of the different variations is indicative of historical and social change. She argues that texts such as the *Ramayana* had a much more open method of preservation. Its oral memorization did not preclude changes and later interpolations such as perorations on good government and the observance of the rules of dharma.

Romila Thapar's persuasive historical perspective on *Rama-katha*, the story of Rama, suggests that a systematic standard version – the north Indian, Hindu Vaishnava version – of the epic is very recent. This has been exacerbated through the powerful government-run medium of television, which has elevated this uniform version to a national status. Its usage has been moulded to contemporary tastes and values, confirming Romila Thapar's view on the changes interpolated in the epics, at specific historical moments, appropriate to the particular social requirements and changing values in society.

Bearing in mind the qualifications noted earlier, Embree's analysis is useful for identifying the core cosmological principles and values that provide meaning to human existence in India. Furthermore, by tracing their relationship to the social and political sphere some general inferences may be drawn. The discussion so far points to the holistic, all-embracing character of the Indian world-view. In the voluminous discourse of Indian religious tradition the religious domain encompasses and is superior to all other domains of life. The claim that this is particular to Indian civilization may not be historically valid. The religious world-view displays significant regional and cultural diversity and has been subjected to historical change and alteration. The questions that emerge are: What is the interplay between religion and modern democratic institutions? What aspects reinforce religious discourse with the political discourse? Where and how do politics and religion meet?

Interplay between religion and modern democratic institutions

Having provided a rough picture of the context of cultural beliefs and practices, we are now ready to consider the historical context in which religion and politics have colluded in India. An analysis of the relationships between religion and politics in India over the past two centuries would have to take into account phenomena of great diversity and complexity. Part of this subject would deal with an examination of the role of the nationalist movement in transmitting religious identities. Another important aspect would involve a closer examination of the political system – the various legal and constitutional structures that resulted because of the success of the nationalist movement. Religious loyalties would have to be examined as a factor in political behaviour, especially during elections and the legislative procedure.

The anti-colonial nationalist movement and the struggle for India's independence

The sanguinary division of the imperial state of British India into the national states of India, Pakistan and Bangladesh heralded the creation of parliamentary democracy in South Asia. The creation of Pakistan as a homeland for Indian Muslims is a demonstration of how the vocabulary of political and social discourse in the subcontinent is rooted in religion. Since the beginning of modern politics in India, in the nineteenth century, the narrative of the nation has been derived from religious identification. This is true for all religious communities in India – the Hindus, the Muslims, the Sikhs and the Buddhists. This characteristic of Indian nationalism had fateful political consequences.

The antipathy that developed between Hindus and Muslims as nationalism gained momentum is vital for understanding the nature of communal politics in India. Central to the anti-colonial nationalist movement was the creation of a specific notion of 'India – the nation'. For most of its history, India was not governed by a single centralized monarchy; instead, there were numerous small princedoms. This made it possible for Muslim rulers from Central Asia and Persia, including the Mogul dynasties that ruled from the sixteenth to the nineteenth centuries, to establish great empires by forming alliances with local kings.

The dominant version of Indian nationalism, articulated by leaders of the Indian National Congress, imagined an Indian nation based on a shared ethnic culture. From its very beginning, the discourse on the Indian nation-state corresponded with discourse on the majority Hindu religious tradition, which was believed to be marked by a tolerant, indigenous religious pluralism. Therefore, one religion formed the basis of national identity. The national anthem, *Bande Mataram* (Hail mother), was selected by the Indian National Congress, despite the poem's strong Hindu emphasis. Indian nationalism is suffused with images that glorify the Hindu Indian past. I will now consider how this notion of India, enunciated by the Hindu nationalists, was a reflection of the nineteenth century misunderstanding about the attitude of the Hindu religion towards other religious faiths.

The question of Hindu tolerance?

The nineteenth century view that Indian civilization was characterized by a tolerant spirituality represents a classic orientalist reading of Indian religion. Influenced by the Enlightenment and seeking the roots of Western civilization in the Vedic scriptures, orientalist historiography introduced the methods and concepts of modern science for interpreting India's past. Sir William Jones discovered the affiliation between Greek, Latin and Sanskrit. This interpretation of early Indian society as being essentially 'pluralist' and 'tolerant' promotes a specific view of religion as a universal characteristic of one great Indian spirituality. Different religions are then seen as manifestations of this universal Indian spirituality. The notion of religion as a spiritual experience and the different religious communities that make up the Indian nation are refractions of one supreme universal Indian spirituality. This unifying essence, which marks the spirit of India, is, however, equated with Hinduism and is regarded as a central feature of the Hindu religion.

This pervasive understanding of Hindu tolerance is a product of a specific orientalist history of ideas, which embrace the older notions of Hinduism as an inclusive religion. As Paul Hacker, an eminent Indologist, observes, 'tolerance' is a weak term for what he refers to as Hindu 'inclusiveness'. The significance of this inclusivist tendency lies in its purpose as a hermeneutic device to serve nineteenth- and twentieth-century social and political circumstances. This view was promoted largely by the great German philosophers and by the Indian nationalists. It laid the foundation for the Hindu nationalist interpretation of Indian history. Furthermore, this scholarly discourse portrays Hinduism as a civilization rather than a religion. This broad definition transcends doctrinal, regional and organizational differences.

This view was espoused by Mahatma Gandhi, the great ideologue of Indian nationalism. His understanding of the universal morality of the Hindu scriptures was based on an orientalist reading. He promulgated the Bhagwad Gita as the fundamental scripture of modern Hinduism. His political style successfully appropriated Hindu ethical values, such as those he referred to as *satyagraha* (the force of truth) and *ahimsa* (non-violence) in situations of political conflict. His particular genius lay in widening the nationalist appeal beyond its sectarian origins. This allowed self-identification of a large section of the Indian population. Mahatma Gandhi endorsed the political ideal of *ramrajya*, the social order of the divine Hindu king Lord Rama, the hero of the Hindu epic *Ramayana*, in the epic city of Ayodhya. Gandhi's tolerant and pluralistic version, cast in the idiom of Hindu spirituality, encompassed different religious traditions. This inclusivist tendency is in turn reflected in modern Hindu nationalism, which incorporates Indians of different faiths – Jains, Buddhists and Sikhs into Hinduism. This is presented as the 'tolerance' that characterizes Hinduism. Yet in practice religious differences are not tolerated.

It was precisely Mahatma Gandhi's inclusivist Hindu tolerance that alienated the Muslim League. On the one hand, it was considered legitimate by leaders of the Indian National Congress to impart a Hindu coloration to Indian nationalism. On the other hand, they denied a similar possibility of a fusion of personal identity with a cultural core to other religious communities. They rejected the idea that Muslims found their identity through membership of a religious community. The two-nation theory, articulated by M. A. Jinnah, suggested that the Muslims and the Hindus were separate nations. This became the ideological basis for the demand for Pakistan and offered the Muslims the possibility of identifying socio-religious community with nationality.

Therefore, the claim that religious strife was a creation of imperialism had fateful consequences. Gandhi's assassination in 1948 for his alleged accommodation of the Muslims by a former member of Rashtriya Swayamsevak Sangh (RSS),[2] a radical Hindu organization, is the most startling example of what is now referred to as the Hindu backlash phenomenon in modern Indian politics. Therefore, the dominant Indian nationalist leaders rejected the idea that religious nationalism was a component of the fabric of Indian culture and historical experience. The question of Hindu tolerance was, therefore, more than an academic discussion of the nature of a religious world-view; momentous political issues concerning the rights of minorities were obscured by the assertion that Hinduism was uniquely tolerant and willing to absorb other systems into itself (Embree 1990: 23).

Association between group identity and political power

What is meant by representative government in the Indian context?

In the preceding section we saw how the emphasis on tolerance of Indian *vis-à-vis* Hindu civilization was a central component of Indian nationalism. The central ideological commitment and legacy of the anti-colonial nationalist movement was the notion of secularism, which corresponded with the discourse on Hindu spirituality and tolerance. That national identity transcended religious identity was the key element in the ideology of the Indian National Congress. In their attempt to create a unifying ideology they denied that religious differences were a source of conflict. We shall now consider how this idea of a secular, tolerant India, which was central to the Indian nationalist movement, was reflected in the legal and political structure of independent India.

The Indian state was to be religiously neutral. The state would not discriminate on the basis of religion. The separation between the church and state in no way denied the significance of religion for society. Religion played, and continues to play, a significant social and political role. The state was to represent different communities in democratic institutions, such as the legal system and the educational system. On the one hand, the Indian constitution gives its citizens the constitutional right to profess and practice their religion. On the other hand, Article 25 of the Indian constitution states that reference to Hindus or to Hindu religious institutions should be construed as incorporating persons professing the Buddhist, Jain or Sikh religions. Not surprisingly, the minorities have expressed apprehension on the arbitrary manner in which they are defined as Hindus under Article 25 of the constitution. In January 1984, the Akali Dal led a campaign during which this portion of the constitution was burnt. They alleged that the cultural domination of the numerically dominant Hindu majority is manifested in politics in India.

The nature of political representation

The form of representative government was first instituted in India in 1909 through the Morley Minto reforms. This preceded a long struggle between the Muslim leadership, who demanded separate electorates to ensure that the Muslims shared the power in the new government, and the Congress

Party. Leaders of the Indian National Congress insisted on the establishment of a representative government based on the Western model, with the will of the numerical majority being the will of the people. This suited the Hindu leadership, as decisions expressed through the legislature would be those of the majority Hindu voters. Under the Morley Minto reforms, separate electorates were established for Muslims and subsequently for Sikhs, scheduled castes, Anglo-Indians and other minority groups. The interests of the minorities could be safeguarded by this constitutional device, which recognized a religious community as a separate political unit. The concept that the groups have rights which cannot be contested by the decision of majority voters as expressed through the legislature expresses the understanding that the nation is an aggregate of groups and not individuals.

Since the attainment of independence in 1947, the government of India, in the constituent assembly, decided to abandon separate electorates and the reservation of seats in legislatures for religious minorities. Reserved constituencies were reallocated to other minorities, such as the scheduled castes and tribes. This antagonized the Sikhs, who had once been the beneficiaries of these constituencies. The implications of the policy of proportional recruitment were strikingly evident in the armed forces, where Sikhs constituted 15 per cent of the military, although they made up just 2 per cent of the total population of India.

Political representation for religious minorities calls into question certain assumptions of democratic representation. The theory of democratic representation assumes that the elected legislators will serve all of their constituents impartially. Since religious minorities in India are not in a position to mobilize a majority of voters, the present imperfect state of India's secularity does not allow some legitimate interests and grievances of minority groups to be voiced adequately.

In the 1950s Indian politics was driven by the movement of linguistic groups seeking statehood. This resulted in a massive territorial reorganization of India's internal political structure in 1956. The formation of separate states transformed many linguistic minorities into majorities. States were established for all linguistic groups listed in schedule eight of the constitution, with the exception of Punjabi, Sindhi and Urdu speakers. The possibility of a Punjabi-speaking state was denied because of the fear that Sikhs would form a majority in that state. This resulted in a 10-year-long struggle by the Sikhs, which finally culminated in the linguistic reorganization of Punjab in November 1966.

So far I have made some general observations about one category of response of Hinduism to the pressures historically associated with the social and political changes generated by the British Raj. This response was institutionally represented by India's Congress party, which has been the major force in the politics of post-independence India. The affinity between the Hindus and the Congress Party existed throughout the 1950s and 1960s, and, in fact, exists even today. This point is forcefully illustrated in an editorial in one of the leading English newspapers after the assassination of Mrs Gandhi on 31 October 1984, 'every time the minorities become assertive, Hindus tend to consolidate behind the Congress despite its professed commitment to secular values' (Graham 1990: 255–56). Bruce Graham, in his book *Hindu Nationalism and Indian Politics* (1990: 255), has argued against the widely held view that competing loyalties of caste, sect, dialect, region and language prevented the Hindus from acting as a political community. Against this he maintains that Hindus, and particularly those in the northern states, did indeed see themselves as a political community but they also saw the Congress Party rather than any one of the Hindu nationalist parties as their principal defender.

The resurgence of religious nationalism in contemporary India

Let us now turn to the second category of response, represented by the Hindu radical right. Bruce Graham (1990) has examined the factors that prevented the establishment of the Hindu political right as the party of the numerically dominant Hindu community in the 1950s and 1960s. He focuses on the emergence and growth of the Bharatiya Jana Sangh (Indian People's Party, BJS), the most robust of the first generation of Hindu nationalist parties. He concludes that the BJS restricted itself to the north Indian brand of Hindu nationalism and failed to transcend the limited appeal of its founding doctrines to broaden its electoral constituency. Graham suggests that in order to develop as a significant force in national politics, the Hindu radical right will have to become more democratic and moderate. The 1980s national politics in India is witnessing precisely this expansion of the religious right. The phase of communal politics in contemporary India is marked by the incredible electoral success of the Hindu radical right, which is close to outflanking the ruling Congress party for the first time in the history of India. Although there is nothing new in the response of the Hindu radical right, the novelty is in its striking success in Indian electoral politics. I shall now consider the philosophy, programme and tactics used by the Hindu radical right in achieving success in electoral politics.

The Bharatiya Janata Party (Indian People's Party, or BJP) was formed in April 1990 and is probably the largest religious nationalist movement in the world. It has an alliance with three other Hindu nationalist organizations, the Vishva Hindu Parishad (World Hindu Council, or VHP), largely comprising religious leaders, the Shiv-Sena, a fanatic Hindu political party, powerful in Bombay, and the Rashtriya Swayamsevak Sangh (National Volunteer Organization, or RSS), a militant youth organization. The VHP was founded in 1964 by the leaders of a Hindu missionary sect and at first was an organization representing marginal religious groups. Only in the 1980s was it transformed into a political organization. It offers connections with religious groups and a network of monastic holy men and other workers in other Hindu political parties. The VHP is probably the strongest transnational movement among Hindus in the world.

The success of the BJP is shown by the number of seats won in the past three general elections: rising from two seats in the Indian parliament in the election of 1984 to 119 out of a total of 545 seats in 1991. It has become the largest opposition party in India. In the recent assembly elections in March 1995, the BJP has established the government in four states and accounts for 107 of the 545 Lok Sabha seats. It is the main opposition party in five other state legislatures, accounting for half of the country's population. The formidable Shiv-Sena–BJP coalition that has emerged in the recent state elections in Maharashtra brought an end to 35 years of uninterrupted rule by the Congress (I) party. Shiv-Sena won nearly half of its seats in Bombay, India's most liberal and cosmopolitan city. The Shiv-Sena derives its name from Shivaji, a seventeenth-century Hindu king of the Marathas from Maharashtra who fought valiantly against the Mogul invaders. Bal Thackeray, the leader of the Shiv-Sena, claimed in an interview that the mobs that attacked the Muslims in Bombay were under his control and that if Muslims 'behaved like Jews in Nazi Germany', there would be 'nothing wrong if they are treated as Jews were in Germany'.

The sharp regional contrasts in India apply to modern electoral politics as well. The overwhelming bulk of the BJP support has, so far, come from the north and west of India, largely Hindi-speaking states. 'Of the BJP members of the Indian parliament chosen in the last election, more than 90 per cent came from just eight states and union territories in the north and west of India (more than 40 per cent from one state – the large Uttar Pradesh alone)' (Sen 1993: 9). Observers of modern electoral politics explain these regional contrasts with regard to the regional variation in the historical experience. It is argued that the Mogul empire never extended to the south and was relatively weak in the east. By contrast, the Hindu rulers in the north and west persistently waged battles against the Mogul empire.

Recent interviews given by the BJP leaders indicate that the BJP is bracing itself for the election year by shedding its traditional image – with emphasis purely on *hindutva*. It wants to broaden its political constituency 'by fighting off casteism, pseudo-secularism, communism, corruption and the criminalisation of politics' (*India Today*, 30 April, 1995).

The Hindu radical right maintains that the Hindus have lived through dark ages for a very long time. The Turkic invaders dominated the political system for 500 years and brought Islamic religion and Persian culture into India. Subsequently, the British established political power in the nineteenth century, and India continues to be colonized by the English-educated establishment, or '*bhadralok*'. It holds that the Hindu ancestral faith is compatible with modern values and ideologies. It plans to modernize Indian society; this, however, they claim will be done in a true 'Hindu spirit' rather than by values and programmes that are Western imports.

The BJP has declared *hindutva* as its ideology. The term *hindutva* is central to their claims that religion is the defining characteristic of the Indian nation. V. D. Savarkar, leader of the Hindu Mahasabha, the most important Hindu nationalist party before independence, advanced the term *hindutva*, which equates religious and national identities. According to this Hindu *rashtra*, or 'Hindu nation' theory, Indian culture has its roots in the Hindu past. 'India is God's chosen land; it's the abode of Hindus.'[3] Hence, the ethical and spiritual values of all Indians who have ancestral roots in India derive from the Hindu culture. In essence all Indians are Hindus. Irrespective of their mode of worship, Christians and Muslims are culturally Hindus. Hindu revivalists seek to incorporate Indians of various faiths into Hinduism. The notion that the Indian nation is the heir to Hindu civilization is a perpetuation of the politics of inclusion discussed in the previous section. On 11 December 1995 the Supreme Court of India passed a landmark verdict on whether or not an appeal on votes based on *hindutva* was permissible in election campaigns. The apex court's judgement was particularly significant as it came virtually on the eve of the general elections in India. The court endorsed the use of the term *hindutva* on the grounds that *hindutva* was a broad philosophical term synonymous with 'Indianization'. The Supreme Court observed that unlike the credal religions, Hinduism does not claim any one prophet, nor does it subscribe to any specific dogmas, or a central authority, or organization. The court's interpretation of *hindutva* has given an impetus to the *hindutva* brigade of the BJP and the Shiv-Sena and has significant electoral implications. L. K. Advani, the party chief of BJP, observed, 'The judgement is a seal of judicial imprimatur to the BJP's ideology of *hindutva*. The BJP believes India is one country and that Indians are one people. We hold that the basis of this unity is our ancient culture. For us this nationalism is not just a geographical or political concept. It is essentially a cultural concept. Whether you call it Hindutva or Bharatiyata or Indianness, the nomenclature does not matter. It is all the same.'[4] The Supreme Court verdict has raised fears that the forthcoming election campaign will witness more communal vitriol and will encourage the use of religion in politics.

Not surprisingly, over the last few years the term *hindutva* has evolved a distinct anti-minorities connotation. By defining other religious faiths, such as the Sikhs, the Buddhists and the Jains, as part of the all-embracing Hindu civilization, they seek to incorporate them within the majoritarian Hindu fold. They claim that Muslims and Christians should accept that they are, in fact, converted Hindus and redeem themselves by joining the Hindu fold. They endorse the movement for the reconversion of Muslims and Christians and for the Hinduization of tribes. The VHP has consistently worked to draw the tribals and untouchables into the Hindu fold. The VHP blames the conversion to Christianity of tribal north-eastern parts of India by Christian missionaries as the cause of insurgency in those areas. It is perhaps worth noting that B. D. Ambedkar had rejected somewhat similar attempts made by Gandhi to improve the status of scheduled castes within the framework of Hinduism.

Another key feature of the radical Hindu right is the assertion of Hindu solidarity. By stressing the solidarity of 'one caste' (*ek jat*) of coreligionists, Hindu nationalists attempt to homogenize themselves against 'other castes', such as the Muslims, the Christians, the Europeans, who they allege pose a grave threat to the survival of Mother India (*Bharat Mata*). Therefore, the Hindu attitude of religious exclusiveness is partly rooted in the traditional social pattern of group exclusiveness, i.e. caste. This attitude of group exclusiveness is legitimized by Hindu religious beliefs. The Hindu nationalists claim that concessions being made to the minority groups threaten the Hindu majority and they seek to redress this imbalance. Crucial to the militant Hindu programme is the demand for a universal civil code that would apply Hindu traditional institutions of family and law to all Indians, including the Muslims. They also demand compulsory national Hindu holidays.

Centres of worship are the foci of religious identities. The Hindu nationalist parties have launched a campaign to reconstitute the sacred space through contests over sacred sites. Referring to the Ayodhya issue, Peter van der Veer has argued that the VHP gained momentum through the use of religious discourse and practice of mass ritual action in the political arena. The centre of the dispute was Babri Masjid, a mosque built by a lieutenant in the army of Emperor Babar, founder of the Mogul dynasty in 1526, in the North Indian pilgrim centre of Ayodhya, the capital of Lord Rama. Its symbolic significance is attested by the fact that the site of the mosque is alleged to be the birthplace of Lord Rama. The campaign consisted of religious processions (*yatras*). A rally organized by the VHP and the BJP resulted in the demolition of this ancient edifice on 6 December 1992. The triumphant aftermath of the Hindu nationalists led to the outbreak of violence in which over 300 people lost their lives. The broadcasting of the *Ramayana* in the form of a serial on national network television, which began in January 1987, dramatized the Ayodhya issue. These attempts further reflect the efforts of the Hindu nationalists to reinterpret India's turbulent Mogul past. They allege that Muslim rulers destroyed many Hindu temples, and the search is now on for historical facts that establish these claims. In states where the BJP is politically powerful, a revision of school textbooks that stress the devastation caused by the Mogul emperors has apparently taken place.

Religious functionaries in politics

Commenting on the pattern of relationship between the church and the state in South Asia, Donald Smith concludes, 'In general, the more highly organized the majority religion, the greater the degree of clerical involvement in politics' (Smith 1966: 4). Until recently, this view was widely held among Western scholars. Given that the Hindu religion was not centred around a powerful church and there was a total lack of centralized ecclesiastical institutions, how was the participation of Hindu saints or monks (*sadhus*) in the political process to be explained? Peter van der Veer makes an interesting remark about this development, 'While politicians have for decades used a saintly facade, only now have saints come to reveal themselves openly as politicians' (Van der Veer 1994: 98). Recent events in India have revealed that clerical participation, both by individuals and organized groups in politics, has assumed national prominence.

Peter van der Veer explains this phenomena by stressing the role of traditional mediators, such as a body of guru lineages and holy men, in articulating and transmitting the beliefs and social practices, in Hinduism as well as in Islam, across a huge and culturally diverse region. In Islam, the significant difference is that all orders endorse a central, sacred authority, the universal revelation of the Prophet, which he suggests allows for more centralization. The Hindu clergy is made up of a wide variety of religious functionaries, comprising temple priests, *gurus* (personal spiritual preceptors), family priests, astrologers and *sadhus* (holy men). Religious identities continue to be transmitted through these holy men working through a network of sacred centres, alongside migration, pilgrimage, print and the visual media. Thus, those features that were believed to preclude the political involvement of priests have evolved means of translating the spiritual authority and social prestige of priests into political influence.

Forms of ritual communication

Ritual discourse and practice are modes of religious communication that transmit ideas of personhood and self. Peter van der Veer contends that religious nationalism in India in the nineteenth and twentieth centuries fuses forms of religious identity and discourse on the nation. This process involves the perpetual transformation of pre-existing forms of religious identity through the ritual construction of identity. Religious nationalism, by introducing the notion of the nation as an extension of the self, therefore reinforces cosmological understandings – dealing with birth and death, illness, etc. According to van der Veer, 'The articulation of religious meaning and practice is part of a historical construction of nationalist identities' (Van der Veer 1994: 84).

The Hindu radical right is increasingly invoking the symbolic universe of community rituals in order to disseminate its message. In this manner, the ritual repertoire engages the accepted Hindu conceptions to communicate the message of Hindu unity. For instance, a basic concern for a modern nation-state is territorial integrity. Religious colouring is imparted to the geographical integrity of India by claiming that it is Hindu cultural identity that unifies the Indian nation. The BJP glorifies the sacred geography of India through *yatras* (pilgrimage in procession). The unity of Hindu India is signified through all the rivers in India, which are symbolically connected with the holy river, the Ganges. The BJP processions followed well-known pilgrimage routes that link major religious centres, suggesting the geographical unity of India (*bharatvarsha*) as a sacred area (*kshetra*) of Hindus.

In this way, pilgrimage was effectively transformed into a ritual of national integration. As part of the temple festival celebrations in India, processions of temple chariots (*rathas*) bearing an image of a Hindu deity are taken for a ride throughout the deity's domain. This ride confirms the territorial sovereignty of the deity. The procession of the VHP invoked a similar use of *rathas* in the form of brand-new trucks. The VHP procession made use of the existing symbolism of Mother India, which is characteristic of the worshipping of Hindu goddesses.

The discussion thus far has attempted to discern the general pattern of religio-political developments in the modern history of India. Some attempts that were made by the élites to reconcile Western (political) ideas to indigenous (religious) values have been noted. This section can be concluded by referring to Donald Smith's succinct comment on the interaction between religion and politics in India. He maintains that politicians attempt to secure the legitimization of Western political ideologies by associating them with religion (Smith 1996: 36). Moreover, we have seen how the Hindu metaphysical principles have supported the dominant political ideology, i.e. democracy in India. These points serve merely to illustrate the many different kinds of relationships between religion and politics in the recent history of India. The factors that account for the explosion of religious nationalism in contemporary India will now be examined. There are three important points to be made here.

The resurgence of religious nationalism at this moment in history

Over and beyond the concrete historical conditions at this given moment in India's history, there are worldwide conditions, such as the state of economic and technological ingenuity prevailing in other parts of the world, that heavily influence the prospects of development of new political ideologies. However, only the specific historical conditions and processes that have exacerbated the use of religion in politics in contemporary India will be examined. The use of the apparatus of the modern state – political parties with mass-disseminated ideologies, legislative bodies, universal adult franchise – in whipping up communal passions using religion has already been discussed.

The weakening of political institutions

The organizational decline of the Congress party

In the earlier sections it has been shown that the Congress party has been the single dominant political party since India's independence until well into the 1980s. There is little scope here for going into the history and development of what scholars label the 'Congress System'.[5] Two general inferences are relevant to this inquiry. First, observers of Indian politics have noted the authoritarianism and centralization promoted by the personal political style of Mrs Gandhi and her predecessors, as part of the Congress Nehru dynastic culture (Brass 1990, Kohli 1990), although other factors linked to the development of the political process, such as constitutional features and the development of central government institutions, i.e. the Planning Commission, have also enhanced the centralizing role of the national government. Second, the Congress Party has often been accused of failing to take adequate political measures before the outburst of ethnic strife. Indeed, critics have said that government actions often precipitated the violence, which was then used by the government to justify the use of force and thereby win popular credit for restoring law and order. In the case of Punjab, these included the attempts of the Congress leaders to exclude the Akali Dal from political power by encouraging Bhindranwale. Indeed, some critics have attributed the conflict in Punjab to the massive Congress government intervention in the state.[6]

Myron Weiner suggests that these criticisms highlight the inability of a weakened governing party to share power with minorities, and the temptation on the part of some government supporters to encourage ethnic strife so as to justify central government intervention and to win support from majority communities (Weiner 1986: 126). His rather pessimistic conclusion is that the weakening of political institutions is likely to intensify ethnic conflict in India.

The state as an arbitrator of ethnic conflict: the strength of the state to respond impartially

In recent years, the minorities have repeatedly accused the administrative services and police of taking a partisan attitude towards minorities. The minorities have accused the police of not ensuring their protection. On the other hand, the media reports confirm that the police have participated in attacks on minorities or have provided support to the attackers. There is considerable evidence that the police in India have become increasingly politicized. The collusion of sections of the Congress party against minorities was starkly evident in the attacks against the Sikhs after the assassination of Mrs Gandhi in October 1984. Independent investigating teams published evidence of organized efforts involving 'important politicians of the Congress (I) at the top and by authorities in the administration' (Roach 1986: 153). Educated Hindus increasingly view the exercise of military force by the Indian government as a necessary reassertion of Hindu authority. This view was evident in the reactions to the pogroms against the Sikhs after Mrs Gandhi's assassination. Rajiv Gandhi defended the Hindu mobs by claiming during the election campaign that when a great tree falls, the ground will quake. The participation of police is evident in the attacks on Muslims in the metropolitan cities of Bombay and Delhi.[7]

Furthermore, the central government has increasingly turned to the armed forces to deal with ethnic conflict. After the June 1984 military assault on the Golden Temple, government sources claimed that 5,000 Sikhs had deserted the army, of which 102 were killed. The mutiny by Sikh soldiers demonstrates the considerable risks entailed in the intense use of the armed forces to arbitrate ethnic strife. Finally, this usually accompanies the suspension of democratic procedures, such as the state government, and the censoring of the press. Punjab provides a test case for the imposition of new ordinances and legislations. The most notable of these are the National Security Ordinance (Second Amendment), promulgated on 14 July 1984, under which Punjab was declared a terrorist-affected area. According to the People's Union for Civil Liberties in Delhi, these acts can be used 'against dissenters and for narrow political ends by the ruling party' (Roach 1986: 153). This is an indication of the considerable erosion of democratic institutions in India.

Loss of faith in secular institutions

The goals of the political and social institutions of the secular state are social justice, democracy and secularism. The anti-colonial nationalist movement in India had promised political freedom, economic prosperity and social justice once India attained independence. James Mayall, in his well-known book *Nationalism and International Society* (1990) has underlined the point that soon after independence the central political concern in the post-colonial world shifted from constitutional to economic issues. The reason for this was that

> Once alien rule had been dislodged, the new rulers faced the oldest question in politics: by what right do you rule? In the heady atmosphere of the anti-colonial struggle, the organisation of a movement for self-government had been sufficient legitimisation; once the goal had been achieved something more was required to underpin the exercise of power.
> (Mayall 1990: 116)

It was in this context that India embarked on the ambitious programme for rapid economic development – the second 5-year plan in 1956. Not only were these programmes of industrial modernization flawed, but the post-colonial states were increasingly marginalized within the Western-dominated international economy. Although India is now close to approaching the fiftieth anniversary of its independence, the fiscal and social crisis has only deepened.

The most prominent feature of Indian political culture in recent years has been the emergence of the hegemonic Indian state. The state not only monopolizes all social resources but usurps a large proportion of its resources. Modern institutions are widely associated with corrupt and inefficient bureaucracy, largely responsible to self-seeking politicians. The inefficiency and lack of public sensitivity of the Indian state is attributed to the working of an unreconstructed colonial-style bureaucracy. The non-performance of the political system is further pinned to overcentralization (Kothari 1976:

25). Disenchantment with modern institutions of the state has induced the urgent need to assert discipline and order.

A new challenge to secular nationalism?

These developments suggest that the resurgence of religious nationalism at this historical moment may be an attempt to usher in an era of a new moral order. The Hindu nationalist movement in India attempts to reformulate the idiom of modern, secular political order by infusing indigenous moral values derived from religion into public life. The Hindu nationalist parties assert that India should be ruled by the Hindu majority as a Hindu state (*rashtra*). Their political agenda seeks a Utopian Hindu nation (*ramrajya*), which they hope will eventually emerge victorious. On the one hand, they morally reject the legitimacy of the modern, secular state. On the other hand, they rely on the accoutrements of Western political structure – political parties and elections – in order to achieve their objectives. Although the Hindu religious nationalists embrace traditional religious values, they are actively involved in the modern electoral process. They use modern techniques in their organization and political campaigns.

Why is the alternative form of political organization based on religion? What is the moral purpose of the nation? I take as my starting point perceptive comments on the nature of the nationalist discourse in India made by two leading South Asian scholars. Mark Juergensmeyer (1994) observes that the nationalism of the colonized countries is a product of the encounter between different conceptions of the socio-political order, one informed by a religious world-view and the other by a secular vision of the world. Likewise, Peter van der Veer succinctly remarks, '...the colonial discourse relates, in one way or another, to the master narrative of progress and modernity, while the indigenous discourses relate to master narratives of salvation' (Van der Veer 1994: 143). The preceding observations are germane to understanding the collusion between religion and politics in India.

Mark Juergensmeyer has explored the dialectic between what he considers to be two competing frameworks of social order. The first is secular nationalism, allied with the national state, and the second is religion, allied with large ethnic communities.[8] Juergensmeyer suggests that both religion and secular nationalism are competing languages of order that claim authority for the social order. Western models of nationhood represent a particular form of political organization in which individuals are linked through a centralized, democratic political system. This political order derives legitimization through common laws, democratic political processes and a sense of identification with a geographical area. The electoral process as a mode of making decisions is the hallmark of democracy and is well established throughout the world. It is based on the modern democratic principle of majority rule.

There is abundant evidence worldwide to show the persistence of natural religious loyalties despite secular politics. Contemporary India is experiencing not an erosion of religion in public life, rather a resurgence. Both religion and national identity fuse personal and social identity. The Utopian vision espoused by religious nationalists appeals because the moral and spiritual goals transcend the materialistic promises of secular nationalists. Religion provides order from the chaos and uncertainty in the world; it is order-restoring and life-affirming. It situates individuals in the great cosmic encounter between sacred and profane, good and evil, life and death. The political system is legitimized by the moral order based on religion. Religious laws form the basis of a moral state.

The interaction between nationalism and religion at a particular historical moment produces social and political conflict. Wherever religious traditions provide the future blueprints for a new social and political order they are opposed by religious groups with equally strong and valid claims upon the future. This inevitably leads to conflict between different groups. These groups also come into conflict with those who espouse the secular or liberal democratic tradition.

Violence in India is not, then, senseless and random. It is a way of changing things, of challenging a recalcitrant political order. In India, as elsewhere in the world, towards the end of the twentieth century religions legitimized violence as people struggled for what they regarded as their just claims upon the future. Frustration and fear may have their roots in identifiable economic and social causes that could be ameliorated by secular remedies within the democratic process, but a religious vision can offer a more readily available solution by legitimizing the violence that is born of hatred and despair.[9]

Religious nationalism as a strategy for change or a form of protest?

It is vital to recognize the vast territorial diversity and the immense historical complexity of India's distinct state formation. It is difficult to arrive at a valid generalization about the appeal of the Hindu radical right. The claim that the Hindu radical right appeals to the urban population who endure the pressures of social change requires some qualification. The electoral results in the various states in India suggest that the Hindu nationalist parties appeal widely to the northern, caste Hindu population.[10] The election results of March 1995 indicate that the Hindu nationalist parties are successfully expanding their regional base and forming coalitions with the more radical, regional variants, such as the recent BJP coalition with the Shiv-Sena in Maharashtra.

Scholars are correct in locating the social base of the Hindu religious right in India's rising middle class, which forms nearly 20 per cent of the total population. Achin Vanaik has taken into consideration the distinct admixture of multi-caste, multi-class and multi-regional diversity to define the term 'intermediate castes'. The 'intermediate castes', according to Vanaik, constitute the agrarian bourgeoisie and the rural and urban petty bourgeoisie (Vanaik 1990: 144).

Indian commentators contend that the resurgence of the Hindu right indicates attempts made by the Hindu middle class for a uniform standard religious discourse. 'On the middle classes there has always been a fringe yearning for a nation-state with one religion, one language, and one culture, for that was what the Western societies seemingly had' (Nandy 1989: 13). The general hypothesis is that the non-European nations yearn to be as successful as the robust, capitalist, European nations. This reflects the notion that capitalism is efficacious only in societies that possess similar systems of cultural praxis to those that define the Semitic religious tradition.[11] This is assumed to explain the desire to emulate the political and social systems of the European nations.

Can the approach discussed above explain why capitalism has flourished in so many non-Christian societies, such as Japan, Korea and Taiwan? Why has capitalism failed in so many societies characterized by the Semitic religious tradition, such as Poland? Although this view is upheld by eminent Indian social scientists, it reflects the propensity to uncritically universalize from European experience that seems to characterize so much of the social science literature.

In this respect, Ainslie T. Embree's emphasis on religion as an ideology of transition that makes change possible and desirable by providing harmony and cohesiveness in society seems to be close to empirical realities. It forcefully reveals how religious nationalist movements bring about appropriate adjustments in society by affirming and transforming traditional values and belief systems. The appeal of the religious right lies in its vision of the future compared with that offered by the forces of social and political modernization.

Various writers have pointed out that the more rapidly industrialization takes place, the more serious the concomitant social and psychological dislocation, and the greater the degree of protest in a society. A critical stimulus to political action is the tension between aspirations and status. 'When education is increasing aspirations, economic growth is enlarging economic opportunities, and political democracy is resulting in increased politicization, then one can expect more, not less competition and conflict among India's many social groups' (Roach 1986: 100).

Political leaders play upon the affective pull of group ties to mobilize a population. This sentiment of combined defensiveness and assertiveness of contemporary Hindus has been tapped by political leaders, particularly by the post-independence Congress leadership. This was evident when for the first time since India's independence the Congress party won a clear majority of votes among caste Hindus in northern India. It was manifest by the support for Congress by the RSS in the December 1984 parliamentary elections. Heightened group consciousness intensifies intergroup conflict only when a group asserts its identity by attacking the identity of other groups, when a claim for political power for the group is perceived as threatening.

The distribution of wealth, education and employment is largely determined by the political process. Ethnic groups seek political power to improve their social status and economic well-being. It is this central feature of political life that induces politicians to mobilize constituencies under the banner of religion. Another factor that makes religious identity a central feature of politics is the notion that other groups are benefiting economically while they themselves are being deliberately excluded. Moreover, politicians have made skilful use of the frustrations of poverty and unemployment to appeal to religious sentiments. The most dramatic example being the carnage of Sikhs in slum areas of Delhi after the assassination of Mrs Gandhi. Both the victims and the killers came from the poorest sections of the community; politicians incited and legitimized the killings in the name of religion. Electoral politics encourages mobilization on the basis of existing identities. As the democratic process has unfolded in India, it has actually retarded the process of secularization (Vanaik 1990: 145). Finally, in a rapidly developing society like India, with her myriad problems, protest inevitably assumes grave proportions.

Conclusion

First of all, the five central cultural beliefs and practices that characterize Indian civilization and harness the involvement of religion in modern politics in India were considered. The historical context, i.e. the social and political changes generated by the British Raj, which provoked the reinterpretation of Hindu religion in the light of Western values, was then examined. The first category of response was institutionally represented by the Congress party. The anti-colonial nationalist movement, articulated by leaders of the Indian National Congress, reconciled Western notions of nationalism and secularism with the Hindu system of thought. In this manner, the nation of India was 'imagined' to have its roots in the ancient Hindu past. The modern structures of the independent Indian state were based on the notion of secularism, which corresponded to the discourse on tolerance of the Hindu religion. This emphasis on tolerance that allegedly characterized Hindu religion, in fact embraced the inclusive attitude of the Hindu religion towards other religious faiths.

The second category of the response of Hinduism to Western institutions and values, represented by the Hindu radical right, was then discussed. The stupendous rise of the religious right in India's national politics in the 1980s was noted. The response of the Hindu radical right was marked by a rejection of the Western secularism embraced by the Anglo-Indian élites. It sought to establish a Hindu state and modernize India in the true Hindu ancestral spirit. The implications of the programme of the religious right for the religious minorities in India were looked at. These are complex matters which have been dealt with in a cursory manner. But even a brief survey of the interaction between religion and politics in India can help one discern the emerging patterns and trends. The problem of religious nationalism will probably result in a period in which majorities and selected minorities become more self-aware; the international ties of some minorities are growing and political coalitions are in flux.

3 The historical roots of Sikh communal consciousness (1469–1947)

This study attempts to locate the genesis of the present-day Sikh ethno-regional movement within the realm of history. In the 1980s the Sikh movement for sovereignty was not a sudden development. This next two chapters look into the deep social and historical roots linked to the growth of contemporary Sikh self-consciousness. This chapter begins with the period of inception of Sikh religion and continues until the collapse of British rule in Punjab. The chapter is broadly divided into three sections. The first section comprises two parts. The first part deals with the evolution of early Sikh tradition (1469–1708), and the second part examines the consolidation of Sikh political power (1708–1849). The second section explores the growth of Sikh communal consciousness during the colonial period (1849–1947). Chapter 1 showed that the social and political changes generated by the British Raj sparked a series of religious reform movements. It was further argued that the exponents of these socio-religious reform movements successfully created a dominant version of Indian nationalism cast in the idiom of the majority Hindu religion. In the final section of this chapter these arguments will be carried forward to examine how this historic development dramatically altered the quality and incidence of relations during the last third of the nineteenth century in Punjab. The aim is to situate the growth of Sikh identity, community and organization within the context of the historic and social forces prevailing during each period of this study. Such an analysis will primarily be concerned with social change and different forms of consciousness.

Early Sikh tradition

The period of the Sikh gurus (1469–1708)

Sikhism has evolved through the succession of ten masters. Sikh tradition informs us that the ten masters are to be regarded as ten manifestations of the same spirit, rather than a succession of mystics. However, a major influence on the development of Sikhism was the interaction between the Sikhs and the Mogul empire. Babur, the first Mogul emperor, ascended the throne during the lifetime of the first Sikh master, Guru Nanak. The Mogul power and Sikh religion developed simultaneously and in close geographical proximity. Thus, the nature and character of Nanak's response must be understood in the context of the prevailing social situation in Punjab during the late fifteenth and the early sixteenth centuries.

Eminent Sikh historian J. S. Grewal (1969) notes that the most significant political development during Nanak's lifetime was the transition from Afghan to Mogul domination in northern India. This he contends had far-reaching implications for politics and administration, the urban and rural economies, and for the prevailing culture and society. During the seventeenth century, North India was afflicted with religious fanaticism, and the Mogul emperors persecuted their non-Islamic subjects. The Mogul emperor Aurangzeb restored capitation tax, or *jizya*, on all non-Muslims and closed Hindu schools in 1669. J. S. Grewal's examination (1969) of the compositions of Guru Nanak reveals that Nanak was familiar with the politico-administrative arrangements and the socio-economic situation that prevailed during his time. Therefore, Nanak's denunciation of much of the religious belief and practice of his times led him to envision a new religious ideology that could become the basis of a new social order.

The first spiritual leader, Guru Nanak, was born in 1469 into a high caste Khatri Punjabi Hindu family at Talwandi, situated 55 miles west of Lahore, now in Pakistan. Nanak's father was a revenue superintendent at Talwandi, and Nanak was educated in Sanskrit by the village *pandit* or Brahmin teacher and learned Persian and Arabic in the village Muslim school. Nanak was married to Sulakhni and had two sons, Sri Chand and Lakshmi Chand. As an educated young man, Nanak thwarted his father's desire for him to become an accountant. Nanak's religious quest or search for a more valuable purpose in life began as a young man while working for an Afghan administrator. During the first quarter of the sixteenth century, Nanak undertook extensive journeys and held deliberations and debates with religious emissaries and holy men of different religious faiths. Nanak was interested in all the major forms of contemporary religious belief and practice.

The *janam sakhi*[1] narratives describe an experience of enlightenment at the age of thirty, when Nanak is believed to have disappeared from the banks of a river. He reappeared after 3 days and pronounced, 'There is neither Hindu nor Mussulman and the path which I follow is God's'. After this profound spiritual experience, Nanak undertook his mission to spread the message of God's name to the world. The *janam sakhi* episodes, which are popular among the Sikhs, proclaim him to be a Guru after this incident and describe him as one who dispels darkness or ignorance *(gu)* and proclaims enlightenment *(ru)*. The following account of Guru Nanak's life has been taken from traditional sources.

The first Sikh master, Guru Nanak, rejected priestly Hinduism and its concomitant rituals and worshipping of idols. He upheld the superiority of moral righteousness over mechanical ritualism. Nanak challenged the authority of Brahmins to communicate divine knowledge and preached the equality of all men. He denounced social differentiation and caste distinctions. Guru Nanak abjured the idolatry of Hinduism and repudiated the veneration of Hindu deities as a means of liberation. He affirmed that none of the Hindu deities could be equated with the Supreme Being because they were in fact the creation of the Supreme Being. He propounded instead the doctrine of strict monotheism. The Supreme Being was formless (*nirankar*) and reveals itself through its creation. Guru Nanak's fundamental teaching was that the path to salvation could be attained through internal religiosity. Salvation could be attained through the remembrance of and meditation on the Divine word. The soteriological teaching of the first master, Guru Nanak, *nam simran*, salvation through the remembrance of the divine word, manifested in the holy words of the Sikh Gurus, became the key doctrine of early Sikhism. Fundamental to Nanak's teachings was the role of the guru. The guru was the mediator between ordinary mortals and God, and meditation on the guru's word, or *gurbani*, was the highest form of worship. Guru Nanak's emphasis on divine meditation does not imply an appeal for renunciation. On the contrary, Nanak emphasizd both the spiritual and the temporal side of human existence. The path of salvation could be pursued while living the life of a householder.

Around 1521, when Guru Nanak was about 50 years old, he settled at Kartarpur with his family. Nanak's emphasis on *gurbani* and not on personal devotion to himself had great significance for the community that he established at Kartarpur. The Kartarpur community was the beginning of the *sangat*, or 'a religious congregation', where all met as equals, irrespective of caste, status or gender. The centrality of congregational singing of hymns, or *kirtan*, represented a new mode of worship. The Sikh tradition of *guru-ka-langar*, or 'a free community meal', in a *gurudwara* dates back to Guru Nanak, and demonstrates his rejection of the caste system and his belief that all human beings are equal. The followers of Guru Nanak came to be known as Sikhs, from the Sanskrit *shishya*, or disciple. Guru Nanak died on 22 September 1539; his work is preserved in 974 hymns.

Guru Nanak was a poet of superb originality and power. Nanak was adept at both Sanskrit and Persian, the north Indian languages of the high intelligentsia of his time, and he evolved a matchless literary expression for his universal message. The very universality of his message required a form of literary expression that was not far removed from ecclesiastical and everyday life. The composite idiom Nanak created not only drew upon his extensive travels, but also incorporated a range of available, existing linguistic resources – his native Sheikhupuri speech and the existing norms of literary expression. This composite Punjabi-based idiom was adopted in prose by his successors and has a degree of uniformity and consistent linguistic pattern. Christopher Shackle (1983) has termed this scriptural language as 'the sacred language of the Sikhs'.

Twenty-four days before his death in September 1539, Guru Nanak appointed his devout disciple Lehina as his successor. Nanak summoned his followers and blessed Lehina with a book of his hymns (*pothi*) and declared that he possessed his spirit and through him God would continue to speak. He bestowed on him the new name of Angad, derived from the word *ang*, literally meaning limb, a pun for a part of his own body. Thus, before his death Guru Nanak ascertained that guruship was to be conferred on the basis of merit in piety and devotion and not passed on solely on the basis of heredity. Guru Nanak was succeeded by nine masters.[2]

The second Sikh master, Guru Angad (born 31 March 1504, guruship 1539–52), propagated the fundamental precepts of Nanak's philosophy for 13 years. He encouraged Guru Nanak's disciple Bala to compile a *janam-sakhi* containing a collection of Guru Nanak's hymns. He further instructed the compilation of the Guru's hymns, and Bhai Paira Mokha wrote them down and prepared the way for a Sikh scripture.

Guru Amar Das (born 5 May 1479, guruship 1552–74) perceived the needs of a numerically and geographically expanding constituency. The third guru divided the congregation into twenty-two communities called *sangatias*, each under the direction of a head. Each division or *manji* referred to the seat of the provincial Sikh leader. The word *manji* stands for bedstead, distinguished from *gaddi*, which means throne and was occupied solely by the Gurus. Women were also appointed to undertake preaching work and were called *peerahs*. Guru Amar Das persuaded the Mogul emperor to abolish the tax imposed on pilgrims visiting the holy city of Haridwar. He also initiated the tradition of Sikh congregation at the spring and autumn festivals of Baisakhi and Diwali.

Guru Ram Das (born 24 September 1534, guruship 1574–81) laid the foundations of the holy city of Amritsar, which literally means 'pool of nectar' and designates the sacred pool. The foundation stone was laid by a Muslim mystic, the Sufi Mian Mir of Lahore. It was Guru Ram Das's successor, Guru Arjan (born 1563, guruship 1581–1606), who built the *gurudwara*, or Sikh temple, at Amritsar and called it Hari Mandir. The Hari Mandir Sahib was designed to possess four doorways, instead of the usual one found in Hindu temples. This was a symbol of the levelling of caste barriers and indicated that Hari Mandir was open to all the four main castes of Hindu society. It was also constructed on a lower platform so that devotees had to step down to enter the temple. This was to remind them that Godliness is attained by humility and bending low in submission.

The prolific and linguistically versatile Guru Arjan is believed to have compiled the Guru Granth Sahib or Adi Granth, the holy book of the Sikhs, and instated it at Hari Mandir Sahib in 1604. A remarkable feature of the Guru Granth Sahib is that it contains the compositions of several mystics who belonged to diverse cultural and social backgrounds. The strong affinity between the beliefs of these mystics and the beliefs of Gurus suggests a pan-Indian stance and an attempt to assimilate a growing popular tradition by Guru Arjan (Grewal 1990: 20). Social and political concerns do not fall outside the scope of the Adi Granth. Social inequality based on the caste system and political injustice in the form of oppression by the rulers is explicitly denounced. The fifth Sikh master, Guru Arjan, conferred the status of guru on the Adi Granth. He also stated specific and elaborate injunctions concerning the mode of behaviour and the code of conduct that were to be observed in the presence of the Adi Granth. It is important to note that although many anthologies of devotional literature were compiled in medieval India, historically neither the compilers nor the readers viewed these texts as statements of a distinct religious tradition. Nonetheless, the Adi Granth is the only Sikh scripture to have been regarded as a substitute guru by the Sikh gurus. No other Sikh scripture has acquired this central position in Sikh religious thought and in Sikh rituals. This is not to deny that the Sikh principle of *nam simran* (meditation of the divine word) enjoins Sikhs to venerate all their holy scriptures.

The Mogul emperor Jehangir was apprehensive of the growing expansion of the Sikh constituency under the powerful influence of Guru Arjan. He ordered the execution of Guru Arjan for, allegedly, supporting his rebellious son Khusrau. Guru Arjan was imprisoned at Lahore and tortured to death on 30 May 1606. Guru Arjan became the first Sikh martyr, and his martyrdom was vital in transforming Sikhism into a more militant faith. It was Guru Arjan's son and successor, Guru Hargobind, who proclaimed the structural bonding of religion and politics, which had by then become a historical necessity. He fortified Amritsar and constructed the Akal Takht, or the eternal throne, opposite the Hari Mandir Sahib. The Akal Takht was to be a symbol of the temporal power of Sikhism,. This complex of buildings became known as the Golden Temple, or the Darbar Sahib, the pre-eminent Sikh shrine. Guru Hargobind assumed authority of the spiritual and the temporal and gave visible expression to them by carrying two swords, *miri* and *piri*: one designating spiritual authority that he had inherited from his predecessors (*piri*) and the other the temporal side of his authority (*miri*).

Guru Hargobind's significant move to militarize the Sikh faith is explained not only by the Islamization of the polity under the Mogul emperors but also by the massive influx of Jats into the Sikh tradition by the time of the fifth and sixth Gurus. The origin of the Jats is shrouded in much uncertainty, but according to the traditions of the Punjab, the Jats are of Rajput descent and emigrated to the Punjab from Central India. The Jats are a people accustomed to bearing arms. This indicates that Guru Hargobind's shift in policy was undertaken in the context of an existing tradition of bearing arms among a significant constituency of the Sikhs.

A few words are necessary here about the caste hierarchy among the Sikhs. Before plunging into an overview of caste among Sikhs, let us note those features of the caste system that are often misconstrued. Caste manifests itself concretely only at the local level, and in actual practice the caste system is very flexible and diffuse. Although the caste has an economic base and a religious explanation, the isomorphism between the two has not entirely been perfect. At the local level, the economically dominant group, particularly the group that owns the land, is also the highest caste. Therefore, the universal superiority of the Brahman is a fiction that has never really corresponded to the actual workings of the caste system.

Likewise, caste among Sikhs presents an apparent conflict between doctrine and actual practice. The Sikh gurus explicitly denounced the caste system and proclaimed that caste status was irrelevant for salvation. Although the basic egalitarian principle of Sikhism rejects caste, a substantial majority of Sikhs observe certain features of caste in practice. However, caste among Sikhs does not have any doctrinal injunction nor does it bear any ritual manifestation; it is a cultural construction. Caste is enforced through local division of labour, the choice of spouse in marriage and the kind of upbringing given to children. The main castes among the Sikhs are Jat, Khatri, Aroras, Ramgarhiya (carpenter and ironworker), Chimba (tailor) and Kumhar (potter) and the Sikh scheduled castes chamar (tanners) and Churah (sweeper). The Jats, being the landed caste, constitute the economically and politically dominant caste group. The Jats are believed to have descended from Scythian tribes who followed the same route as the Aryans across the Hindu Kush and settled in Punjab. They were brought into the fold of Sikhism during the time of Guru Arjun. They spearheaded early Sikh armies and Sikh Jats became a land-owning aristocracy during the rule of Maharaja Ranjit Singh. Recruitment into the British Army further consolidated their power. The mercantile caste group among Sikhs are the Khatris and the Aroras. The Ahluwalias are identified closely with Khatris and Aroras, although they are by origin distillers. An overview of caste among Sikhs presents a complicated situation that becomes even more complex when we notice that most Khatris have dominant Hindu affiliations. The custom of having one son baptized as a Khalsa[3] Sikh while the other children remain Hindus is widespread among Khatris.

In a bid to stamp out the religious and political threat of Sikhism, Muslim rulers carried out a relentless policy of repression against the Sikhs. In May 1675, a deputation of Brahmins met the ninth Sikh master, Guru Tegh Bahadur (born 1621, guruship 1664–1675), and begged for his help to save them from religious persecution by the Mogul governor of the Kashmir valley. Guru Teg Bahadur offered to court martyrdom. On his refusal to accept Islam, he was beheaded in Chandni Chauk, the central market square near the Red Fort in Delhi on 11 November 1675. Guru Tegh Bahadur's unique sacrifice to uphold the freedom of conscience and protect the Brahmins, to whom he was ideologically opposed, assumed great symbolic and ideological significance among the Sikhs.

By the time of the ninth master, the Sikhs possessed several important accoutrements of a separate religious practice. These included a major sacred text, the Adi Granth, a collation of devotional anthology compiled by the fifth master, Guru Arjan in 1603–4, the convention of a communal meal (*langar*), the foundation of religious congregations (*sangat*), and the setting up of elaborate pilgrim centres. However, it was the initiatives of the tenth master, Guru Gobind Singh (birth 1666, guruship 1675–1708), that endowed the Sikhs with a distinctive religious identity. For it was he who instituted the new Khalsa normative order on the day of the spring festival of Baisakhi in 1699, which distinguished the Khalsa Sikhs from others in Punjabi society. The word Khalsa is derived from the Arabic-Persian word *khalis*, meaning pure. The distinctions were inscribed through a novel form of initiation, *khande di pahul*, which affirmed a new identity through a complex and powerful set of symbols.[4] Those who chose to join the Khalsa brotherhood were to abandon all links with the caste system and worship the one immortal God. The adoption of the common surname of 'Singh' or 'lion' for men and 'Kaur' or 'princess' for women was aimed at levelling caste distinctions and to instil courage in the faithful. Ideologically, the institution of the Khalsa was intended to combine spiritual excellence and militant valour of the highest order. Guru Nanak's doctrine of equality was translated by Guru Gobind into the militant defence of the rights of all men. He proclaimed that it was legitimate to draw the sword in the defence of righteousness when all other methods of redress had failed. Historically, it was a response to the perilous situation facing the Sikh community and an attempt to resolve external as well as internal dissension. The Khalsa brotherhood was founded in order to join the Sikhs into a cohesive and homogeneous entity.

The great warrior-hero of the Sikhs Guru Gobind Singh had lost his father and four younger sons to Mogul tyranny. Before his death, Guru Gobind Singh announced an end to the line of human gurus. Henceforth, the sacred book of the Sikhs, the Guru Granth Sahib, was to be regarded as the spiritual authority. The temporal aspects of the authority of the Guru were vested in the collective wisdom of the Sikh community, the Khalsa Panth. Thus, the line of human gurus ended in 1708, when the tenth master, Guru Gobind Singh, died.

After the time of Guru Arjan, Braj[5] and Persian, the great North Indian literary languages of the later Mogul period, dominated Sikh writing. Guru Gobind was equally at home with Persian, although the preferred medium was Braj. Some 2,000 hymns composed by Guru Gobind Singh are contained in the Dasam Granth, or 'book of the tenth master'. Thus, Braj written in Gurmukhi script came to dominate Sikh writings in the eighteenth- and early nineteenth-century. Sanskrit, preserved for 1500 years in the archaic mould established by Panini, offered privileged access to ontological truth and had served as the language of the high intelligentsia until the Islamic invasions. The Muslim conquests resulted in the replacement of Sanskrit by Persian, although its use was restricted to literary and administrative purposes. Here it is useful to bear in mind that during the Mogul period the use of many regional Indo-Aryan languages, Braj in particular, for religious poetry resulted in their becoming widely used unlocalized languages.

After the death of the last Sikh guru, two doctrines were to guide and provide cohesion to the Sikh community. First was the highly complex doctrine of *guru granth* or scriptural guru: the apotheosis of the Adi Granth, a repository of the utterances of the Sikh gurus, popularly known as *bani*, as an embodiment the figure of a Sikh guru. In other words, the Adi Granth was to serve as a point of contact between God and ordinary mortals. The second was the relatively simpler doctrine of *guru panth*, which ascribed religious authority to the corporate assembly. It proclaimed that God could be found within the *sangat*, or religious congregation, and decisions made by the *sangat* were to represent the will of the guru. The essence of these doctrines was that the Adi Granth, containing the sacred writings of the gurus, was the sole successor of the gurus. Salvation could be attained through meditation and ritual incantation of the Sikh scripture, which was endowed with miraculous powers for solving existential dilemmas and was efficacious in overcoming mundane problems. Any person who claimed the status of a living guru was a heretic.

The separate Sikh identity was further reinforced through the *rahit-nama* literature – the new code of conduct manuals that enlisted moral duties and covered all domains of life. The *rahit-namas* laid down specific injunctions for a Sikh way of life based on distinct life-cycle rituals, modes of behaviour, tabooed actions, dietary injunctions, and a whole new classificatory code concerning the body and distinct rites of passage to mark birth and death, which defined a unique Khalsa personhood. By the time of the last Sikh guru, the Sikhs possessed a distinct set of religious doctrines and practices. J. D. Cunningham, who was the first to document the Sikh population after British rule in Punjab, writes on the distinct cultural and religious tradition of the Sikhs:

So Nanak [the first Guru] disengaged his little society of worshippers from Hindu idolatry and Muslim superstition and placed them on a broad basis of religious and moral purity; Amar Das [the third Guru] preserved the infant community from declining into a set of asceticists; Arjun [the fifth Guru] gave his increasing followers a written rule of conduct and a civil organisation. Hargobind [the sixth Guru] adds the use of arms and a military system and Gobind Singh [the tenth Guru] bestowed upon them a distinct political existence and inspire them with the desire of being socially free and nationally independent.

(Cunningham 1849: 80)

To recapitulate thus far: we have attempted to situate the metamorphosis of the pacifist followers of Guru Nanak to the militant brotherhood of the Khalsa within the context of the historical and social development of Sikh religion. During this process, the contribution of each Sikh Guru in consolidating the doctrinal discourse of Sikhism has been noted. We have also delineated the key additions of a distinct and separate practice that characterized early Sikh tradition. Whether the Sikh gurus intended to create an independent faith is a subject of theological debate and lies outside the scope of this study.

The political triumph of the Sikh movement: the post-guru period until the British annexation of Punjab (1708–1849)

The dramatic political triumph of the Sikh movement in the second half of the eighteenth century and the establishment of the vast Sikh empire under Maharaja Ranjit Singh between 1799 and 1839 must be viewed in the wider context of the historical decline of the Mogul empire and the rise of successor states in the eighteenth century in India. The eighteenth century witnessed the political emergence and consolidation of Khalsa principalities. The Khalsa Sikhs attempted to establish their power by regrouping into political units called *misls*.[6] By the mid-eighteenth century there was a total of twelve Sikh *misls*. Each *misl* was an independent confederacy, although they acted in unison when faced with a common danger. It was the khalsa principle of *guru-panth* that provided cohesion for their political struggle and bound them together when faced with internal dissension.

The leading representatives of each *misl* gathered twice annually during the festivals of Baisakhi and Holi, which correspond with the agrarian cycle of harvest and spring in the Sikh religious calendar. These occasions had been customarily marked by festivities at the two pre-eminent Sikh sacred centres, Anandpur Sahib and Amritsar, right from the period of the gurus. Sikhs assembled on the occasions of these bilingual meetings to discuss problems facing the Sikh Panth and to decide on collective action to resolve these problems. The resolutions passed by these gatherings were called *gurmattas*, literally meaning resolutions endorsed by the guru. The holy site and the presence of the Adi Granth endowed the *gourmets* with a sacred character. These proceedings were regarded as those of the *sarbat-khalsa* or corporate body of the Khalsa. The biannual convergence of Sikh pilgrims at Amritsar for the festivals of Baisakhi and Diwali instilled in them a corporate spirit. Moreover, it was on these occasions that the Sikh chieftains would co-ordinate the deployment of the Dal Khalsa, or the Khalsa army, when faced with serious political turmoil.

It is curious that the reign of Maharaja Ranjit Singh seems to have disappeared from conventional Sikh histories, and that the element of intercommunal relations during this period has been attenuated to the point of caricature. Nonetheless, the striking feature that determined the policies adopted by Maharaja Ranjit Singh was that at least 80 per cent of the population in the territory that he ruled were Muslims, 10 per cent were Hindus and the remaining 10 per cent were Sikhs. It is astonishing that even in the palmiest days of the Khalsa, Sikhs made up only a small proportion of the total population of Punjab.

Consequently, Maharaja Ranjit Singh's policies were directed to building up a core of support among all religious communities. Therefore, state patronage was extended equally to Punjabi Muslims, Hindus and Sikhs. Many of his measures, such as a ban on cow slaughter throughout his domains, the celebration of Muslim festivals and an order to desist from public calling to prayers in the Sikh holy city of Amritsar, emphasize the point that all religious communities enjoyed considerable patronage and power. However, Maharaja Ranjit Singh ruled in the name of the Khalsa, issuing coins in the name of its central council of chieftains. Also, the title of Maharaja was conferred on Ranjit Singh by the Khalsa Panth. But at the same time he was careful to have Muslim learned men present in the court when he assumed the royal title, which implicitly rejected the Mogul's authority, in 1801. He fulfilled all the necessary criteria so that Punjab could remain a land in which Islam could be publicly practised. He secured tributes from Muslim holy men and from those who recognized his legitimacy. At the same time, Maharajah Ranjit Singh made generous endowments to *gurudwaras* and built the upper floors of the Akal Takht. He lavishly designed and decorated the Darbar Sahib, transforming it into the 'Golden Temple'. Under the patronage of the monarch, Amritsar became a flourishing trade centre.

The symbolic memory of Sikh rule is infused with images of Maharaja Ranjit Singh as a truly secular sovereign. Given the bitter memories of religious persecution during the Mogul period, the Sikh monarch did not seek revenge against the Muslims. The Maharaja is believed to have once told his foreign minister, 'God intended that I look upon all religions with one eye; that is why I was deprived of the other eye'. The monarch's accommodating attitude was reflected in the heterogeneous power structure. Maharaja Ranjit Singh's Prime Minister was Dhian Singh, a Hindu, his Finance Minister was Dina Nath, a Hindu Brahmin, and his artillery commander was Mian Ghausa, a Muslim, who was given the title of 'Commander and Faithful Friend'. The noted Sikh commanders of his army were Hari Singh Nalwa and Phoola Singh Akali. His army formed the backbone of his empire, and he promoted the reorganization of his armed forces along European lines by inviting French, Italian, German and Greek officers to train his army. His formidable empire was the largest segment of India that remained beyond colonial control. The language of Maharaja Ranjit Singh's court was Persian, the North Indian language of the high intelligentsia. Maharaja Ranjit Singh was the owner of the famous Koh-i-Noor, or 'the mountain of light', diamond.

Thus far a somewhat embellished picture of the growth and consolidation of Sikh identity in pre-colonial Punjab has been given. In the discussion in Chapter 1 on whether Sikhs constituted a 'nation' under Maharaja Ranjit Singh, it was noted that social mobilization and political organization were indispensable elements for establishing a distinct Sikh self-identification. The creation of an institutional framework that successfully articulated Sikh political aspirations in the 1900s played a decisive role in the development of a modern Sikh nation. The nineteenth century, a much vaunted period of religious revival and purification, displayed quite contradictory features in religious practice. For this reason it is important to consider some of the striking features of religious conflict that can be found scattered throughout the record of this period and to put them into some sort of interpretative framework.

Socio-religious reform movements and the growth of communal consciousness in British Punjab: the colonial period (1849–1947)

The most striking feature of nineteenth century Punjab is the degree to which religion, on the one hand, and language, on the other, came to determine social and political identities. The perfect isomorphism between linguistic and religious identities that exists in contemporary South Asia has its historical antecedents in the social and political upheaval that took place in the nineteenth century in Punjab. This section will focus on examining these profound historical developments.

The historical context

Sikh political power collapsed on 29 March 1849, when Punjab was annexed by the British after two sanguinary Anglo-Sikh wars. After the annexation of Punjab, the last Sikh monarch, Maharaja Dalip Singh, was exiled and the formidable Khalsa army was disbanded. After centuries of Hindu rule, followed by over 500 years of Islamic dominance and half a century of Sikh rule, the compact geographical area that constituted British Punjab was a region of cultural and religious diversity unsurpassed in the entire subcontinent. The Punjab was historically the meeting point of three major world religions, Hinduism, Islam and Sikhism, and three languages (Hindi, Urdu and Punjabi), each with its own distinct script, coexisted within its borders.

However, the population of British Punjab was distributed in a manner that did not allow numerical domination by a single community: Muslims were found in a majority in the west, Hindus in the east; Sikhs were most prevalent in the centre. The number of Hindus and Sikhs roughly equalled the number of Muslims. Another unique feature of British Punjab, noted by Kenneth W. Jones (1968), was its lack of a single dominant social system. Whereas the rest of the subcontinent was characterized by the dominant Hindu social system, British Punjab was characterized by the existence of three separate but interconnected social systems, one in each religious community. Therefore, when approaching the subject of the growth of communal consciousness in British Punjab, we confront a situation of unusual complexity that has a richness of phenomena which simultaneously intrigue and perplex.

The missionaries, the print media and the creation of new spheres

The Christian missionaries advanced with each new British annexation. Soon after the annexation of Punjab on 29 March 1849, missions were opened in the provincial capital, Lahore. The first Christian mission beyond Delhi was established in Punjab at Ludhiana in 1834. By the 1880s a network of mission establishments covered virtually the entire Punjab province. In order to expand their base, the Christian missionaries introduced new methods of communication. The first printing press was set up at the Ludhiana mission in 1835. The introduction of the printing press generated tracts, pamphlets and religious newspapers in vernacular languages, such as Punjabi, Hindi, Urdu and Persian, with enormous speed.[7] With the advent of the printing press, these languages became the medium of written communication among the literate sections of the population. Later on in this chapter under the section 'Print communication and the creation of a new public sphere', the vital role of the vernacular press in reinforcing the linguistic basis of religious identity, thus heightening religious dichotomies in Punjab, will be examined. Further, in Chapter 6 the critical role of the historic rivalries between the Hindi and Punjabi press will be explored; these rivalries sharpened in the late 1970s, when the movement for a separate Sikh state first arose.

Besides the introduction of the printing press, an extensive network of mission schools was established. The content of the school curriculum was soaked in crypto-Christian ideas, and Bible classes were included in the curriculum. C. A. Bayly (1994: 6) notes that 'Some of the earliest Bengali and Hindi printed history books for schools contain accounts of the Jewish people and the Christian Church'. The education imparted first at mission and then at state schools combined a knowledge of Western subjects with instruction in English and the vernacular, and the term 'anglo-vernacular education' designates this hybrid educational system. Moreover, the British conquest of Punjab had generated an urgent need for English-educated Indians to staff government offices, and the mid-nineteenth century witnessed a rapid increase in state bureaucracies. The education imparted at mission schools was a prerequisite for coveted government jobs. The aim of the colonial educational policy was to produce a carefully calibrated quantum of English-educated Indians to serve as a politically reliable, grateful and acculturated indigenous élite, who filled the subordinate echelons of the colony's bureaucracy and larger commercial enterprises.

In their drive to gain converts, the missionaries also instituted orphanages and medical missions. They introduced the *zenana* mission, which was intended to reach women in the privacy of their homes. The missionaries not only conducted their proselytizing activities through the introduction of Western institutions, they also transmitted their message through indigenous channels of communication, such as *shastrarths* (a form of traditional religious debate), and they took to preaching the gospel publicly in streets, in bazaars and at village fairs.

The activities of the Christian missionaries were backed and supported by the colonial state. The number of Christian converts rose rapidly from 3,912 in 1881 to over 19,000 a decade later, an increase of 410 per cent (Jones 1989: 87). The rise in Christian converts was perhaps not as alarming as the success of modern communication methods and the formidable alliance between the Christian Church and the British administrators. A constellation of ideas developed around the notion of surreptitious conversion and was very significant in sparking a series of reform–revival movements in Punjab.

Punjab was rife with religious reform movements in the nineteenth century. A comprehensive description of the long social history of these movements lies outside the scope of this study. The focus will be on examining how these religious reform movements yielded conflict between members of India's major religions. This theme has generated considerable scholarly interest and the following analysis draws on the perspective developed by Kenneth W. Jones, an eminent historian of South Asia. The pioneering studies by Kenneth W. Jones (1976, 1989) about the growth of communal consciousness in British Punjab provide valuable insights into the history and development of nineteenth-century reform movements.

The Arya Samaj movement

The Arya Samaj movement was the foremost Hindu reform movement in the nineteenth century in North India. The Arya Samaj movement represented the response on the part of the newly anglicized Hindu community to reformulate a modernized Hindu religious tradition. It also represented the first modern efforts to link Hindu religious values with modern life. Although this movement was not overtly political, it later formed the basis for the development of radical Hindu political parties, such as the RSS and the BJP. Emphasizing that the Punjab province was a core area of support for the RSS, Christophe Jaffrelot (1996: 74) notes that the '...organization's membership as Partition approached: between January and June 1947 the number of *swayamsevaks* in the province rose from 46,000 to 59,200.'[8]

The ideology of the Arya Samaj was enunciated by Swami Dayanand Saraswati (1824–83), a Brahmin from central Kathiawar in western India. Swami Dayanand, a peripatetic ascetic, proclaimed a 'purified' form of traditional Hinduism and insisted on the infallibility of the Vedas. He proclaimed that the only true Hinduism was to be found in the Vedas. He envisioned a purified Hinduism free of contemporary Hindu practices, such as polytheism, idolatry, child marriage, and the ban on widow marriage; he also questioned the role of Brahmin priests. These principles were not in conflict with Sikh tradition and many Sikhs participated in the Arya Samaj campaigns in the formative years. In order to disseminate his message of a revived Hindu tradition, Dayanand Saraswati founded the Arya Samaj, or 'Aryan Society', at Rajkot, in the western state of Gujarat. In 1875, Dayanand published his major polemical work the *Satyarth Prakash*, or *The Light of Truth*, in which he elaborated the concept of true Hinduism.

It was in Punjab that Dayanand Saraswati's vision evoked an enthusiastic response. Dayanand Saraswati's 15-month sojourn in Punjab (starting in 1877) had lasting effects on Punjabi society. The Lahore Arya Samaj was instituted in 1877. Within a month of its foundation, its membership had shot up by 300 per cent. By the time Dayanand completed his tour of Punjab in July 1878 he had founded eleven Samajs.

After his death in 1883, his followers drafted plans to honour their departed teacher by setting up modern institutions that would impart and propagate Arya tenets and counter the challenge posed by Christian missionaries. This resulted in the founding of the first centralizing organization within the Samaj – the Dayananda Anglo-Vedic Trust and Management Society. The first meeting of the Dayananda Anglo-Vedic Trust and Management Society was held on 27 February 1886 and led to the institution of the first Arya school on 1 June 1886. The educational activities of the Samajis received a boost on 18 May 1889, when the Punjab University granted affiliation to the new Dayananda Anglo-Vedic College. The Dayananda Anglo-Vedic High School and College did not receive support from the government and English people did not participate in the running of the faculty. These schools and colleges were highly successful, as demonstrated by the results of the students in the annual examinations. The success of these educational institutions stimulated discussions to impart education to women. By the early 1890s a girls' school, the Arya Kanya Pathshala, was established at Jullunder, and on 14 June 1896 a women's college, Kanya Mahavidyalaya, the very first of its kind, was established at Jullunder. Thus, the spectacular success of the Dayananda Anglo-Vedic educational movement, which began in 1883, led to the establishment of educational institutions throughout North India. In addition, the *Vedic Magazine* was founded in 1877 and became a powerful channel for launching bitter attacks on other faiths. In 1877, the first Arya Samaj orphanage was opened in Ferozepur. The Arya Samaj promoted the use of Hindi as a medium of education.

The primary thrust of the militant Aryas was on proselytization and *Ved Prachar*, or 'preaching of the Vedas'. C. Jaffrelot (1996: 76–7) argues that the efforts by the Arya Samaj to reform Hindu society through a selective reinterpretation of cultural traditions subsequently led to the invention of a Vedic Golden Age. Although, traditionally, Hinduism lacks a conversion ritual, plans were made to hire professional missionaries to preach Arya tenets. A stream of tracts, pamphlets and newspapers were printed in English as well as the vernacular languages to supply the Samaj missionaries with a wide variety of literature. In November 1895, six full-time professional preachers were hired to preach and work with the local Arya Samaj branches. The entire province was divided into circles, or *mandalis*. Mindful of the success of Christian missionaries in converting the lower castes, militant Aryas developed their own ritual of conversion, *shuddhi*. The Arya Samaj activists used *shuddhi* to reconvert any Muslim or Christian whose ancestors were alleged to have been Hindus and to purify the untouchable Sikh and Hindu castes. In 1900, the Arya Samaj activists reconverted some outcaste Rehatia Sikhs using a similar ceremony. The Sikh community was outraged by the ceremony, and protest meetings were held to denounce the efforts of Hindu religious reformers to bring Sikhs back into the Hindu fold.

The proselytism of the Arya Samaj activists and the Arya Samaj message of an aggressive Vedic Hinduism intensified the religious conflict. The writings of several Arya Samajis repeatedly attacked other faiths, and arguments were developed to destroy the credibility of other religions. The goal, which was repeatedly articulated, was one of defeating all opponents and, in the process, of establishing the superiority of Vedic Hinduism. The Samjis did not talk of ethical equivalence or of all religions being true. Dayananda's extensive critique of Christianity elaborated in Chapter 13 of *Satyarth Prakash* laid the foundation for anti-Christian writings and later became the source for Arya criticism of Christianity.[9] The most dramatic instance was the writings of a militant Arya Samaji Pandit Lekh Ram (1858–97) and his portrayal of Islam as a religion of slavery, murder and bigotry. This infuriated the Muslim population and led to the assassination of Pandit Lekh Ram. The three main targets of the Arya Samaj were the *kernanis,* or 'Christians', *kuranis,* or 'Muslims', and *puranis,* or 'orthodox Hindus'. C. Jaffrelot (1996) has stressed the strategy of emulation and stigmation of the 'threatening Others' pursued by the ideologues of the Arya Samaj movement. He argues that the extreme differentiation into castes and sects that characterizes Hinduism makes it particularly prone to such feelings of vulnerability and hostility to the presence of the Other.

In addition, there was considerable anti-Sikh propaganda throughout the late 1880s. In 1888, the Arya 'fire-brands' mounted an attack on the Sikh faith. The Arya critique of Sikhism was elaborated in a lengthy article entitled *Sikhism Past and Present*. This article ridiculed the infallibility of Guru Nanak and Sikhism was presented as a degenerate and decadent religion. Public attack and criticism of Sikhism by Arya protagonists during the Lahore anniversary celebration on 25 November 1888 resulted in immediate loss of Sikh support for the Arya Samaj, whereas earlier young reformist Sikhs had collaborated with Arya activists so as to stem the tide of the success of the Christian missionaries. A sense of shared goals and similar ideological commitment had formed the basis of the alliance between the Arya Samaj and the Sikh reformers. Sustained attacks on Sikhism appeared in the Arya press throughout 1887 and 1888, which further embittered relations between Aryas and Sikhs. Thus, developments within the Arya Samaj, the rising radicalism of the Samaj, the insistence on the unique and superior qualities of Hinduism and its expanding organizational strength intensified existing communal cleavages.

The Arya Samaj movement appealed particularly to the newly educated segments of the Hindu population. The Arya Samaj movement derived its force from its ability to appropriate and invert Christian doctrines and to use the Christian media and aggressive proselytizing against them. Consequently, the Arya Samaj instituted modern institutional forms in order to propagate Arya tenets successfully. Broadly speaking, one of the critical changes to come about during this period was the conception of a novel version of a public, all-India Hinduism, which was under attack from Western interference. Commenting on this critical change, C. A. Bayly writes,

Whereas, in the past, *dharma* (piety), had always been qualified by a region or type – for instance, Raj Dharma, or Maharashtra Dharma – the Dharma Sabha became a generalized public arena for a Hindu nation, opposed both to the unreformed brahmanical hierarchy and the foreign *mlecchas*.

(Bayly 1994: 8)

The Singh Sabha movement (1870–1919)

Young, educated Sikhs found themselves caught up in a similar historical process as their Hindu counterparts. By the late 1880s they had become disillusioned with the Arya Samaj and they sought to re-evaluate the Sikh identity. Although different groups within the Sikh community sought to redefine the Sikh identity, attention will be focused on the activities of the most powerful of Sikh reformers – the Singh Sabha ideologues. The Singh Sabha social reform movement marked a new phase in the evolution of modern Sikhism.

Attempts to come to terms with the cultural forces unleashed by the British Raj resulted in the setting up of numerous voluntary bodies and socio-religious associations in Punjab. Chief among these were the Anjuman-i-Punjab, or 'the society for the diffusion of useful knowledge', founded in 1865 with the backing of the Lieutenant-Governor of Punjab, Donald McLeod, and the Brahmo Samaj, set up at Lahore during 1862–3 by Navina Chandra Rai, an accountant with the North-Western Railway. The activities of these native bodies received incessant interest from the Sikh gentry. The Brahmo Samaj received wide patronage and endowments from Dyal Singh Majithia (1849–98), a Jat Sikh aristocrat, who founded *The Tribune*, a twelve-page English weekly paper first published on 2 February 1881. *The Tribune* became a powerful channel for broadcasting Brahmo ideology in Punjab. Likewise, many prominent Sikhs lobbied in forums organized by these associations.

Participation in the activities of the Anjuman and the Brahmo Samaj spurred the Sikh leaders to launch new initiatives. This heralded the formation of Sri Guru Singh Sabha at Amritsar in 1873. The leadership of the early Sikh reform movement, referred to as the Singh Sabha or Tat Khalsa movement, comprised the Sikh princes, the landed gentry and the traditional intellectuals. It became a forum for canvassing public opinion on such social issues as mass education, reform of social customs, changes in customary behaviour, such as female infanticide, widow remarriage, rights for women, the development of the economy and wider theological issues. Hailing from the established social classes, these leaders had been loyal to the British authorities and were poorly equipped for confronting the rapidly changing cultural milieu. After the expansion of British administration during the first two decades of the twentieth century, influential new figures entered the political arena and were to play a vital role. This embryonic class of young

Sikhs outflanked the landed Sikh gentry, many of whom looked down upon the parvenus. Thus, the role of articulating the flux in social attitudes was assumed by the newly educated, bilingual, young Sikhs. Hence there came about a split between the Sikh landed élite and the commercial classes, which had very significant political consequences.

The functionaries of the Lahore Sabha were committed to the mechanics of print culture. This period saw a flurry of activity resulting in the founding of the Khalsa Press in 1883. Two newspapers, the *Khalsa Gazette*, an Urdu weekly, and *Khalsa Akhbar*, a Punjabi weekly, were founded in 1884 and in 1886 respectively. However, compared with the Hindu press, Sikh journalism remained sporadic and varied in its appeal.[10]

In 1879, another Singh Sabha was set up in Lahore, and by 1899 some 121 Singh Sabhas were operative (Kapur 1986: 17). The rapid expansion in the number of Singh Sabhas necessitated the formation of a central organization to coordinate their activities. In 1902, Chief Khalsa Diwan was instituted, and Sunder Singh Majithia (1872–1941), a prominent member of the Sikh landed gentry, became the first secretary of the Diwan. One of the factors that contributed to the ascendancy of the Lahore Singh Sabha (1879) was the patronage it received from the British. In 1881, Sir Robert Egerton, the Lieutenant Governor of the Punjab, accepted the office of patron of the Lahore Singh Sabha, which enhanced its position considerably.

The interest of the Singh Sabha in establishing modern-style educational institutions led to the foundation of the Khalsa College at Amritsar in 1892. The Khalsa College became a premier Sikh educational institution providing knowledge of Western science and literature, along with imparting *gurmat*, or 'Sikh religious education'. Soon branches of Khalsa Colleges and Khalsa Schools were established all over Punjab. This affirmed a growing acceptance of the moral importance of Western knowledge. Thus, Western-style education became more acceptable, not only because it provided cadres for governmental and corporate hierarchies, but also because it was believed to be morally significant. Moreover, the aim was to create an Anglo-vernacular education that placed emphasis on Punjabi language instruction, with English taught as a second language. The movement for the establishment of a Sikh college received enthusiastic support from the government. Endowments were received from the Viceroy, the Commander-in-Chief of the Indian Army and Sir James Lyall, the Lieutenant-Governor of Punjab. Sikh leaders expressed their gratitude by naming the college Lyall Khalsa College in honour of the Lieutenant-Governor of the province.

The courage shown by the Sikhs during the Anglo-Sikh wars had won great admiration from the British. Commenting on the Second Anglo-Sikh War (1848–9), General Thackwell, a British commander, observed,

> Seikhs caught hold of the bayonets of their assailants with their left hands and closing with their adversaries, dealt furious sword blows with their

right....This circumstance alone will suffice to demonstrate the rare species of courage possessed by these men.

(Kapur 1986: 213)

A similar declaration, that 'Sikhs were the finest martial races in the subcontinent' by S. S. Thorburn (1844–1924), a British civilian, underlined the attitude of a considerable number of British officials. Admiration for Sikh valour turned to gratitude when they remained loyal to the Raj during the Indian mutiny of 1857. Sikhs had come foremost to the defence of the Raj during the mutiny. As a result of Sikh loyalty during the mutiny, recruitment in the army was opened to the Sikhs. The outbreak of the First World War further marshalled the resources of the Punjab province, and Sikh loyalty was once again expressed during the war. Of the twenty-two Military Crosses awarded for gallantry to Indians, fourteen were received by Sikh soldiers (K. Singh 1989). Consequently, the Sikhs were recipients of considerable official patronage. English publishing companies took a keen interest in the Sikhs during the nineteenth and twentieth centuries. During the 31 years following the beginning of the Singh Sabha movement in 1873, a large number of books were published emphasizing the Sikh martial tradition and their loyalty to the British crown.[11]

The ideological issues

Before the key ideological issues concerning the Singh Sabha movement are examined, let us note that there was a diversity of opinion about specific issues among Sikh reformers. There was also a variety of expressions associated with the Lahore Sabha and later the Chief Khalsa Diwan. However, the major thrust was on internal issues. The growing concern was about clear demarcation of Sikh communal boundaries and the defence of the Sikh religion from attacks by other religions. As will be seen in Chapter 4, this process of demarcation of religious boundaries, which began during the nineteenth century, had important ramifications for the demands for Sikh autonomy during the twentieth century.

By the late 1880s the question of Sikh identity became a controversial legal and public issue. In 1877, the first partial English translation of the Adi Granth was published. The translator, Dr Ernest Trumpp, was a controversial German philologist and missionary. This translation was rebutted by the Sikh leadership on the ground that Trumpp had repeatedly made disparaging remarks about their religious tradition. The Sikh leadership was dismayed by Trumpp's claims that he could explain the contents of the Adi Granth better than any Sikh intellectual and that the Sikhs did not know the contents of the Adi Granth. The controversy generated by this issue evoked considerable interest in the interpretation of Sikh scriptures and traditions.

In 1898, the question of Sikh identity became a legal issue. The widow of Dyal Singh Majithia, a Sikh aristocrat and philanthropist, contested his will on the plea that the Hindu law of inheritance under which her husband had bequeathed his fortune to a trust did not apply because he was a Sikh and not a Hindu. The Punjab High Court was left to determine whether Sikhs were or were not Hindus. To the dismay of the Sikh community, the court ruled that Dyal Singh Majithia was, in fact, a Hindu. This sparked controversy in public meetings and in the press over the issue of Sikh identity. Earlier, in 1853, the conspicuous conversion to Christianity by Maharaja Dalip Singh, the last Sikh monarch, had outraged the Sikh public.

The issue of Sikh identity was further sharpened by vociferous Arya Samaj attacks on the Sikh faith. In 1899, two widely circulated pamphlets entitled *Sikh Hindu Hain*, or 'Sikhs are Hindus', claimed that Sikhism was a reformist strain within Hinduism. In response, Bhai Kahn Singh published his classic tract *Ham Hindu Nahin*, 'We are not Hindus', which laid the basis of a distinct Sikh identity. Thereafter, Arya Samaj polemicists engaged in sustained attacks on the Sikh religion and attempts were made to incorporate it within the Hindu fold.

The Sikh reform movement of the 1880s was opposed to the 'inclusivistic' tendencies of the Hindu movement. Scholars of the Sikh religion unanimously accept that Sikhism had historically evolved as an 'exclusive' religion. The Sikh gurus established specific rules of conduct, prescribed rules of membership, preached adherence to specific dogmas and purged the heterodox in the Sikh tradition. This partly explains why the Sikh reform movement of the 1880s was 'exclusive' in contrast to the 'heterodox' and reformist Hindu Arya Samaj movement of the 1880s, which sought to incorporate other religions. It was precisely this logic of Hindu-inclusive tolerance that induced a section of the Sehajdhari[12] Sikh leadership to declare that they were Hindus, and to support a resolution that Sikhs were part of the Hindu community, at a large public meeting to commemorate Queen Victoria's diamond jubilee at Lahore in 1897.

Let us now consider how far the Sikh reform movement succeeded in establishing a new episteme. The central theme of Harjot Oberoi's book *The Construction of Religious Boundaries: Culture, Identity and Diversity in the Sikh Tradition* (1994) is an examination of the processes of construction and transformation of religious identities among the Sikhs during the eighteenth and nineteenth centuries. Harjot Oberoi seeks to question the use of universal, monolithic religious categories such as 'Hindus', 'Sikhs' and 'Muslims' by examining the pluralism of religious traditions, which, he contends, was a distinct central feature of early Indian religion. Against this he maintains that the history of early Sikh tradition, firmly rooted in the diversity of Indic culture, was in fact marked by the absence of a concern for demarcating religious boundaries, which remained fluid and ambiguous. Only later, with the social and political changes generated by the British Raj, was a systematic discourse of Sikhism established.

Harjot Oberoi's book is a classic example of what may be termed the 'hegemony' approach to the study of religious reform in colonial India. The 'hegemony' approach seeks to explain how the rising middle class, empowered by its position in modern capitalism, used religious reform to gain cultural hegemony by gaining control over sacred centres and by defining a uniform, undifferentiated religious discourse with discrete boundaries. The hegemony approach maintains that the urbanized, semi-English-educated middle class attempted to reform their religion by purging it of superstition, irrational and magical beliefs and condemning folk practices such as the veneration of local saints and sorcery. This response was partly to save the indigenous religion from attacks by Christian missionaries, who believed that the present decadence of Indian civilization was due to the belief in superstitions and polytheism.

This view holds that in pre-colonial India the boundaries that marked the beliefs and practices of Indian religion were open, allowing room for local practices. Participation of different religious communities in the worship of local saints is interpreted as a sign of in-built tolerance. But, what did this mean to the different religious communities involved in these shared practices? What was the nature of their interaction with each other? What were the constraints on this interaction? These questions have been persistently ignored.

Harjot Oberoi maintains that the Tat Khalsa leadership comprised a new class, which established a new discourse of modern Sikhism. This new class needed a meaningful, standard cultural idiom to universalize its aspirations. They articulated and disseminated the discourse of modern Sikhism by generating new texts and by selecting symbols, ceremonies and customs. Through a series of innovations the Tat Khalsa provided the Sikhs with a distinct and separate Sikh identity by endowing them with a standard history, text, ritual calendar, life-cycle rituals, sacred space and festivities. The process involved the selection of specific traditions, beliefs and practices that provided key features to the formulation of a codified, corporate Sikh identity. According to Oberoi, the new doctrine of monotheism and scripturalism constituted 'a gross transgression of Sikh doctrine' (Oberoi 1994: 323). The new doctrine established a fundamental change in the definition of a Sikh, and the new discourse was universalistic, positivist, rational and heavily imprinted with a Protestant-style ethic. Thus, in the course of the nineteenth century, a profound and irreversible transition from an earlier pluralist Sikh tradition into a highly uniform Sikh identity took place. The Sikhs began to see themselves as a separate, undifferentiated religious community.

But the approach adopted by Oberoi provides only a partial understanding of the historical process of identity formation. This view is based on the contention that the Singh Sabha reformers enunciated a fundamentally new Sikh doctrine which dramatically transformed the Sikh identity. Harjot Oberoi argues that in order to establish a separate Sikh identity, the Khalsa Sikhs formulated 'their own code of conduct, a novel form of initiation and some new rites of passage' (Oberoi 1994: 89). What was so novel and profound about this message remains unexplained in Oberoi's book and contradicts his earlier observations. For instance, he argues, 'But in the eighteenth century the Khalsa Sikhs became keenly aware of the absence of distinct life-cycle rituals and took urgent steps to rectify the situation by introducing new rites, particularly to mark birth, initiation and death' (Oberoi 1994: 63,65–7). This is in stark contrast to his later claim, 'Similarly, in the area of life-cycle rituals, Sikhs had not as yet formulated distinctive marriage and mortuary rituals' (Oberoi 1994: 90). On the one hand, he argues that the Khalsa Sikhs had established their distinctive rites of passage, initiation ritual and rites to mark birth and death by the eighteenth century. On the other hand, he claims that a novel form of initiation and exclusive Khalsa life-cycle rituals were constituted by the Tat Khalsa reformers only during the nineteenth century. It is evident that there was nothing innovative about the Sikh initiation ritual, and the rites to mark birth and death. Oberoi surprisingly does not consider the systematic and rigorous religious and moral codes an initiated person was required to follow. This is one of the reasons why the percentage of Sikhs who undergo an initiation rite remains fractional, even among the *Kesdhari* Sikhs (Sikhs who retain uncut hair). The Sikh initiation rite is consonant with the teachings of Guru Nanak. Oberoi empties the Sikh initiation rite of its profound, ritual and symbolic significance, and reduces it merely to its overt function as an ethnic marker. But religious rituals aim at transforming the self by overcoming the forces that threaten personal and cosmic harmony, and cosmological understandings are communicated in religious rituals.

In other words, Oberoi's suggestion that the beliefs and practices of the Tat Khalsa movement in the nineteenth century marked a fundamental transformation in Sikh identity and were radically different from earlier Sikh tradition is not only difficult to sustain empirically, but also self-contradictory. The iconoclastic monotheism and egalitarian social values were precisely the principal teachings of the Sikh gurus.

Another basic limitation of the approach adopted by Oberoi is that only a small section of the middle class subscribed to this distinct and standard version of religious identity. In Oberoi's discussion this assumption is thrown into sharp relief. For instance, did a majority of the Sikhs uphold the standard Khalsa paradigm since it regained hegemony in the nineteenth century? If so, how can the plurality in the Sikh tradition since the nineteenth century be explained? Similarly, was the Sikh initiation ritual endorsed by all individuals who embraced the Khalsa tradition? If so, why has the number of baptized Sikhs remained fractional in the Sikh community? By the same logic, if the urban mode of religious experience was dominated by the Sanatan paradigm (see below), did all urban Sikhs subscribe to the Sanatan tradition?[13]

Thus, the Singh Sabha expended much of its energy on defending Sikh identity from the inroads of Christian missionaries and from attacks by Hindu proselytizers. Early Sikh organizations were, therefore, involved in the process of defining group boundaries and differentiation from other groups. As Kenneth W. Jones notes, 'Sikhs in future years might debate who they were, but they knew with increasing certainty who they were not: *Ham Hindu Nahin!*' (Jones 1973: 475).

The struggle over reconstitution of sacred space

In the period between 1920 and 1925, Sikh reformers launched a series of agitations in order to gain management and control of sacred Sikh shrines. The running of Sikh temples had for centuries been entrusted to *mahants*, or priests. The *gurudwara* reform movement of the 1920s had profound implications for the consolidation of Sikh communal consciousness.

Under Sikh rule (1801–49), the Sikh aristocracy and the landed gentry required religious specialists to perform ritual functions for them, and the religious intermediaries received generous endowments from their élite clientele in pre-colonial Punjab. Thus, since the eighteenth century, a body of guru lineages and other holy men – the Sanatan Sikhs – had gained control over Sikh shrines. There were fundamental differences in the doctrines and religious practices of Khalsa Sikhs and the Sanatan Sikhs. Whereas the Khalsa normative order required Sikhs to maintain the external symbols of the Sikh faith and to adhere to the *rahit* injunctions, the Sanatan Sikhs did not consider it mandatory to maintain unshorn hair and believed that salvation could be attained through their own esoteric methods. The Sanatan Sikhs considered that they were not bound by the *rahit-namas*, and they took to idol worship, the worship of living gurus and accepted the caste system as being fundamental to the Sikh faith.

The Sanatan Sikh tradition was generated and transmitted primarily by the priestly class. Three categories of men acted as religious intermediaries: members of guru lineages, holy men (*bhais, sants, babas*) and traditional intellectuals (*gianis, dhadhis*). Thus the Sanatan Sikhs gained control over Sikh shrines and articulated Sikh theology and tradition. Harjot Oberoi contends that although in principle the role of the guru was exclusively reserved for the holy word of the Sikh gurus and the scripture served as a channel between man and God, in actual practice this doctrine was too abstract. This principle was successfully invoked by the religious specialists to consolidate their position.

The influence of the priestly *mahants* was enhanced under the British by the colonial state granting large revenue-free estates to the *gurudwaras*. As a result, the revenue derived from Sikh ecclesiastical property increased enormously. Further, elaborate land-settlement records were compiled by the British authorities and *mahants* were granted proprietary rights over the *gurudwara* estates, which they maintained on behalf of the Sikh community. The *mahants* began to regard the *gurudwara* lands and revenue as their personal property. Allegations of licentious living, misappropriation of funds, debauchery and sacrilege were made against the *mahants* of several *gurudwaras*. Some local congregations marshalled popular pressure against them and tried to make them relinquish control. But the large revenue derived from *gurudwara* estates empowered them to resist popular pressure.

Moreover, the *mahants* were accused of 'Hinduization' of Sikh customs and of flagrant abuse and debasement of the Sikh faith. *Gurudwara* priests were accused of committing sacrilege by instating Hindu idols in the precincts of the Golden Temple, the premier Sikh shrine. Reformers pointed with growing bitterness to the prevalence of 'non-Sikh' practices and customs in Sikh worship. Controversy over the mismanagement of sacred Sikh shrines led to a sustained campaign to reconstitute the sacred space by gaining control over the management of Sikh temples. One of the key objectives of the nineteenth-century Sikh reform movement was to purge the pervasive influence of Brahmanical beliefs by expelling the priestly *mahants* or *pujaris*. Other Brahmanical beliefs that had crept into the Sikh tradition were idolatry and polytheism.

Changes in the larger political arena

Spurred on by their particular grievances and by the contagion of the prevalent spirit of national consciousness, the Sikhs initiated a campaign of non-violent, non-cooperation against the colonial authorities. Matters were brought to a head on 13 April 1919, when a peaceful public gathering at Jallianwallah Bagh in Amritsar was brutally suppressed by Brigadier General R. E. H. Dyer. Troops were ordered to open fire without warning on the unarmed crowd, killing 379 and wounding more than 2,000 others. The Jallianwallah Bagh massacre became a landmark in the history of India's independence movement. The unsolicited comments to General Dyer by the priest in charge of the Golden Temple, Arur Singh, provoked a furore in Tat Khalsa circles. The disturbances in the Punjab in 1919 heightened the urgency for the Sikh community to gain control of the *gurudwaras*.

Perturbed by these events, the Punjab government appointed a provisional committee to formulate proposals regarding the running of the Golden Temple. The thirty-six-member committee was composed entirely of reputable Sikh landed and aristocratic families. The Singh Sabha leadership expressed disapproval of the committee and convened a large gathering at the Golden Temple on 16 November 1920. A new committee of 175 members was elected. However, the new committee included members of the committee appointed by the government. The Punjab government allowed the formation of the committee and pursued a policy of non-interference and neutrality. In December 1920, the new committee in charge of the *gurudwara* was named as the Shiromani Gurudwara Prabahandak Committee (SGPC). The SGPC resolved to liberate all *gurudwaras* from the corrupt *mahants*. The SGPC was assisted by the Shiromani Akali Dal, a centralized body instituted at Amritsar in December 1920, in coordinating the activities of local bands of volunteers known as Akali *jathas*. The Akalis, or 'soldiers of the *akal*, or immortal', was a militant order, adhering strictly to the Khalsa precepts and ascribing its origin to the tenth Sikh master, Guru Gobind Singh. The Akalis had risen to a position of considerable prominence under Phula Singh Akali, one of Maharaja Ranjit Singh's able commanders. Subsequently, after the death of Phula Singh the order lost its authority and virtually disappeared. The bands of volunteers in the army of Maharaja Ranjit Singh were called *jathas*. The SGPC and the

Shiromani Akali Dal, became the foremost Sikh institutions of the twentieth century and were to play a vital role in Sikh affairs.

After the success of Akali reformers in gaining control of the Golden Temple, attention was focused on the *gurudwara* at Nankana. Nankana Sahib, the site of the birthplace of Guru Nanak, was associated with several shrines marking various events in the guru's childhood. The *mahant* of the *gurudwara*, Narain Das, had a reputation for immorality and licentiousness and had been accused of misappropriating *gurudwara* funds. The misconduct of the *mahant* of the *gurudwara* had elicited sharp condemnation from the local congregation, but the considerable revenue derived from the *gurudwara* estates made the *mahant* immune to the censure of the public. The Akali struggle to gain control of the Sikh shrines was gaining rapid momentum. Public meetings were held and resolutions were passed by the reformers condemning the conduct of Narain Das. Apprehensive about being ousted by Akali reformers, the *mahant* approached the government for protection. While the government would not of its own accord take direct action, the incumbent managers of the shrine were encouraged to make private arrangements. Narain Das took matters in his own hands. The *gurudwara* was fortified and some eighty mercenaries were hired to defend the shrine. Arms and ammunition were stockpiled to defend the *gurudwara*. On 20 February 1921, an Akali *jatha* made an unscheduled trip to Nankana without any intention of taking it over. Moments after the *jatha* entered the precincts of the *gurudwara*, the *mahant's* men opened fire upon them without warning. Those who attempted to seek refuge within the shrine were chased and slaughtered. The dead and the wounded were then collected in heaps and burnt on the spot in an attempt to obliterate evidence of the massacre. On hearing the news of the cold-blooded massacre at Nankana, thousands of Akalis hastened towards Nankana Sahib. The local authorities restricted access to the shrine. The government was forced to concede, and on 3 March 1921 the running of the shrine was handed over to a temporary committee of Akalis. Narain Das and twenty-six of his henchmen were arrested.

The hideous massacre at Nankana brought several prominent nationalist politicians, including Mahatma Gandhi, to the site. They exploited prevalent anti-government sentiment to imbue Sikhs with a vital nationalism. Meanwhile, the Sikhs were exhorted to join in the nationalist movement of non-cooperation and appeals for boycotting the official inquiry into the Nankana massacre were made. In May 1921, the Shiromani Gurudwara Prabandhak Committee passed a resolution in support of a campaign of non-cooperation and issued an appeal to the Sikh community to commence civil disobedience.

In October 1921, the executive committee of the SGPC passed a resolution asking the *mahant* of the Golden Temple, Sunder Singh Ramgarhia, to hand over the keys to the *toshakhana*, or 'treasury', of the shrine to the committee. The SGPC insisted that Sunder Singh Ramgarhia, being an official nominee, represented government control over the sacred treasures of the Golden

Temple. In November 1921, relations between Sikh activists and the local government deteriorated further, and the Punjab government took possession of the keys to the *toshakhana*. The Punjab government's action evoked a sharp reaction from the SGPC. The committee accused the government of interfering in the religious affairs of the Sikh community. In response to an appeal from the SGPC, Akali *jathas* began congregating at Amritsar and protest meetings were organized. In a gesture of defiance the Punjab government fixed their own locks to the *toshakhana*, escalating the bitterness among Sikhs at the attitude of the Punjab government.

The recurring conflict between the Sikhs and the government was not only imposing strains on Anglo-Sikh relations but also the alliance between the Akalis and the nationalists was being consolidated. Public opinion concerning allegations of government interference in religious affairs was permeating Sikh troops and the Sikh peasantry, the two staunch bastions of the British Raj. In a conciliatory gesture, the Punjab government decided to hand over the keys of the *toshakhana* to the SGPC and agreed to the release of all Sikhs arrested in connection with the affair. Mahatma Gandhi telegraphed the SGPC on their success over the key issue, 'Congratulations, first decisive battle for India's freedom won' (*The Tribune* 17 January 1922). Sikh unrest over the key affair witnessed active cooperation with nationalist politicians and saw Sikh involvement in the mounting nationalist campaign of non-cooperation with the government. Thus, Sikh communal concerns became linked to wider Indian demands.

In August 1922, another shrine, Guru-ka-Bagh (the garden of the guru), the site of a small shrine built to mark the visit of Guru Arjan, situated some 12 miles from Amritsar, was the scene of fresh confrontation between the Sikh activists and the government. Controversy over the control of this shrine had resulted in a settlement between the Akalis and *mahant* Sunder Das, under which the *mahant* remained in charge of the shrine under the supervision of a managing committee of which he himself was a member. However, in March 1921 the *mahant* revolted against this agreement, forcibly occupied the office of the committee and destroyed its records. On 9 August 1922, the Akalis at Guru-ka-Bagh had chopped wood on land adjoining the *gurudwara* for use as fuel in the *guru-ka-langar* (free community kitchen) provided at the shrine. Sunder Das had them arrested on charges of theft. The arrests at Guru-ka-Bagh sparked off what is regarded as the most famous Akali struggle for control over Sikh shrines. The bitter controversy was over the larger problem of *gurudwara* management. The Akalis contended that the *mahant*, a mere custodian of the shrine, could not claim private possession of sacred property, which they insisted belonged to the Sikh Panth. The Akalis warned the government that by denying the Sikhs their religious duty of collecting fuel for the *guru-ka-langar*, the government was evidently determined to undermine their faith.

News of the arrests at Guru-ka-Bagh attracted other Akali volunteers who marched towards the disputed shrine. The SGPC launched a sustained campaign and dispatched Akali *jathas*, or 'a band of volunteers', daily to Guru-ka-Bagh. Each *jatha* would take a vow of non-violence at the Golden Temple before proceeding to march towards Guru-ka-Bagh, where they were arrested daily by the local authorities. By October 1922, the number of Akalis arrested was more than 2,450. As waves of *jathas* kept coming, the authorities began to resort to violent tactics. Nationalist leaders rallied to support the Sikh cause by making speeches at the site of confrontation. C. F. Andrews, who visited the Guru-ka-Bagh in September 1922, was shocked by the brutality of the British administration and noted that the Akali tactics were a 'new lesson in moral warfare' (Grewal 1990: 161). He protested to the Lieutenant-Governor of Punjab, Edward Maclagan, and the dispute at Guru-ka-Bagh was finally settled and the *mahant* was persuaded to sell the disputed land to Sir Ganga Ram, a notable Hindu philanthropist. During the 5-year Akali campaign, nearly 400 men had lost their lives, over 2,000 were wounded and more than 30,000 had gone to jail (Kapur 1986: xv).

The Government of India had grave misgivings regarding the escalating controversy over the control of sacred Sikh shrines. The Sikh Gurudwaras and Shrines Bill of 1925 conceded the management and control of all Sikh religious institutions to the Sikh community. On 7 May 1925, the Bill was introduced in the Punjab Legislative Council and was implemented on 1 November 1925. This Act brought Sikh *gurudwaras* and shrines under the jurisdiction of the SGPC. The Sikh Gurudwara Act was of immense significance for the Sikh community. The guardianship of all Sikh religious institutions in the Punjab conferred a unique religious authority on the SGPC. The income derived from religious property and the daily offerings of devotees provided the SGPC with access to enormous financial resources. The annual budget of the SGPC from these sources was considerable and was estimated at Rs 841,952,258 for 1995–6 (*The Tribune*, 23 March 1996). Access to substantial funds enabled the SGPC to establish numerous schools and colleges, hospitals and medical dispensaries. The surplus income enabled the SGPC to recruit a body of *grandhis*, or 'scripture readers', to propagate Sikh tenets. Moreover, the SGPC could exercise its unique sacred authority through which Akal Takhat could issue *hukamnamas*, or 'edicts', binding upon all Sikhs through the head priests of important Sikh *gurudwaras*. The staffing and management of various institutions under the control of the SGPC created a significant network of patronage for the SGPC. This gave the SGPC a formidable platform from which to reach the Sikh community. The SGPC rapidly became a forum and a power base for Sikh political action. Thus, the 1925 Act provided the Sikhs with an unparalleled, highly organized institutional structure in the form of the SGPC. The formation of the SGPC, an elected, representative organization of the Sikhs, further emphasized the demarcation between Sikhs and Hindus.

After the 1925 Act had been passed, the Shiromani Akali Dal emerged as an important political party. As a result of the close historical evolution of the SGPC and the Akali Dal, close links between the highly organized cadre of Akali workers and the SGPC's cadre of religious functionaries have been maintained until the present day. The Akali Dal derives significant strength from its ability to dominate the SGPC.

Despite the drawing of communal boundaries between the Sikhs and Hindus over several decades, the bonds between the Sikhs and a large body of Punjabi Hindus were strong. Common identification with social and historical traditions, a shared spoken language and culture bound the two communities together. After the 1925 Act had been passed, the persistent concern of Sikh leaders became the maintenance of a separate Sikh communal identity. The primary political objective of the Akali Dal was to safeguard Sikh religious liberty by maintaining and promoting separately the political existence of the Sikhs and securing greater political leverage for Sikhs. Under the Montagu-Chelmsford constitutional reforms introduced in 1921, the Sikhs were granted separate electorates in the Punjab legislature.

In the decades before India's independence, the Akalis had urged Sikhs to participate in the nationalist campaign. The population of Punjab province under British rule was 52 per cent Muslim, 30 per cent Hindu and 14 per cent Sikh.[14] The Sikhs supplied a significant contingent to the Indian army, and, although only some 14 per cent of the provincial population, they contributed almost one-third of the provincial land revenue. The Akalis insisted that Sikhs were not adequately represented in the provincial legislative bodies and pressed for greater Sikh political representation. This was opposed by the Hindu politicians on the grounds that Sikhs were Hindus. In all, the Sikhs had thirteen seats at both the Council of States and the Legislative Assembly between 1919 and 1947. The Akalis demanded that if separate electorates were maintained, the rights of the Sikhs could only be protected if they were granted a one-third share in any scheme of provincial administration. In 1932, the British administration announced its decision to maintain separate electorates and to reserve seats in legislatures for minority communities. This decision granted the Sikhs thirty-three of 175 seats in the Punjab Legislative Assembly and special representation at the centre. Thus, only 18 per cent representation was granted to the Sikhs in the Punjab legislature. The Akalis were bitterly critical of this decision, the communal award as it was called.

When the possibility of a sovereign Muslim state of Pakistan was imminent, the Akali Dal proposed the creation of a new territorial unit called Azad Punjab, or free Punjab, through a redemarcation of the boundaries of Punjab. The Azad Punjab scheme of the Akali Dal was a defensive strategy to create a province in which the Muslim population was 40 per cent, the Hindu population also 40 per cent and the Sikhs 20 per cent. The dynamic Akali leader Master Tara Singh declared that although Sikhs were a nation they did not constitute a majority and did not have the right to demand a Sikh state. Therefore, the proposed state was not intended to be a separate Sikh state, but a province that would curtail the constitutional domination by a single community and thus bolster Sikh influence. Such a demand was rejected by the Indian political leaders. A Sikh conference was held in August 1944, and a committee was set up to look into the possibility of the creation of an independent Sikh state. The Akali leaders maintained that if the demand for Pakistan was conceded, the Sikhs would insist on a separate Sikh state, with the right to federate with either India or Pakistan. In March 1946, a resolution adopted by the Akali Dal stated,

> Whereas the Sikhs being attached to the Punjab by intimate bonds of holy shrines, property, language, traditions, and history claim it as their homeland and holy land and which the British took as a 'trust' from the last Sikh ruler during his minority and whereas the entity of the Sikhs is being threatened on account of the persistent demand for Pakistan by the Muslims on the one hand and of the danger of absorption by the Hindus on the other, the Executive Committee of the Shiromani Akali Dal demands, for the preservation and protection of the religious, cultural and economic rights of the Sikh nation, the creation of a Sikh state.
>
> (H. Singh 1964: 302)

However, even when the Sikh leaders talked of a Sikh state, what they still had in mind was an area in which no single community would form a majority. This they believed would give the Sikhs a secure political position, which was necessary to safeguard and guarantee Sikh religious freedom. At the time, the Akali leaders contended that they had been persuaded to give up this demand after promises from Congress leaders that the Sikhs would be granted special status in independent India.

The striking question with regard to Sikh political demands is: why was there no Sikh nationalist movement in the 1880s in spite of a rising Sikh bourgeoisie and an energetic intelligentsia? Further, why did the Sikhs not aspire to form an independent Sikh state despite the acquisition of a cohesive Sikh identity in the nineteenth century and the historic fact of Sikh rule? It would be misleading to give any definitive answers, but, broadly speaking, Sikh leaders did not demand a separate Sikh state because Sikhs were territorially dispersed and were a permanent minority in the Punjab province. They, therefore, reasoned that Sikh political demands had to be confined primarily to questions of representation rather than a separate political status. Here it is useful to remember that Sikh folk memories are infused with bitter struggles against the tyranny of the Mogul rule. In contrast, the bonds between Sikhs and Hindus remained strong, despite the development of inter-communal consciousness. A common identification with the same social and historical traditions, a shared spoken language and culture, and similar caste identifications weld the two communities together. Even in religious matters, Sikhism had roots in Indic philosophical tradition; therefore sociologically Sikh and Hindu religious thought had much in common. Moreover, Hindu and Sikh rulers had frequently formed alliances against Mogul domination, and Sikhs had a history of defending the Hindus from Muslim persecution. It is for this reason that when the Akali Dal shifted its mandate from religious reform to political action in the 1940s, Sikhs collaborated with Hindus throughout most of the nationalist period. This highlights the tangled and contradictory relationships between Sikhs and Hindus. Thus, Sikh political aspirations are characterized by ambiguity and uncertainty, and by the need for political compromise with other groups.

In effect, the most important role played by the Singh Sabha was the introduction of new associational forms, such as the SGPC – a central committee for the control of Sikh shrines and its political wing – and the Akali Dal, which moulded the growth of modern Sikhism. However, the establishment of a modern institutional framework was concomitant with the strengthening of existing traditional institutions of power and patronage, such as the traditional intellectuals and the landed gentry.[15] Also, Sikh shrines continued to be the foci of Sikh activism. Another critical contribution of the Singh Sabha was the establishment of educational institutions and the introduction of printing press which published newspapers, books and religious tracts in the Gurmukhi script. Thus, the foremost impact of the energetic activities of Singh Sabha reformers, which spanned a period of 55 years, was that it forged the formation of institutions which were critical in the recasting and revitalization of Sikh communal consciousness.

New leaders and new arenas: recasting social identities

There is a growing body of sophisticated literature which demonstrates that in the eighteenth and nineteenth centuries some forces were creating areas of greater ideological and practical uniformity within the broad boundaries of religious affiliation.[16] In this section, the processes that gave rise to specific social and ideological formations in colonial Punjab will be delineated. How examine these profound social transformations energized and hardened pre-existing religious affiliations will be examined.

In the preceding sections it has been shown that the vital orchestrator of these reform movements was the editor, or the publicist, or the writer, or the clerk or the subordinate public official. Despite their sectarian orientation, these bodies of men belonged to broadly similar social backgrounds.

Richard G. Fox (1985) has examined the religious reform movements in Punjab in the nineteenth century within the context of longer term socio-economic transformation. He explores the processes that fostered the expansion of a particular social class under the aegis of British colonialism. He explains how the penetration of the capitalist world economy into British Punjab harnessed agricultural production to the world system without radically transforming rural productivity or capital investment. This, Fox argues, altered the existing relations of production in such a way that it led to an expansion of indigenous mercantile interests. A collectivity of Punjabi money lenders and merchants received their share from the colonial appropriation of rural surplus and combined to form the growing urban lower middle class. The factors that predisposed the fostering of this caste of commodity traders in colonial Punjab has been the subject of some highly stimulating work.[17] That the commercial communities survived into and even expanded their dealings during the colonial period is concluded by C. A. Bayly (1992) in his pioneering study.

The category of leaders who proclaimed moral leadership of communities belonged overwhelmingly to the mercantile castes – Aroras, Baniyas and Khatris. However, efforts to represent this community conceptually run into difficulties. The major difficulty is that these classes did not arise out of an industrial revolution as was clearly the case in Europe. Therefore, labels like 'lower middle class (petty bourgeoisie)' used by C. A. Bayly and R. G. Fox to define this social group are unsatisfactory.[18] No matter which conceptual category we prefer to use, we must bear in mind the distinctive pattern of class formation in India. Thus, the social situation of these reformers allowed them access to the medium of anglo-vernacular education, which enjoined them to acquire bilingual skills and gain hegemony over the print medium. To sum up, by the 1880s a distinct commercial class had risen in India. It was these influential commercial and professional classes who spearheaded the anti-colonial, religious reform movements in British Punjab.

Print communication and the creation of a new public sphere

We will now consider how the 'revivalist' streams of Hinduism, Islam and Sikhism, which originated in the late eighteenth or early nineteenth centuries, were energized by the spread of print communication. A significant aspect of the British Raj was the impetus it gave to the development of indigenous press and publishing. In 1905, of the approximately 260 newspapers and journals published in Punjab, twelve were in English, eighteen in two or more languages, seventeen in Punjabi (Gurmukhi script), fifteen in Hindi and the remainder in Urdu.[19] Clearly the bulk of printed communication was in regional languages, and these newspapers were circulated among a growing audience of literates. These publications accelerated the spread of vernacular scripts, unintentionally helping to turn them into a popular medium of expression of religious and cultural solidarity. The educational and printing activities of the Hindu, Muslim and Sikh reformers either promoted or used Hindi, Urdu and Punjabi respectively as a medium of communication. Fellow readers to whom they were connected in print experienced a feeling of growing communality. Thus, the vernacular press became a powerful medium of correct knowledge and behaviour. As will be seen in Chapter 6, by the 1970s the vernacular press and radiocassettes had become foremost in transmitting religious messages that had mass appeal.

The account by Kenneth Jones (1992) of the philological-lexicographic revolution in nineteenth-century Punjab presents evidence which shows that polemical religious literature served to debate differing opinions in tracts, journals and plays. Sacred texts supporting movements were translated and made available in inexpensive editions. Even texts from the well-established oral tradition were put into print. The philological incendiaries relied extensively on polemical literature and exploited cheap popular editions for the new literate public in order to mobilize them for politico-religious purposes. While internal religious polemics pitted social and religious reformers against orthodox members of the same religious community, external polemics was directed between defenders of one faith and the opponents of other faiths. The overall positions articulated in polemical literature were uncompromising and sparked religious controversies between different religious communities.

The writings of Hindus, Muslims and Sikhs acted to redefine group identities and heightened the sense of boundary-defining identity. So by 1900, Sikhs 'knew with increasing certainty who they were not: Ham Hindu Nahin!'(Jones 1973: 475). The most important consequence of the dialectic process of questioning and redefining the past was the recasting of ideological systems, which altered the existing relations among different religious groups. The ideological positions and polemical techniques forged in the nineteenth century led to politicized expression of religion in the twentieth century.

To recapitulate thus far: the massive social transformation generated by the British Raj comprised the commercialization of the rural economy and revolution in communications. Both these changes favoured the mercantile, trading castes, who gained access to anglo-vernacular education and acquired new skills in the mechanics of print culture. These bodies of men were employed by the British had had an English-style education. It is widely accepted that the rise of the literate, bilingual professional commercial class, and the resulting interlock between specific education and administration, was central to the growth of communal consciousness in nineteenth century Punjab. The reformers were based primarily in urban settings where publishing facilities were available and newspapers and journals served to create bonds among members of the receptive audience. This affirms the arresting formulation of Benedict Anderson, 'Thus in world-historical terms bourgeoisies were the first classes to achieve solidarities on an essentially imagined basis' (Anderson 1991: 77).

The development of standardized vernacular languages of state

The outstanding communication skills of Christian missionaries not only helped in securing converts but also played a vital role in the standardization of north Indian languages.[20] The printing process encourages homogenization by standardizing scripts, lexicons and grammatical rules. The general growth in literacy, communications and the expansion of colonial machinery that characterized nineteenth century Punjab created powerful impulses for religion-based linguistic uniformity.

Administrative requirements alongside the spread of vernacular education allowed the development of selected Indo-Aryan varieties as administrative vernaculars. The British conquest of Punjab witnessed the spread of Urdu, the Persianized form of the lingua franca based on the Khari Boli dialect of Delhi.[21] However, the Urdu norms of Delhi and Lucknow were to come under increasing challenge from its Sanskratized variant, Hindi, the newly formed medium promoted by the Benaras and Allahabad enthusiasts. In 1837, the North Indian administrative language, Persian, was replaced by the pre-eminent world imperial language English. In north India, this meant that Persian was replaced by Urdu as the official language of the province in 1855. Thus, Urdu, along with English, was the officially established medium of provincial administration, whose seat was at Lahore. Urdu was introduced as the medium of primary education. Since Urdu became the hegemonic language of general communication, all three religious communities in Punjab comprised a considerable proportion of Urdu literates.[22]

The subordinate position of Hindi and Punjabi in government courts and offices contrasted with Urdu, which was well entrenched in the higher reaches of administration. Hindi and Punjabi were promoted by the Arya Samaj and by the Chief Khalsa Diwan respectively through the establishment of an extensive network of private educational institutions and through publishing efforts. The Arya Samaj protagonists challenged the preponderance of Urdu, which represented the Persianate mixed culture of North Indian élites and sought to displace Urdu by Hindi as the official vernacular language. The Hindi–Urdu controversy in nineteenth- and twentieth-century Punjab resulted in the association of Urdu with Muslim dominance, whereas Hindi was associated with past resistance to Muslim rule and became the edifice of Hindu nationality. Further, the Arya Samaj polemicists also denounced the use of Punjabi.

It was only in the 1900s that modern standard Punjabi (MSP) developed as a standardized medium of formal literary expression, although the vast bulk of the sacred and literary literature of the Sikhs has been recorded in the distinctive Gurmukhi script, and some form of Punjabi spoken by a majority of Punjabis. The Sikh reformers championed the introduction of Punjabi in Gurmukhi script as the medium of education and administration on the grounds that Punjabi was the dominant language of the province. They reasoned that Punjabi was the dominant spoken language in the province.

What makes the evolution of modern standard Punjabi so striking is that unlike Urdu, which had enjoyed an unbroken pattern of evolution as a literary language, and Hindi, the new Sanskritized variant whose firmly entrenched heritage provided a solid linguistic base, Punjabi had none of these innate advantages. Moreover, it is interesting to note that Hindi and Sanskrit are written in the Devnagari script, whereas Urdu and Persian are in the Persian script. Print capitalism did not change the script but popularized a language. In the case of Gurmukhi it was the reverse. Print popularized the script but the language remained the same. This was because Punjabi had earlier been written in the Persian script.

Thus Urdu, written in a modified form of the Arabic script, came to symbolize the Qur'an, the core of Islam, whereas Hindi in the Devanagri script became associated with Sanskrit and the Hindu scriptures, and Punjabi in the Gurmukhi script became a marker of Sikh identity. The identification of each of the three major literary languages with one of the three main religious communities in Punjab generated a struggle among all religious communities to secure a place for their language for administrative purposes. Thus, the struggle over religio-linguistic identity fostered the development of a standardized language of state. The dramatic political effects of this historic struggle culminated in the establishment of Hindi and Urdu as the national languages of India and Pakistan respectively. Thus, print languages were of central ideological and political significance in equating script and a separate linguistic identity which underpins contemporary religious identities.

It is important to note that Hindi and Urdu were used by a small proportion of the literate population, the great bulk of the illiterate population spoke the regional or local dialects. How far the urban and rural masses shared in the new vernacularly imagined communities depended to a large extent on the relationship between the masses and the spokesmen of nationalism.

The revolution in print communication and the spread of education also affirmed a transition from the traditional form of learning based on a privileged personal relationship between the teacher and student to a more public and impersonal form of education, imparted in formally organized schools and aided by the availability of printed books. Access to traditional forms of learning, in a ritual setting, had earlier been restricted to a privileged few, and the new educational institutions also widened the access of the population to new forms of learning. Here it is useful to remember that although these bodies of men came to promulgate the revitalized religious tradition they were not traditional intellectuals – the heirs of the historically transmitted traditional learning.

Interpretations of this historic shift stress its dramatic nature. Historians argue that this historic shift to a new form of learning entailed a dramatic levelling of caste barriers. People prohibited by birth from receiving education now had access to learning. In a somewhat similar vein, Harjot Oberoi (1994) claims that this new class displaced the traditional cultural bearers such as the *nais*, bards, minstrels, genealogists, healers, local saints and shamans. The traditional mediators like the *nais* and *mirasis* had key ritual roles in customary matrimonial practices and in transmitting social values. They were entitled to customary obligations from their patrons in exchange for their services. Oberoi argues that the 'New élite that cut across kin ties, neighbourhood networks and even caste affiliations' (Oberoi 1994: 265). In the process, the traditional social order based on kinship was destroyed and replaced by a standard, highly uniform Sikh tradition, and allegiances based on kinship were replaced by religious solidarity in colonial Punjab.

In the light of these accounts, which conjure a dramatic historical transformation, let us now consider some historical facts. In 1881, approximately 87 per cent of the population of Punjab province lived in the 34,000 villages[23] and a further 93 per cent of the population of Punjab – an overwhelming majority – was still illiterate![24] Between 1891 and 1921, the proportion of the provincial population living in urban areas was 9.5 per cent of the total population.[25] Thus, only a minuscule, privileged minority was directly affected by these historical processes. Nonetheless, even if only 7 per cent of the Punjabi population was literate by the late 1880s, this was a proportion unprecedented in the history of Punjab. Moreover, these literates were committed to a rapid increase in their own numbers.

Therefore, Oberoi's description of the sudden and radical displacement of one set of cultural bearers by another group and the destruction of a social order at a specific historical moment is oversimplified and deficient. Even if we are to accept Oberoi's suggestion, how can we explain the striking presence of cultural mediators, such as *pirs, bharais, mirasis, ojhas* and saints, who were meant to have perished in the nineteenth century in contemporary Punjab? It seems implausible that teachers, journalists, lawyers and clerks displaced the traditional mediators. Oberoi contends that marriages were now arranged through new networks and (reformed!) marriage rites. The Anand Marriage Bill introduced in the Imperial Council in October 1908, which conferred legal recognition on the Sikh marriage ceremony, made the role of traditional social groups (i.e. *nais*) redundant. One wonders how all the marriages could possibly have been arranged through newspapers, when the majority of the population resided in rural tracts and was not literate. Colonialism did bring about a profound social transformation in Indian society. But Oberoi's restricted view only describes the social transformation among the Sikhs; he thus overlooks the profound implications of the wider changes in the socio-economic sphere in colonial Punjab.

If the outcome of the revolution in print culture and founding of modern style educational institutions was confined to the new urban élite, how might we explain the extraordinary success of the reform movements? What were the factors that conduced to mass mobilization? The founding of the printing press went together with the establishment of an extensive social network that successfully intervened at the level of everyday life. Traditional methods of transmitting and disseminating information through personal and institutionalized relationships continued to remain equally influential. Moreover, improved mobility by train, bus and rail facilitated the rapid increase in the number of pilgrims visiting pilgrim centres, where they could be informed about reform movements. Further, the bulk of the population of the province was occupied in agricultural pursuits. Early in this account, we have seen how the vast horde of unlettered Sikh peasantry was mobilized through the Akali *jathas* on specific issues, such as control over Sikh sacred shrines.[26] Undoubtedly, the politically vigorous Sikh bourgeoisie of town dwellers spearheaded the anti-colonial Sikh reform movement, which also linked them with the peasantry. Although important, a comprehensive analysis of the historical circumstances within which the fateful alignment between the Sikh bourgeoisie and the massive reservoir of Sikh peasantry arose lies outside the scope of this account. However, in very general terms, a substantial section of both strata of the population felt cramped by the British Raj, driving them into a coalition.

In contrast, Hindus predominantly resided in urban areas and were engaged in the commercial activities of the bazaar. This facilitated the vigorous permeation of the aggressive message of the Arya Samaj to Punjabi Hindus.

Conclusion

We have been dealing with a long period of north Indian history and with a society in great turmoil in which ideas and structures were constantly being contested. Any generalizations must, therefore, be avoided. An examination of the historical and social development of early Sikh tradition shows that along with an evolving inventory of Sikh separatist symbols and a doctrinal discourse, the Sikhs possessed the key concomitants of a distinct and separate practice. Further, the political triumph of the Sikh movement and the establishment of the powerful Sikh empire under Maharajah Ranjit Singh imbued Sikh identity with the symbolic memory of Sikh rule. Finally, the social and religious reform movement among Sikhs during British colonial rule resulted in the establishment of an institutional framework that provided the arena and base for Sikh separatism.

However, this study attempts to locate the growth and consolidation of Sikh identity within the wider context of historic and social forces prevailing during each period of the study. Let us now recapitulate important aspects of the nineteenth-century reform movements that resulted in the revitalization of religion and the emergence of sharper group boundaries. The transfer of new forms of organizational structure and techniques such as printing, modern style associations and education by the British introduced new arenas of power and competition, which unwittingly created a political context that permitted and even invited communal competition. However, the new institutional framework, revitalized and restructured existing patterns of public debate and knowledge rather than create anything new. Thus, print capitalism energized the existing tendencies towards differentiation between the diverse religious communities rather than, as in Benedict Anderson's formulation, creating a radically new consciousness. The growing cleavages among religious communities in Punjab were partially a continuation of existing patterns of hostility, accented by the emergence of new institutional framework for communal competition.

C. A. Bayly (1994) has stressed the conflict and amalgamation of the British and the indigenous elements in the formation of classes and dominant ideologies in colonial India. He argues that although every area of Indian life was subjected to the powerful and distorting influences of colonial rule, structures and ideologies of the Indian past remained vital. The nature of colonial and modern India has to be determined by the collusion of these two elements. He further argues that the history of political events in colonial India demonstrates that some of these economic and ideological formations came into conflict with the colonial state. Remarkably, the rising commercial classes spearheaded the anti-colonial, religious reform movements in British Punjab, although there is considerable evidence to support the view that the rise of new social formations also provided allies, infrastructures and compatible ideologies for the colonial and post-colonial state.

It may now be possible to challenge influential explanatory interpretations of change in India, which impute it to British policy. One such view is Richard G. Fox's (1985) formulation that it was the British view of the Sikhs that projected the British army as the saviour and guardian of the Sikh 'martial race' and the recruitment policies based on that view which created a distinct Sikh identity. Another is the view espoused by Harjot Oberoi that the Sikh commercial class of town dwellers was an indispensable element in the growth of Sikh communal consciousness, and it was, in fact, the vigorous Sikh bourgeoisie who created a new episteme, a standard discourse of modern Sikhism. So also the widely influential claim that the 'divide and rule' policy of the British, in fact, nurtured and incited religious communalism as a counterweight to emerging Indian nationalism.[27]

Rather, I have argued that the interplay between the general growth in literacy, communications and the expansion of imperial bureaucracy, on the one hand, and the socio-religious reform movements, on the other hand, gave birth to religio-linguistic nationalisms at the end of the nineteenth century in Punjab. Print capitalism facilitated the historic formation of languages of everyday life to the sacred languages of scriptures. Thus, Hindi, Urdu and Punjabi became the languages of sacred communication of Hinduism, Islam and Sikhism, and this heightened communal consciousness. These nationalisms were primarily responses by power groups, but not exclusively. Finally, these religio-linguistic nationalisms laid the bases for national consciousness, from which arose the anti-imperialist national resistance.

4 The rise of Sikh national consciousness (1947–95)

In Chapter 3 the evolution of the Sikhs from a religious congregation in the sixteenth century into a fully formed ethnic community during the period of the British Raj was traced. In this chapter the examination of the growth of Sikh separatism from the period of India's independence (1950–66) until the last period of Sikh unrest (1970–95) will be continued. To start with, some key questions will be posed. These questions emerge from trying develop a conceptual framework for understanding the emergence of Sikh ethno-nationalism. How is the emergence of a movement that during the 1980s aimed to create the separate Sikh state of Khalistan explained? What are the factors that gave rise to a fierce Sikh ethno-nationalism in the 1980s?

This chapter will focus on the growth of Sikh national consciousness. It is divided into two sections. The first section considers the Akali movement for a Punjabi *suba,* or 'a Punjabi-speaking state'. The nature of the demand for a Punjabi-speaking state and the tactics and strategies used by the Hindu and Sikh élites will be studied. The falling out of the Punjabi *suba* movement over communal consciousness is further examined. The second section examines the processes that gave rise to the Sikh armed resistance for the formation of a separate Sikh state of Khalistan. To start with, the historic Anandpur Sahib resolution, which outlined the policy and programme of the Akali Dal in independent India will be examined. This is followed by an examination of the meteoric rise of the charismatic Sikh preacher Sant Jarnail Singh Bhindranwale and the subsequent army assault on the Golden Temple in 1984. The rise and disintegration of the Sikh guerrilla movement, focusing on the impact of the policies of the central government on regional demand will be examined. Finally, the role of the Sikh diaspora in the movement for the formation of a separate Sikh state of Khalistan will be discussed.

The demand for a 'Punjabi *suba*', or a Punjabi-speaking state, in independent India (1950–66)

The foremost controversy that pushed India to the brink of civil disorder soon after independence was the language issue. While the burning issue in the 1950s and 1960s was a linguistic one, it is the religious issue that poses the gravest threat to India's secular foundations since the 1980s. The debate over the question of an official language before partition was centred around the Hindi–Urdu controversy. Mahatma Gandhi advocated Hindustani, as a neutral between Hindi and Urdu, as an official language. However, when the reality of partition became apparent, Hindustani was voted out as the official language by a margin of one vote in the Constituent Assembly in 1946. Hindustani still remains the *lingua franca* of a large part of South Asia. After independence, the question of the determination of a national language and an official language was based on the choice between Hindi and English. The people who framed the Indian Constitution accorded constitutional status to most of the major regional languages of India, but Hindi, the language of the dominant north-Indian Hindu majority, was chosen as the official language of India. English was to coexist alongside Hindi for official purposes.[1]

The nationwide movement of linguistic groups seeking statehood resulted in a massive reorganization of states according to linguistic boundaries in 1956. However, Punjabi, Sindhi and Urdu were the only three languages not considered for statehood. This prompted the Akali Dal to launch its first major agitational movement in August 1950, which spanned over two decades. Thus, the language dispute in post-partition Indian Punjab has to be viewed within the wider context of controversies prevailing throughout India during the 1950s and 1960s.

The independence of India in 1947 and the sanguinary partition of British Punjab between India and Pakistan on the basis of Hindu and Muslim majority areas altered the demographic composition of Indian Punjab dramatically. As communal riots broke out, the entire Hindu and Sikh population of the western districts of Pakistani Punjab fled to India. Similarly, Muslims in Indian East Punjab moved to Pakistan. The Sikhs were divided into two groups, each made up of 2 million people, on either side of the Punjab province: one scheduled to go to India and the other to Pakistan. As a result of the emigration of the Sikh population in 1947, the Sikhs lost Lahore, the capital of Maharaja Ranjit Singh and 150 historic Sikh shrines including Nankana Sahib, the birth place of Guru Nanak. They also had to leave their richest lands in the canal-irrigated zones of west Punjab. Indian Punjab secured thirteen out of twenty-nine districts, which amounted to 38 per cent of the land area (Ali 1993: 91). The mass migration of refugees altered the communal composition of Indian Punjab significantly. Punjab became a dual community province. The displacement of Muslims increased the Hindu majority, and the Sikhs were transformed from a small, dispersed minority into a substantial, compact minority in Indian Punjab. Further, the urban–rural demographic pattern of post-independence Punjab was such that the Hindu population was concentrated largely in urban areas. In 1948, Punjab was again divided into two administrative units. The small Sikh princely states were merged to form a new state of PEPSU (Patiala and East Punjab States Union). The Sikhs and Hindus were in equal numbers: 49.3 per cent and 48.8 per cent in PEPSU.

The emigration of the Muslim population in 1946–7 meant that the status of Urdu was no longer a major issue in Punjab. Conflict was over the status of the Punjabi language. The Akali Dal formally presented its case for the creation of a Punjabi *suba,* or a Punjabi-speaking state, to the States Reorganization Commission established in 1953. The Akali Dal appealed for the amalgamation of Punjabi-speaking areas of existing Punjab, PEPSU and the neighbouring state of Rajasthan. The Hindi-speaking areas of Punjab and PEPSU were to merge with neighbouring Hindi-speaking regions. The Akali Dal reasoned that a unilingual state would provide education and administration in the language of the area and this would allow for the development of Punjabi culture. The position of the Akali Dal is stated in a manifesto:

> The true test of democracy, in the opinion of the Shiromani Akali Dal, is that the minorities should feel that they are really free and equal partners in the destiny of their country…to bring home a sense of freedom to the Sikhs, it is vital that there should be a Punjabi speaking language and culture. This will not only be in fulfilment of the pre-partition Congress program and pledges, but also in entire conformity with the universally recognized principles governing formation of provinces….The Shiromani Akali Dal has reason to believe that a Punjabi-speaking province may give the Sikhs the needful security. It believes in a Punjabi speaking province as a autonomous unit of India.
>
> (K. Singh 1991: 296)

The Akali Dal projected the demand for the formation of a Punjabi-speaking state, or a Punjabi *suba,* overtly as a linguistic issue, shadowing the domain of centre-state relations in India. However, the fundamental issue was not so much a linguistic one as a question of the rights and claims of a minority community. In 1951, 61 per cent of the total population of Punjab was made up of Hindus, and the Sikhs made up 35 per cent (Kapur 1986: 208). The abolition of separate communal representation in independent India raised Akali apprehensions about the survival of the Sikhs as a separate entity. In colonial India, Sikh communal representation in the political bodies had ensured a degree of political representation to the Sikhs. The prospect of having little political leverage as a minority community raised Akali apprehensions as they sought to protect their language and religion in a Hindu-dominated society. Thus, the language controversy became a symptom of a deeper quest for recognition and power by a minority community in a multi-ethnic state.

In post-partition Punjab, the Arya Samaj protagonists spearheaded the campaign of aggressive promotion of Hindi among the Hindus. They opposed the adoption of Punjabi as an official language in the Punjabi-speaking region and launched a successful campaign exhorting Punjabi Hindus to repudiate Punjabi as their mother tongue and to declare themselves as Hindi speakers.

As a consequence, the Hindus declared Hindi as their mother tongue in the 1951 and 1961 censuses. Since the census enumerators were instructed not to verify the response of the respondents and record whichever language the respondents gave as their mother tongues, Paul Brass notes, 'There is good reason to believe, therefore, that the 1961 census accurately reflects the language preference of the people of the Punjab, although certainly not the actual mother tongue spoken' (Brass 1974: 293). More striking still is Paul Brass's (1974) inference that the existence of a widely spoken or written idiom does not necessarily generate linguistic consciousness. He has emphasized the distinction between the capacity to communicate and the willingness to communicate a particular language. He further notes, 'The dominant Hindu majority, unable to assimilate the Sikhs, adopted the tactic of avoiding their language so that the Sikhs, a minority people by religion, might become a minority by language as well' (Brass 1974: 298).

By 1971, only one-half of the 5 million Hindus in the state declared Punjabi as their mother tongue. The Hindus raised the slogan of 'Hindi, Hindu, Hindustan', evoking the dangerous trinity of Hindi language, Hindu religion and Hindu India. Paul Brass has discussed the Punjabi *suba* movement at considerable length in his book *Language, Religion and Politics in North India* (1974). He points out that although the process of linguistic identification based on the religious component was at work since the nineteenth century, the repudiation of the mother tongue by the Punjabi Hindus in the 1951 and 1961 censuses was ever more dramatic because 'it was an overt and deliberate political act designed to undercut the linguistic basis of the Punjabi *suba* demand' (Brass 1974: 327). Hindu organizations accused the Akali Dal of emphasizing the linguistic argument as a camouflage for the eventual creation of a state in which the Sikhs would form a majority.

The Akali demand became the subject of a major controversy between the Sikhs and Hindus of Punjab and between the Akali Dal and the Congress government. In its report, the States Reorganization Commission rejected the demand for Punjabi *suba* primarily on two grounds. First, in its report the Commission did not recognize Punjabi language as distinct grammatically or spatially from Hindi. The second reason given for the rejection of the demand was that the movement lacked the general support of the people inhabiting the region. The lack of support referred to the Punjabi Hindus who opposed the formation of a Punjabi-speaking state.

The dismissal of the demand by the Commission did not outrage the Sikhs perhaps as much as the rejection of a separate status for the Punjabi language. Sardar Hukum Singh, then associated with the Akali Dal wrote, 'While others got States for their languages, we lost even our language' (Brass 1974: 320). The Akali Dal maintained that the refusal to concede their demand by the States Reorganization Commission constituted discrimination against a religious group that spoke a distinct language. They claimed that Punjabi was a grammatically and lexically distinct language from Hindi. As Fateh Singh stated, 'No status is given to the Punjabi language, because Sikhs speak it. If non-Sikhs had owned Punjabi as mother tongue then the rulers of India would have seen no objection in establishing a Punjabi State' (Brass 1974: 325–6). Further, the Akalis contended that had Hindus formed a majority in the proposed Punjabi *suba*, the demand would have been conceded without any question. The refusal of the central government to accept the demand was primarily because it would reduce the Hindu majority in the province.

The rejection of the Akali demand by the States Reorganization Commission prompted the Akali Dal to launch the Punjabi Suba Slogan Agitation of 1955. In an attempt to pressurize the government to concede their demands, the Akali Dal undertook widespread political demonstrations. The agitational tactics of the 1920s were resurrected. In response to a call by the Akali Dal, Sikh volunteers from all over the province gathered at Darbar Sahib, Amritsar. As Akali *jathas* marched out of the Golden Temple shouting slogans in favour of Punjabi *suba*, they were arrested. The Akali campaign continued unabated and 12,000 Sikhs had been arrested in nearly 2 months (Kapur 1986: 213). The agitation was terminated twice by negotiations with the Congress. The Prime Minister of India, Jawaharlal Nehru, was adamant in rejecting the demand on the grounds that it was a communal demand. This somewhat dampened the Akali Dal's campaign, in which an estimated 26,000 Sikhs were arrested (Kapur 1986: 215).

The development of internal differences over strategy and tactics between Akali leaders resulted in the displacement of Master Tara Singh by one of his lieutenants, Sant Fateh Singh, in 1962.[2] Sant Fateh Singh, a Jat Sikh, commanded a substantial following among the peasantry and held a base in the *gurudwaras*. In 1965, Sant Fateh Singh succeeded in gaining control over the SGPC.[3] The strength and success of the Akali Dal depended considerably upon the ability to appropriate the resources of the SGPC, which provided an arena and base for Sikh political activity. The involvement of large masses in public demonstrations is illustrated by 'the Punjabi Suba Slogan Agitation of 1955, in which an estimated 12,000 Sikhs were arrested, and the massive Punjabi Suba Agitations of 1960–1, in which an estimated 26,000 volunteers were arrested and which was marked by two epic fasts, first by Sant Fateh Singh and then by Master Tara Singh' (Brass 1974: 317).

In the meantime, the death of Jawaharlal Nehru brought new leaders in the central government who were more receptive to regional demands. The outbreak of war between India and Pakistan in September 1965 provided the Indian government with the opportunity to express their appreciation for the contribution of the Sikhs in war efforts to defend India. In March 1966, the Indian parliament finally accepted the Akali demand for Punjabi *suba*. The state was trifurcated in September 1966 under the Punjab State Reorganization Bill. The southern, Hindi-speaking, plain districts were formed into a new state of Haryana; the other Hindi-speaking hill districts to the north of Punjab were merged with neighbouring Himachal Pradesh; the remaining Punjabi-speaking areas formed the new state of Punjab. The new Punjabi *suba* thus created was nearly 54 per cent Sikh and 44 per cent

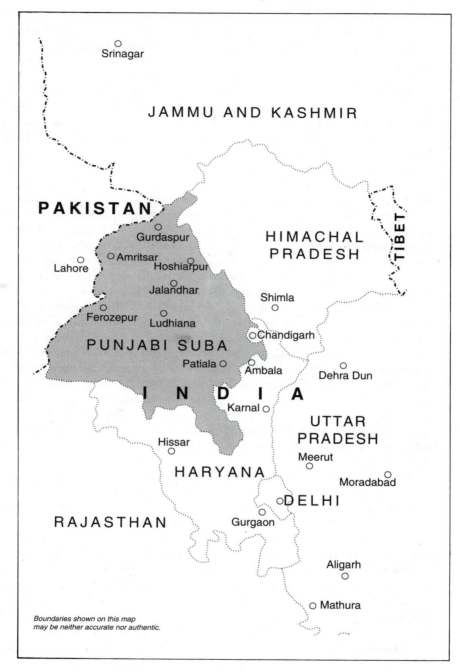

Map 4.1 The Punjabi *suba* and neighbouring provinces

Hindu (Kapur 1986: 216). The new city of Chandigarh, designed by the French architect Le Corbusier and built in the 1950s to replace Lahore, was declared the joint capital of Punjab and Haryana, until Haryana could create a new capital.

The main driving force of the Punjabi *suba* movement was that the Sikh leadership saw a separate political status for the Sikhs as being essential for preserving an independent Sikh entity. Thus the Akali leader Master Tara Singh noted in 1945, 'there is not the least doubt that the Sikh religion will live only as long as the *panth* exists as an organized entity' (S. Singh 1945: Foreward). The Akali Dal presented itself as providing this critical organization, the Khalsa *panth*, which elicited allegiance from its Sikh constituency. It was further argued that the *panth* was based on the common ideology of Sikh religion. A prominent Akali leader argued that the ideology of the *panth* binds its adherents together in 'Kinship which transcends distance, territory, caste, social barriers and even race' (S. Singh 1945: 10). By this logic the *panth* was coeval with the Sikh nation. On the question of participation in politics, the Akali Dal claimed that the Sikh community acting as a single political group was imperative for the existence of Sikh religion. It was argued that participation in politics by the Sikhs acting as a community was built into Sikh religious ideology, for Guru Gobind Singh established the Khalsa *panth* in order to organize his religious followers into a political community. Apart from this, he hardly made any other changes in the doctrines formulated by the first Sikh master, Guru Nanak. Thus, the Akali leadership drew on an interpretation of Sikh history and traditions in order to enhance and legitimize their authority in the struggle for critical political leverage. The Akali leaders believed that it was essential to provide the Sikhs with political leverage in order to preserve an independent Sikh entity. This could be possible if the Sikhs had a territorial unit in which they were the dominant population. By this logic the Akali Dal came to identify itself with the Sikh *panth*.

After the achievement of the Punjabi *suba*, the Akali Dal emerged as a governing party and this marked a new phase in electoral politics. The fear of the Punjabi Hindus at the prospect of a Sikh-dominated society and the apprehension of the central government in creating a Sikh-dominated state were to prove equivocal. Although the various agitational campaigns had amply demonstrated the strong support for Akali Dal by the Sikh community, the Sikh electoral support was not confined to the Akali Dal. The Sikhs did not vote exclusively along communal lines. The Congress Party had enough Sikhs in positions of power to make it a powerful contender for support from a significant body of Sikh voters. Thus, in the first elections in reorganized Punjab, the Congress party succeeded in electing more Sikh legislators than the Akali Dal (Brass 1974: 360). As a consequence of this cross-communal following of the Congress Party, the Akali Dal managed to obtain not more than 30 per cent of the total votes in the five elections to the Punjab legislative assembly held between 1967 and 1980 (Kapur 1986: 217). Thus, the Akali

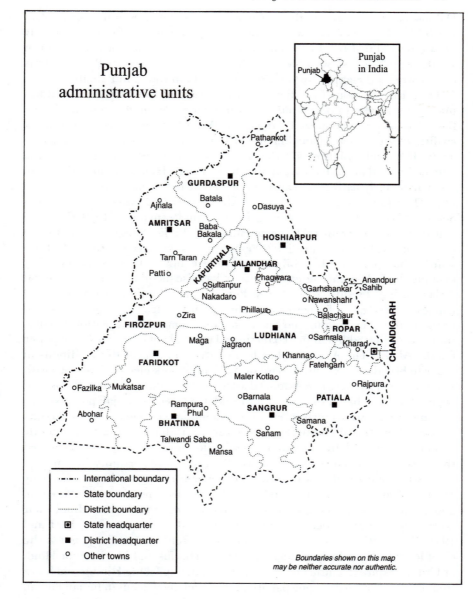

Punjab
administrative units

Punjab in India

Map 4.2   Post-1966 Punjab.

Dal has had to compete with the Congress Party for electoral support from the Sikhs. The Akali Dal was ousted from power in the Punjab Assembly elections held in 1972. In the elections to the lower house of Parliament in 1980, the Congress won twelve out of thirteen seats in Punjab. This demonstrates the appeal of the Congress party to voters in Punjab.

From the creation of the Punjabi *suba* in 1966 to 1980, the Akali Dal has managed to come to power only by forming a coalition government. In the first elections in reorganized Punjab, the Akali Dal succeeded in forming a coalition government in an alliance with the Jan Sangh and the Communist Party. The Akali alliance with the Jan Sangh, the political arm of the Arya Samaj, founded in 1951 and a party with essentially Hindu communal appeal, was particularly baffling because its president had gone on record to state that, 'The Jana Sangh regards the Sikhs as part and parcel of the Hindu Society' (Brass 1974: 333). Once again in the midterm poll of 1969, the Akali Dal came to power only with the assistance of the Jan Sangh. The history of party politics in Punjab thus vividly demonstrates that if competitive electoral politics has permitted mobilization along communal lines, remarkably enough, the Indian parliamentary system has also facilitated intercommunal collaboration. In this context, the Punjab case illuminates how political parties, in their quest for power, collaborated in the electoral process, thereby bringing together Hindus and Sikhs on a common political platform. Thus, the creation of a Sikh-dominated territorial unit did not ensure political power for the Akalis. The Akali Dal has had to strive to appeal to the Hindus in order to broaden its electoral base or has had to seek electoral alliance with other political parties. The Akali Dal's control over the SGPC and its political appeal have combined to make it a formidable force in Punjab politics.

Census operations also intensified communal consciousness in Punjab. Census officials and enumerators in their desire for uniformity frequently had preconceived definitions and classifications of groups, which influenced the census results considerably. This also gave an opportunity for interest groups to organize efforts to influence the census returns. Such efforts by Muslim organizations urging Muslims to declare their mother tongue as Urdu, and by Arya Samaj protagonists to persuade Hindus to declare Hindi their mother tongue are noted by Paul Brass in the censuses of 1911, 1921 and 1931 (Brass 1974: 292–3). In the Hindi–Urdu controversy, Punjabi was the chief loser because Punjabi was forfeited by Hindus and Muslims for Hindi or Urdu. Despite the influx of millions of Punjabi-speaking Hindus and Sikhs from Pakistani Punjab during partition, the Hindi movement in Indian Punjab reduced the number of Punjabi speakers in the 1961 census to a minority for the very first time in the history of the census. Although Punjabi was the language of Muslims, Hindus and Sikhs, it became increasingly identified with the Sikhs alone. Thus, Punjabi was transformed into a minority language in the successive censuses.

The history of the Punjabi *suba* movement throws light on the significance of language as a symbol of group identity. We have seen how language became a symbol of contest for political power between the Hindu and Sikh élites in post-independence Punjab, as religious meaning was infused into language identification. Thus, the Punjabi *suba* movement consolidated the process of linguistic differentiation between the Hindus and the Sikhs on the basis of religion. In this chapter I will contest Paul Brass's view that the '...standing of a language in relation to particular social groups is not something fixed, but may evolve and change over time and may be subject to deliberate direction. Such has been the case at least with regard to language in the Punjab in modern times' (Brass 1974: 292). All of the preceding evidence indicates that the historic process of equating linguistic and religious identity was facilitated by the creation of the modern administrative state and by print capitalism in the nineteenth century in British Punjab. Further, modern institutions, such as the state and the census reports, reinforced the fusion of linguistic and communal identities. Thus, Hindi came to be identified ever more strongly with the Hindus, and Punjabi became synonymous with Sikh identity. These arguments are developed further in Chapter 6 to examine the role of the popular mass media, such as the vernacular press, in intensifying religious divisions between the Hindu and Sikh population through the transmission of religious messages of mass appeal to a rapidly expanding, literate population in the 1970s. Thus, in Punjab the identification of a language with a particular social group has only intensified over time.

Background to the present conflict (1970–95)

The Anandpur Sahib resolution

Between 1981 and 1984, the Akali Dal led a series of peaceful mass demonstrations to present a set of grievances to the central government. The core of the Akali Dal's demands were based on a resolution adopted by the working committee of the Akali Dal at Anandpur Sahib in October 1973, outlining the policy and programme of the party. The issues raised in the historic Anandpur Sahib resolution were political, economic and social.[4] The primary political objective stated in the Anandpur Sahib resolution was the 'pre-eminence of the Khalsa through creation of a congenial environment and a political set up' (K. Singh 1991: 346). The political goal stated in the resolution, the Akalis pointed out, was not in itself new but a reiteration of the Akali Dal's earlier objective, before India's independence, to preserve and maintain the distinct and independent entity of the *panth*. In order to achieve this political goal, the resolution outlined seven key objectives. These were,

1   The transfer of the federally administered city of Chandigarh to Punjab. It was argued that although the Punjabi *suba* had been conceded in 1966, Punjab still shared its capital, Chandigarh, with the neighbouring state of Haryana.

2   The readjustment of the state boundaries of Punjab to incorporate certain
     Sikh-populated Punjabi-speaking areas, presently outside and contiguous
     to Punjab.
3   The re-examination of the centre-state relations under the existing
     constitution of India so as to grant a measure of provincial autonomy to
     all Indian states. The powers of the central government should be
     confined to external affairs, defence and communications.
4   The call for land reforms. Loans to be provided to farmers at the rates
     given to industrialists and non-remunerative prices be fixed for
     agricultural produce. The rights of weaker sections of the population be
     safeguarded. Further, all key industries should be brought under the
     public sector. The central government should invest in setting up heavy
     industry in Punjab, in order to alleviate the industrial stagnation of the
     state.
5   The enactment of an all-India *gurudwara* act that would bring all the
     historic *gurudwaras* in India under the control of the SGPC.
6   The Sikh minorities living outside Punjab be provided protection.
7   By reducing the recruitment quota of Sikhs in the armed forces from 20
     per cent to 2 per cent, the Indian government was keeping the Sikhs out
     of their traditional professions in its new recruitment policy.

The text of the Anandpur Sahib resolution became a subject of considerable
controversy. Although rival factions of the Akali Dal adopted different versions
and different interpretations of the Anandpur Sahib resolution, it was
endorsed by a significant body of Sikh intelligentsia, Sikh servicemen and
politicians. On the question of Sikh political autonomy, the Akalis denied
that the Anandpur Sahib resolution envisaged an autonomous Sikh state of
Khalistan. As the President of the Akali Dal declared, 'Let us make it clear
once and for all that the Sikhs have no designs to get away from India in any
manner. What they simply want is that they should be allowed to live within
India as Sikhs, free from all direct and indirect interference and tampering
with their religious way of life. Undoubtedly the Sikhs have the same
nationality as other Indians' (Tully and Jacob 1985: 50). Addressing a Sikh
conference, a prominent leader proclaimed that, 'Sikhs were still struggling
for asserting our rightful claim to our identity and nationhood' (Kapur 1986:
221).

The meeting of the Akali Dal in 1978 endorsed the principles and objectives
of the Anandpur Sahib resolution. In February 1981, the working committee
of the Akali Dal reiterated that the party would strive for the implementation
of the Anandpur Sahib resolution. Between August 1980 and September 1981,
the Akali Dal organized a succession of seven peaceful agitations in which
25,000 volunteers courted arrest, in order to accentuate their demands (K.
Singh 1991: 350). A set of forty-five demands was submitted to the central
government in September 1981. These demands reflected the core objectives
of the Anandpur Sahib resolution and two new demands were added. These
were:

1   The halting of reallocation of available river waters of riparian Punjab
    to other non-riparian states (under the arrangement regulated by the
    central government, 75 per cent of the river waters of Punjab were being
    allocated to other states; Pettigrew 1995: 5) and a further reduction in
    government control over hydro-electric installations.
2   The recognition of Sikh personal law.[5]

As negotiations between the Akali leaders and the central government
began in October 1981, the list of forty-five demands was reduced to fifteen.
The core of these demands concerned the socio-economic grievances over
the centralization policies of the Indian government, which were adversely
affecting the rural sector of the society. The manner in which the
centralization policies of the Indian government, concerning control over
the productive and development processes, propelled agrarian unrest in
Punjab in the late 1970s is examined in detail in Chapter 5. There seemed
nothing unconstitutional about the Akali demand to seek greater autonomy
for all Indian states. However, these negotiations continued sporadically for
a period of 2.5 years, with the Akalis accusing the government of intransigence,
bad faith and deliberate delaying tactics.

Once again, the Akali Dal organized mass agitations in order to pressurize
the government. In April 1982, the Akali Dal organized the *nahar-roko*, or
'block the canal', campaign to obstruct the construction of a canal that would
divert river water to the neighbouring state of Haryana and would deprive
the Punjab's peasantry of vital water resources. Agrarian interests seem to
be at the heart of the issue. Peasants were also urged to refrain from repaying
the loans due to the government as a protest. The characteristic Akali
agitational style of passive resistance was resurrected. Each *jatha* would
proceed daily to the site of construction and be subsequently arrested. The
Akali campaign continued unabated and by September some 20,000 agitators
had been arrested. This campaign was suspended briefly for negotiations
with the government, which were unsuccessful. In response, the Akali Dal
announced a new 1-day *rasta roko*, or 'block the roads', campaign in April 1983
to disrupt vehicular traffic on Punjab's national highways. Similarly, the Akali
leaders announced a 1-day *rail roko*, or 'block the rails' campaign, to stop
railway services in the state. In August, the *kam roko*, or 'halt the work',
campaign to hamper functioning of the state administration was organized.
These political demonstrations were inundated with volunteers from all over
the province and proved remarkably successful. The Indian government had
grave apprehensions of widespread Sikh unrest. In October 1983, the Punjab
legislative assembly was dissolved bringing the state under the complete
control of the central government. These developments coincided with the
rise of a charismatic Sikh preacher, Sant Jarnail Singh Bhindranwale. A
detailed account of Bhindranwale's message and his mass appeal is given in
Chapter 6.

Meanwhile, after the historic nationwide defeat of the Congress party by the Janata party, the Akali Dal had formed a coalition government with the Janata party in 1977. The Akali Dal had launched powerful campaigns to protest against the imposition of a state of emergency by Mrs Indira Gandhi. The Akali Dal was the most successful opposition party in India and it opposed the promulgation of the draconian Maintenance of Internal Security Act, which gave the police the power to arrest and to detain people without trial. The Congress party, therefore, was desperate to break up the formidable Akali Dal. It was looking for someone who could challenge and put an end to the traditional Akali hegemony over the SGPC. Bhindranwale's position as head of the historic Damdami Taksal and his increasing popularity as a religious preacher made him a formidable political ally. In the vital SGPC election in 1979, Bhindranwale was promoted and supported by the Congress leaders and encouraged to put up candidates against the Akali Dal.[6] Nonetheless, Bhindranwale was to become an outspoken critic of the Congress party. In 1980, the Congress party was returned to power in the Punjab State Assembly elections.

Throughout this period, the vernacular press in Punjab had been critically engaged in fomenting the religious divide between the Hindus and the Sikhs, and this is the subject of discussion in Chapter 6. In its study on the role of the press in inflaming communal passions in Punjab, The Editors' Guild of India reported:

> Responding to the general climate of sectarian confrontation and polarization, it is disturbing to note that newspapermen in Punjab by their own admission are divided all the way down on communal lines. We were repeatedly told this quite candidly in Chandigarh, Jalandhar and Amritsar by a variety of journalists, both Hindu and Sikh. This is a sad commentary and a matter for deep professional and social concern. If the press becomes partisan, the images it reflects will be distorted. The reporters who met us preferred to discuss matters individually and separately rather than collectively in an open forum.
>
> (Singh and Nayar 1984: 41)

It was in this charged atmosphere that Lala Jagat Narain the proprietor of the Hind Samachar group of newspapers was assassinated in September 1981. As an Arya Samaj leader he had played a prominent role in exhorting Punjabi Hindus to declare Hindi as their mother tongue. His editorials had consistently attacked the Akali leaders, and attacked the Congress party for promoting Bhindranwale. After the assassination of Lala Jagat Narain, there were incidents of violence as a mob of Hindus set fire to Sikh shops and burnt the offices of a Punjabi newspaper, *Akali Patrika*, at Jalandhar. The government acted hastily and arraigned Bhindranwale in the assassination of Lala Jagat Narain.

At the time, Bhindranwale was giving a sermon at the Chando Kalan *gurudwara* in Haryana. The government ordered his arrest and a contingent of Punjab policemen was dispatched to Chando Kalan. The armed entourage took 7 days to cover the 300 kilometres from Punjab to reach Chando Kalan at Haryana (K. Singh 1991). By the time they arrived at the *gurudwara*, Bhindranwale had already left. The frustrated police officers committed acts of arson. The villagers testified that the policemen set fire to vans and burnt Bhindranwale's sermons. Bhindranwale was outraged, not because of his alleged complicity in the murder of Lala Jagat Narain but because of the burning of his sermons by government officials. He alleged that these actions amounted to the '...insult of my Guru' (Tully and Jacob 1985: 68).[7] On 20 September 1981, Bhindranwale voluntarily offered his arrest at his headquarters at Mehta Chowk, near Amritsar. He was detained for 25 days, and after intensive interrogation and at the behest of senior Congress leaders he was released because of lack of evidence. The indiscreet actions of the government generated much sympathy from the Sikh community and the Akali Dal. After this incident, Bhindranwale disassociated himself from the Congress party and subsequently moved to Guru Nanak Nivas.[8]

In the meantime, in order to highlight their grievances, the Akali Dal launched the *dharam yudh*, or 'battle for righteousness', under the leadership of Sant Harchand Singh Longowal in August 1982.[9] Bhindranwale and the Akali Dal joined hands for the first time. A batch of Akali volunteers would march out of the Darbar Sahib every day and would be arrested for violating the order banning the assembly of more than five persons. The agitation proceeded unabated and in a period of 2.5 months, 30,000 Sikhs had been arrested (Singh and Nayar 1984: 60). Many women too joined in the agitation. As the number of arrests surged it became very difficult for the authorities to accommodate the protesting volunteers in the existing jails. The government was apprehensive about the widespread response to the Akali agitation. In a conciliatory gesture the central government released all Akali volunteers and resumed negotiations with the Akali Dal. The conspicuous presence of Sant Bhindranwale during the discussions was another factor in the discussions. A settlement is believed to have been virtually reached, but Bhajan Lal, the Chief Minister of Haryana, played a critical role in sabotaging the talks. Mrs Indira Gandhi failed to find a settlement and this was to have grave consequences.

Meanwhile, serious differences between Bhindranwale and the Akali leadership headed by Sant Longowal began to surface. Bhindranwale was sceptical of the Akali leaders' capacity for compromising with the central government, lured on by the prospect of power. He also mistrusted the intentions of the Congress government to resolve the grievances of the Sikhs. These differences accentuated the divisions between the Akali Dal, headed by Sant Harchand Singh, and the hardliners, who were supported by young Sikhs through the All India Sikh Students Federation (AISSF), which was under the patronage of Sant Jarnail Singh Bhindranwale. While the Akali Dal was vulnerable to the carrot and stick policies of Mrs Indira Gandhi, Sant Bhindranwale was adamant that nothing short of the Anandpur Sahib resolution would be acceptable.

In November 1982, the Akali Dal announced that it would hold peaceful demonstrations in Delhi during the Asian Games. The government wanted to avoid any disturbances in the capital during an occasion of international significance. Great efforts were made to prevent Akali agitators from reaching Delhi. All buses, trains and vehicles heading for Delhi were stopped, and every Sikh travelling to Delhi was hauled out and searched. Among those who suffered this indignity were senior, retired Sikh army officers. Two Sikh army generals, Shahbeg Singh and Jaswant Singh Bhullar, stated that the humiliation suffered during the Asian Games was a factor in their decision to join Bhindranwale.[10] This was the first time that Sikhs as a community felt discriminated in independent India. On 23 December, the Akali Dal organized a convention of Sikh ex-servicemen at the Darbar Sahib, which evoked a good response. Of the 5,000 ex-servicemen who attended the convention, 170 were retired officers above the rank of a colonel. There were reports of discrimination against Sikhs in government service.

The situation in Punjab was steadily worsening as the number of violent incidents escalated. These incidents included bank robberies, bombings, burning of railway stations, selective killing of public men and politicians, indiscriminate firing on religious congregations and desecration of religious places.[11] In October 1983, the activities took a more violent form and a number of innocent Hindu passengers travelling on a Delhi-bound bus were taken out of the bus and murdered in cold blood. In order to curb the wave of violence, Punjab was brought under the complete control of the central government through the imposition of President's rule in October 1983. Nonetheless, the violence continued unabated. Ramesh Chander, the son and successor of Lala Jagat Narain, was assassinated in May 1984. As the violence escalated, the Akali Dal and the SGPC blamed the central government for the bloodshed. In May 1983, the president of the SGPC stated that the turmoil in Punjab was a 'sustained conspiracy of the Punjab Government to foment communal trouble' (Kapur 1986: 228).

In February 1984 the Akali Dal led a campaign protesting against the wording of Article 25 of the Indian constitution. Article 25 of the Indian constitution pertains to the freedom of religious worship that is given to all citizens. The Akali Dal objected to the Sikhs being defined as Hindus in clause (2) (b) of Article 25. A pamphlet circulated by the Akali Dal stated,

> India is a multi-lingual, multi-religious and multi-national land. In such a land, a microscopic minority like the Sikhs has genuine foreboding that…they may also lose their identity in the vast ocean of overwhelming Hindu majority. Their misgivings are heightened by arbitrary manner in which they are defined as Hindus under Article 25 of the Constitution.
>
> (Kapur 1986: 228)

Several Akali leaders were arrested when they burnt the portion of the Indian constitution containing Article 25 (2) (b) in protest.

Operation Bluestar and Operation Woodrose

The Akali Dal threatened to launch a new campaign of mass non-cooperation on 3 June 1984. The Sikh peasantry was exhorted to prevent the movement of food grain out of Punjab and to stop the payment of land revenue and water rates to the government. The Akali Dal chose 3 June, the anniversary of the martyrdom of Guru Arjun, the founder of the Golden Temple, to launch this mass non-cooperation campaign against the government. Ironically, this was the day that Mrs Indira Gandhi gave orders to the army to launch an attack on the Darbar Sahib. Operation Bluestar was the codename given by the Indian army to the assault on the Darbar Sahib in June 1984.

The government prepared itself for the final assault. The borders of Punjab were sealed off from the rest of the country and censorship was imposed on the press in Punjab. A curfew was imposed at Amritsar and the army cordoned off the Golden Temple complex. The supply of water and electricity to the Golden Temple was cut off. Troops equipped with tanks and heavy armour took up strategic positions around the Darbar Sahib. A large number of pilgrims had gathered at the temple to pay obeisance and participate in the special services at the Golden Temple to mark the martyrdom anniversary of Guru Arjun. According to one estimate, there were some 10,000 pilgrims in the temple on 3 June. This included a large *jatha* of about 1,300 people who had come to court arrest for the *dharam yudh morcha* of the Akali Dal (K. Singh 1991: 366). In the first phase of Operation Bluestar, the Akali leaders who were inside the temple complex were flushed out and detained. The impending military action in the bastion of Sikhism prompted the agitated Sikh peasantry to converge upon Amritsar in large numbers. Army tanks blocked the movement of some 30,000 Sikhs near Amritsar; many were killed in the action (Singh and Nayar 1984: 100). Helicopters were brought in to identify the mobs, and tanks and armoured vehicles were used to disperse the heavy crowds. The government feared the outbreak of a Sikh uprising and decided to launch a full-scale attack on Darbar Sahib.

Grenades, tanks and armoured vehicles were used to attack the Temple on all sides, and helicopters flew overhead to attack the temple and guide the armoured vehicles inside the temple complex. The army took control of the temple on 6 June. A large number of innocent pilgrims, including women and children, officially described as 'the enemy', were killed in the heavy barrage of cross-firing. The troops shot scores of young Sikh men with their hands tied behind their backs at point-blank range.[12] Most accounts put the number of civilian casualties at 5,000, and 700 officers are estimated to have lost their lives during the army action (Grewal 1990: 227). The shells fired by the tanks brought down the edifice of the Akal Takht, the seat of Sikh temporal power. The bullet-ridden bodies of Bhindranwale, General Shahbeg Singh and Amrik Singh were found in the basement of the Akal Takht. Officers of the Indian army commented that Bhindranwale and his followers had fought with courage and commitment. Similar assaults were carried out by the army on forty other *gurudwaras* where Sikh activists were alleged to be hiding.

It took the army several days to gain control of the temple, resulting in heavy casualties on both sides and substantial damage to the sacred property. Many rare manuscripts and archives housed in the Sikh reference library located inside the temple were burnt during the army action. D. S. Duggal, the director of the Sikh reference library, categorically stated that no damage had been done to the research library until the evening of 6 June when he left the library. He accused the troops of deliberately setting fire to the Sikh archives (Pettigrew 1995: 35). The soldiers were accused of desecrating the temple and of looting and robbing the temple.

Sant Longowal had warned the government of the serious consequences of launching an army operation on Darbar Sahib. He had written, 'every bullet fired at the Golden Temple will hit every Sikh wherever he be in the world' (K. Singh 1991: 363). The entire Sikh community was outraged, not so much by the death of Bhindranwale but by the all-out assault on their premier shrine by the Indian army. On hearing the news of the Indian army's action, Sikh troops deserted their regiments in several parts of the country, and many Sikh soldiers attempted to march towards Amritsar to defend their faith. They were intercepted by the authorities and scores of them were killed and others were court-martialled. Several Sikhs resigned from top government posts, eminent Sikh intellectuals returned honours bestowed on them by the government, and many Sikh politicians resigned from parliament in protest.

The government acted in haste and speedily rebuilt the Akal Takht before handing control of it to the temple high priests, and not to the SGPC, in October 1984. This perpetuated resentment among Sikhs, who felt that the government had snatched the prerogative from the Sikh community to rebuild their historic shrine through the customary *kar seva*, or 'voluntary service in accordance with Sikh tradition'.[13] The actions of the central government gave credence to the widespread belief that Operation Bluestar was a deliberate attempt to humiliate the Sikhs. It was alleged that the Congress party had itself brought Bhindranwale to prominence and that the government could have chosen some other way to arrest Bhindranwale and his followers. The government could have laid siege to the temple complex and persuaded Bhindranwale and his followers to surrender. The result that the army action had on the Sikh community is described by Khushwant Singh. He notes, 'The army action widened the gulf between the Hindus who had welcomed it and the Sikhs who had not, and gave the movement for Khalistan its first martyr in Jarnail Singh Bhindranwale' (K. Singh 1991: 378).

In the months after the attack on Darbar Sahib, between June and September 1984, the government conducted Operation Woodrose in an attempt to prevent the outbreak of widespread public protest in the province. All prominent Akali leaders were detained and a ban was imposed on the All India Sikh Students' Federation (AISSF). The army combed the countryside and thousands of Sikhs, especially young men, were detained for interrogation and many were tortured and killed. It was during this period that a substantial number of rural Sikh youths crossed over to neighbouring Pakistan.[14] The government instituted draconian ordinances, which enabled the authorities to arrest persons without warrants and to detain people without a trial in the province. Under the Terrorist and Disruptive Activities (Prevention) Act, or TADA, of 1985 the accused were presumed guilty unless they could prove their innocence. Further, confessions extracted under torture were treated as evidence. The government established extraordinary judicial procedures under the Special Courts Act, which allowed trials to be conducted *in camera* and the accused were given no right to appeal. Many Sikhs, among whom were several retired army officers, were charged with sedition and detained under the National Security Act (NSA) of 1987. The NSA allows a person to be detained without trial and to be given no legal representation. The central government was accused of introducing draconian legislation in order to repress a minority community.

On 31 October 1984 the Prime Minister of India, Mrs Indira Gandhi, was assassinated by two of her Sikh bodyguards, seemingly as an act of revenge. After the assassination of Mrs Indira Gandhi, anti-Sikh riots broke out in several parts of the country. Sikhs were singled out, lynched and burnt alive. The capital city of Delhi was worst affected, and Sikhs became the targets of brutal mob violence. Of the 10,000 Sikhs massacred in the pogroms, some 6,000–8,000, including thirty officers in uniform, were killed in Delhi alone. Sikh property worth Rs 300 crores was looted and burnt, and in Delhi over 50,000 Sikhs were rendered refugees (K. Singh 1991: 385).

Reports published in the Indian press accused the civil administration, the police and the Congress party with complicity in the mob violence against the Sikhs. An independent inquiry by two human rights organizations reported that,

> the attacks on members of the Sikh community in Delhi...far from being spontaneous expressions of "madness" and of popular "grief and anger" at Mrs Gandhi's assassination as made out by the authorities, were the outcome of a well-organized plan marked by acts of both deliberate commission and omission by important politicians of the Congress...and by authorities in the administration.[15]

The report further stated, 'the police all over the city uniformly betrayed a common behavioural pattern marked by (i) a total absence from the scene, or (ii) a role as passive spectators, or (iii) direct participation or abetting in the orgy of violence against the Sikhs.'[16] Further, the refusal of the central government to order an official inquiry into the anti-Sikh riots enraged the Sikh community. Eleven years after the anti-Sikh riots, the government has not arrested any person in connection with this. The actions of the government dramatically compounded the alienation felt by the Sikhs and gave ample credence to the widespread belief of an official conspiracy against the Sikhs.

In the parliamentary elections held in December 1984, the Congress party secured an overwhelming victory and an absolute majority in parliament.

Mrs Gandhi's son, Rajiv Gandhi, who had earlier been unanimously selected as the leader of the Congress party, became the Prime Minister of India. However, elections were postponed in Punjab, and the province continued to be governed by the central government. In the meantime, the Akali Dal and the SGPC threatened to launch another agitation if the government did not institute an official inquiry into the pogroms against the Sikhs in November 1984 and urged the government to release senior Akali leaders detained since Operation Bluestar. In March 1985, Akali leaders were released, and in May 1985 Sant Harchand Singh Longowal was reinstated as the head of the Akali Dal. Soon after his release, Sant Harchand Singh Longowal began an extensive tour of Punjab. He addressed a series of public meetings enlisting the Akali Dal's demands for a peaceful settlement in Punjab. The more important of these demands were that the central government should apologize to the Sikh community for storming Darbar Sahib, and that it should conduct an official inquiry into the Delhi massacres, withdraw draconian judicial procedures and anti-terrorist legislation in the province, rehabilitate Sikh soldiers discharged from the army and release innocent Sikh detainees. He, however, categorically stated that the Akali Dal did not favour a separate Sikh state of Khalistan. He further reiterated that the grievances of the Akali Dal were with the central government and that his party was committed to Hindu–Sikh harmony. The government invited Sant Longowal for secret unilateral negotiations, and on 24 July 1985 an eleven-point memorandum of settlement was signed. This came to be known as the Rajiv–Longowal Accord.

The Rajiv–Longowal Accord did not directly concede any of the Akali Dal demands. Just three points of the settlement dealt with substantial issues. First, the issue of greater autonomy for Punjab was referred to a commission that was to make recommendations on centre-state relations with the central government. Second, it was agreed to transfer Chandigarh to Punjab on the condition that some territory belonging to Punjab would be transferred to Haryana, and a commission was set up to determine which areas of Punjab would be transferred to Haryana. Other territorial disputes between Haryana and Punjab were also referred to a boundary commission. Third, the question of reapportionment of river waters was similarly addressed and referred to a tribunal. Other issues stipulated in the memorandum of settlement were that the central government would provide compensation to victims of violence in Punjab since August 1982, although the terms and conditions for determining the extent of compensation and to whom it was to be paid were not specified. The memorandum stated that Sikh soldiers discharged from the army would be reinstated but no leniency would be shown towards Sikh troops charged with mutiny and waging war against India.

A broad cross-section of the Sikh population did not endorse the Accord. Some Akali leaders denounced the accord as a 'sell out' and expressed reservations regarding the central government's commitment to implement the accord. Others criticized the agreement on the grounds that unilateral negotiations on Sikh demands with the central government undermined the confidence in the Sikh constituency. Moreover, resentment towards the traditional Akali leaders accentuated divisions in the Akali Dal. This subsequently led to the formation of a rival Akali Dal. The United Akali Dal was headed by Baba Joginder Singh, father of Sant Bhindranwale. In the meantime, the growing unrest in Punjab was compounded by the migration of some 20,000–30,000 Sikh refugees from different parts of the country to Punjab (K. Singh 1991: 385). In May 1985, transistor bomb explosions in Delhi, allegedly orchestrated by Sikh migrants from Delhi, killed nearly eighty people. On 20 August 1985, Sant Harchand Singh Longowal was assassinated, reportedly by Sikh extremists. The central government called early elections in Punjab to deflect the growing dissension over the Rajiv–Longowal Accord.

The elections were boycotted by the United Akali Dal in protest against the settlement with the central government. Thus, the elections became a straight contest between the Akali Dal and the Congress party. The Akali Dal emerged victorious and secured seventy-three seats and the Congress only thirty-two seats in the State Assembly. Finally, the Akali Dal had achieved its dream to form a provincial government independently. The election results revealed the growing polarization between the Sikhs and the Hindus in Punjab. The Akali Dal received broad support from the Sikhs, whereas the Hindus voted in favour of the Congress party. 'Never were the Punjabis split so clearly on communal lines as in the elections of September 1985' (Grewal 1990: 230–231). However, the newly formed provincial government was faced with the formidable challenge of ensuring the implementation of the Rajiv–Longowal Accord. The various commissions set up by the central government to determine the terms of settlement either failed to give a verdict or their recommendations were unacceptable. Chandigarh was not transferred to Punjab on 26 January 1986, as promised by the Prime Minister, Rajiv Gandhi. The Chief Minister of Punjab accused the central government for delaying the implementation of the agreement, and the central government accused the state government for not dealing firmly with the deteriorating law and order situation in the province. In January 1986, the Damdami Taksal, supported by the United Akali Dal and the AISSF, resumed the reconstruction of the Akal Takht. At a meeting in Amritsar on 29 April 1986, a resolution was adopted proclaiming the state of Khalistan, after which the Akali government was pressurized into sending security forces into the Golden Temple Complex. The acrimony between the Akali government and its Sikh opponents was causing serious dissension within the Akali Dal. In May 1986, President's rule was imposed in Punjab and the province was once again brought under direct control of the central government.

Thus, far from curbing extremist activity, Operation Bluestar and Operation Woodrose fomented considerable alienation among a broad cross-section of the Sikh population. Further, the massacre of the Sikhs after the assassination of Mrs Indira Gandhi and the failure to implement the Rajiv–Longowal Accord culminated in a fresh outburst of violent activity in the province. It is in this context that the campaign for Sikh separatism developed into a guerrilla movement, posing a grave threat to the unity of India.

State violence and the rise and fall of armed resistance

What are the factors that propelled a significant body of young Sikhs into an armed struggle for national independence against the Indian state in the 1980s? The limited and fragmentary nature of source material poses special problems in answering the above question. Considerable risks were involved in securing access to the militants during the period of active armed resistance and, at present, most of the Sikh activists have been eliminated by the Indian paramilitary forces. My primary source material draws on my field work experience, conducted between October 1992 and April 1993, during which I met several people who were involved with the guerrilla movement. I have also relied on the account presented by Joyce J. M. Pettigrew (1995), which is based on recorded interviews with guerrilla activists of the Khalistan Commando Force (KCF) conducted on her behalf by Ajit Singh Khera.[17]

Both the above accounts delineate two phases of recruitment to the guerrilla movement: recruitment of Sikhs captivated by Bhindranwale's message and personality and recruitment of the survivors of the aftermath of Operation Bluestar and Operation Woodrose. As Joyce J. M. Pettigrew notes, 'all guerrillas mention that it was the behaviour of the security forces towards them and their families that finally drew them into the struggle' (Pettigrew 1995: 139). She further observes that issues of injustice and inequality were foremost themes reiterated by her interviewees. Further, the religious context was invoked by the guerrillas to legitimize the armed resistance. They explained the centrality of social and economic justice in Sikh religious tradition and armed resistance as a moral response to restore justice and to fight oppression.[18] They claimed that the first Sikh master, Guru Nanak, repudiated the divinely ordained Brahmanical hierarchical structure of power and wealth. At this historic moment, they believed that the central government represented the interests of the Brahmins, and that the guerrilla resistance represented a transposition of the fundamental precept of Sikh faith, which challenged the Brahmanical belief system.

The movement had suffered a major setback at an early stage. A significant number of its political leaders had been eliminated in Operation Bluestar and Operation Woodrose, and many survivors went underground for fear of harassment and torture by the paramilitary forces. Attempts to resurrect the guerrilla movement were initiated by those with some trade union experience, or members of the splintered AISSF or those associated with the religious seminary, the Damdami Taksal.[19] Between 1987 and 1988, resistance began to proliferate and the strength of guerrilla groups surged. However, until 1987, guerrilla activities were sporadic and uncoordinated, largely confined to the Amritsar and the Gurdaspur regions.

The official policy towards Sikh unrest was to suppress the movement by brute force and seemed little concerned with remedying the causes of the violent conflict. To subvert the movement, it was vital to create a wedge between the guerrillas and the civilian population. Therefore, the government perpetuated a major counter-insurgency operation in order to destabilize the movement. Guerrilla cadres were infiltrated by undercover policemen and criminals were inducted in the police force to malign the guerrillas. This led to an outburst of violent incidents, such as looting, extortion, murder and rape. It was common for an entire village to be evacuated for house-to-house searches, during which the security forces freely indulged in brutal acts of violence, rape and arson. Armed bands stalked the countryside and the distinction between a policeman and a militant became blurred. The difficulty in distinguishing the policeman, the militant and the criminal is also noted by Joyce J. M. Pettigrew:

> A large part of the problem for ordinary villagers was that they had no means to identify a genuine militant. At one stage a family would be visited by persons masquerading as militants....At another stage, the same family would be confronted by the same persons dressed as police who accused them of feeding and sheltering militants overnight and then either killed them outright or took from them a large sum of money. Innumerable families could report events of such nature.
>
> (Pettigrew 1995: 114)

Between 1989 and 1991, civilian casualties rose from 54 per cent to 73 per cent of the total number of killings, and ordinary Sikh villagers were targeted in an unprecedented orgy of violence (Pettigrew 1995: 77). The wealthier families migrated to cities, often abandoning their land holdings in fear of abduction or extortion. A situation of general lawlessness prevailed, and the scale and nature of violence suggests the wider breakdown in social relationships in the province. The 'lumpen' or those referred to in India as the 'anti-social' elements of society, such as smugglers and criminals, exploited the intimidation of the people by the guerrilla groups and the paramilitary forces. Armed bands plundered the land of farming families, and the rural masses were subjected to brutal attacks on their lives and property.

By 1988, a serious rift occurred between the main guerrilla organizations over issues of policy and tactics. The core of the ideological difference was whether to raise the issue of social reform, notably an anti-dowry and an anti-alcohol campaign, during the armed struggle. Divisions in the resistance increased between 1990 and 1991.[20] Once the paramilitary forces had succeeded in eliminating the ideologically committed cadre, the weakness in the organizational structure of the guerrilla groups became evident. The average life span of a militant was no more than 3 years, and this induced the guerrilla organizations to draw in fresh recruits continually.[21] Moreover, in an attempt to broaden their mass base, the guerrillas had inducted recruits without proper scrutiny and many recruits had not undergone any ideological training or training in surveillance tactics. This perpetuated an overall lack of discipline among the guerrilla cadres. Further, the guerrilla groups had instituted a decentralized organizational structure in order to minimize the risk of infiltration.[22] All these factors encouraged many guerrillas to secure a local power base and in the process many of them accrued considerable financial assets. Another factor that propelled the guerrillas to seek self-limited goals through violence was the failure of the prevailing institutional structures, both modern as well as customary, to give them a measure of power.

Another noteworthy feature of the movement is that the rural population of the province sought the intervention of militants to settle disputes, primarily land disputes, and render justice. In many areas the militants instituted Khalsa panchayats, which ran parallel to government courts. This indicates the disenchantment of the masses with the prevailing institutional structure of India. At this stage, many Sikh youths were drawn into the movement by the Robin Hood image and the glorification of slain activists.

So far the growth of the guerrilla movement has been studied, now the factors that contributed to the disintegration of the guerrilla movement will be investigated. The course of the movement depended on support from other sections of the Sikh population. The rapid growth of armed resistance in the countryside and its effect on rural society has already been examined.[23] Being socially and economically vulnerable, the rural population became soft targets and victims of both state and guerrilla violence. But the viability of the guerrilla movement depended on the cooperation of the local population to provide them with food, shelter and a safe hideout. Thus, the withdrawal of support to the guerrillas by the rural population was a decisive factor in determining the course of the movement.

The first phase of the guerrilla movement evoked a sympathetic response from the Sikh professional classes – teachers, doctors, engineers and lawyers. Their response, however, was not manifested in an overt political form. Many Sikh professionals and office workers reiterated the fear of state repression as a key factor that prevented them from getting involved in political protest. Moreover, many Sikh professionals believed that any confrontation with the central government would not only ruin their prospects of social promotion but would also put their jobs in jeopardy. Thus, many strings tied the Sikh professional class to the central government. These institutional ties were critical in preventing the guerrilla activists from finding allies among the Sikh professional class.

The handful of discontented Sikh professionals who overtly protested against government actions included one retired justice, two retired army generals and two members of the Indian Civil Service. 'Of the politically committed cadres involved with the KCF, none save two came from families of status' (Pettigrew 1995: 56).[24] The second phase of the guerrilla movement was marked by an outburst of violence that antagonized the liberal minded. On 15 June 1991, seventy-four Hindus were killed in cold blood when a train was attacked, and on 10 March 1992, in a similar incident, sixty people were massacred. Attempts were made to dissuade the masses from participating in democratic procedures, and in the run-up to the aborted Punjab Assembly elections June in 1991 thirty-two candidates were assassinated. The tactics and activities of the guerrillas lost their ideological credibility among a broad section of the Sikh population. Thus, the failure to establish a mass base was a vital factor in the disintegration of the guerrilla movement. Consequently, the lack of institutional means to coordinate guerrilla activities also facilitated the break up of the movement.

Moreover, the central government rendered political groups ineffective by creating divisions within them through incarceration or harassment of members. Simranjit Singh Mann, a former officer in the prestigious Indian Police Service (IPS), tendered his resignation in protest against the assault on Darbar Sahib.[25] Thereafter, he was dismissed from service and charged with treason and with waging war against the Indian state and for inciting a Sikh rebellion in the Indian armed forces. He was among the few Sikhs from his social background to share with the guerrillas the experience of torture and psychological degradation during detention. In November 1989, he won a massive majority in the Punjab elections, and on 26 December 1990 all the major factions of the Akali Dal united under his leadership to form the Shiromani, or 'united', Akali Dal. However, within 4 months of its formation, the Shiromani Akali Dal fragmented into various factions, but at the turn of the twentieth century Singh Mann was still president. The political goal of the Shiromani Akali Dal is to claim the right to self-determination for the Sikhs. The central government regards it as a militant party and many of its workers have been incarcerated, harassed and killed. It is perhaps the only political party to have preserved and documented the activity of paramilitary forces in the province.[26] At one level, the party has attempted to highlight the Sikh case and elicit support for Sikh self-determination at an international level; at the local level its workers and activists are in direct contact with the activities of the guerrillas.[27] Also, the Shiromani Akali Dal is closely associated with the DamDami Taksal. Although the President of the Shiromani Akali Dal is widely regarded as a man of commitment and integrity, his party has not been successful in securing mass support.

The nature of political organization in the province is critical for determining the electoral pattern. After the assassination of Sant Harchand Singh Longowal, the prominent Akali leaders before Operation Bluestar had been discredited by the Sikh masses. However, the traditional Akali Dal has been successfully resurrected under the leadership of Parkash Singh Badal and is now referred to as Akali Dal (B). The Akali Dal (B) has considerable control over the resources of the SGPC. In February 1992 the Punjab state assembly elections were boycotted by all the major political parties in the province. The Congress Party won 8 per cent of the popular vote and formed the state government. By 1992, the guerrilla network was believed to have been virtually eradicated. However, on 31 August 1995, the chief minister of

Punjab was killed by a suicide bomber, who was reported to be an activist in the Babbar Khalsa, a guerrilla organization with links abroad. As the state geared up for the nationwide assembly elections in 1996, the contest was expected to be between the Akali Dal (B) and the Congress party. While the Akali Dal had the vital resources of the SGPC, the Congress party had the resources of the state and central government at its disposal.

The Sikh diaspora

So far in this chapter we have examined the growth of Sikh national consciousness and the rise of armed resistance in favour of the formation of a separate Sikh state in the 1980s. The movement for the formation of an independent Sikh state of Khalistan has also found support in the large Sikh expatriate community. Recent estimates suggest that out of 18 million Sikhs, nearly 2 million live outside India, and of 3,000 *gurudwaras* almost 500 are situated outside India (K. Singh 1991: 409). By the mid-1980s, the Sikh community in England was by far the largest, estimated to be nearly 300,000, followed by the Canadian Sikh community, numbering between 120,000 and 200,000; over 125,000 Sikhs were estimated to be living in the United States. Moreover, the majority of Sikh emigrants have peasant origins. That is why an appraisal of Sikh unrest must take into account the attitudes and activities of Sikhs based outside India.

In this section we will attempt to explain the role of the Sikh diaspora in the Sikh ethno-nationalist movement. This entails a brief account of the process of emigration from rural Punjab. Although no scholar has covered the entire field, there are several historical accounts of Sikh settlement in different countries, focusing on different aspects of this emigration. Sikh emigration overseas is a relatively recent phenomenon, the first phase of which began in the early nineteenth century. Despite the adverse and hostile surroundings encountered by the pioneer founders of overseas Sikh settlements, and despite stating at the lowest level of the industrial work force, they have managed to achieve considerable prosperity, just as other upwardly mobile minorities have done.

Sikhs in England

The pioneer founders of Britain's Sikh settlement were Sikh soldiers who had fought in Europe during the First World War and had decided to remain in Britain instead of returning to India. Most of the early pioneers belonged to the Jat caste, from which the Indian Army drew many of its recruits. They were soon joined by a different caste, the Bhatras, whose traditional occupation as peddlers enjoined them to deploy their traditional skills and work as peddlers, selling clothes and other goods from door to door, thereby establishing an occupational toehold in Britain. During the 1930s the inflow of Sikh migrants grew steadily through the process of chain migration. The onset of the post-war economic boom transformed the opportunities that were available to the Sikh immigrants. Since British industry was acutely short of workers, there was a shift from peddling to industrial employment, and the Sikh immigrants increasingly became part of the industrial labour force. By the early 1960s there was an ever-increasing inflow of migrant workers from Punjab until the imposition of immigration controls in 1962.

Throughout the 1970s there was a constant inflow of Sikh settlers from East Africa. Sikh emigration to East Africa had begun in the late nineteenth century. The early Sikh pioneers to East Africa belonged to the Ramgarhia caste, whose traditional occupation as artisans ascribed to them a relatively low social status. They were recruited by the British colonial authorities as construction workers, and they used their traditional skills in bricklaying and carpentry to lay railway lines in Nairobi. Many East African Sikhs achieved position of power in trade and industry. But soon after many colonized African countries had attained independence, the employment opportunities for East African Sikhs dwindled or were curtailed. Members of the Indian community were regarded as colonialists, and for many Africans it became their mission to regain control of the economic sphere of their country from the supposed stranglehold of the Indians. As a consequence, many East African Sikhs migrated to Britain because some of them already held British passports. Of the 300,000 Sikhs currently living in Britain, more than half are Jats (Ballard 1994: 95).

The onset of industrial recession during the 1980s resulted in shrinkage of opportunities in the waged labour market, and according to one estimate 'as many as half of all middle-aged Asian industrial workers had lost their jobs' (Ballard 1994: 100). The imminent collapse of the labour market has prompted many Asian industrial workers to search for alternative means of making a living. This has prompted more and more Sikh industrial workers who have been made redundant to increasingly turn towards self-employment and small-scale manufacturing. As we have seen, the first-generation Sikh immigrants predominantly found employment in the waged labour market. However, because of the changes in occupational and economic situations, the second generation of British Sikhs are steadily becoming more middle class.

The political activities of early Sikh settlers were centred around promoting their interests as an industrial labour force. Many of the Sikh industrial workers, especially the Jat Sikhs, had links with the Communist Party of India. During the late 1950s and early 1960s Indian Workers' Associations (IWAs) were instituted in many industrial towns to articulate workers' grievances and to challenge their subordinate position in the labour market. Membership of the IWAs was confined overwhelmingly to Jat Sikhs.[28] Moreover, it is critical to note that this egalitarian orientation reflected as much a commitment to Sikhism as to socialism. That is why local *gurudwaras* provided a vital arena for social and industrial solidarity. Despite the success of IWAs in challenging the marginalization of Punjabi industrial workers, there has been a gradual decline in the once thriving network of IWAs. Further, the onset of industrial recession had contributed to the collapse of the IWAs by the 1980s.

It was only after the turbulent events of 1984 that the attitude of the British Sikh community underwent a transformation. Thereafter, the movement for the formation of an independent Sikh state of Khalistan found vociferous support among the British Sikh community, although earlier, in September 1971, Jagjit Singh Chauhan, a former minister in an Akali government, had announced the formation of a sovereign Sikh state of Khalistan in a press statement issued in London. It was only after 1984 that many Sikh organizations abroad, such as the Dal Khalsa and the Babbar Khalsa, canvassed support from the expatriate Sikh communities in Canada, the United States, Germany and Great Britain. Many Sikh guerrilla organizations maintain international political wings involving politically active expatriate Sikhs. Since they are unresponsive to local conditions, they engage in hatching long-term strategy for the Sikh struggle.[29] They maintain contacts with human rights organizations in Punjab, and human rights cases are frequently taken up through the Sikh Human Rights Internet, and by Amnesty International. These organizations also lobby support for the Sikh cause in the United Nations. Thus, we see that serious violations of human rights no longer fall within the purview of internal affairs of the state and further influences relations among states. The Indian intelligence service has attempted to curb the activities of various Sikh individuals and organizations based outside India through propaganda and subversive activities.

Sikh emigration to Canada and the United States

Among the early Indian settlers in Canada were Sikh ex-soldiers who had participated in Queen Victoria's diamond jubilee celebration in British Columbia. Within a few years, a large number of Sikh immigrants had settled along the west coast of Canada, and by 1908 there were 6,500 Sikh workers in British Columbia. Most of them found employment as lumbermen or miners, or were engaged in building railroads. In a bid to stop further Indian immigration to Canada, the Canadian government enforced a number of restrictive immigration measures enacted through legislation. In 1910 a law was passed that severely restricted Asian immigration into Canada. Stricter immigration control in Canada resulted in an increase in the number of immigrants to the United States. By 1910, nearly 6000 Indians had moved southwards to California's Sacramento and San Joaquin river delta lands, where they found employment as farmhands or as labourers.

The response of the older immigrants from north-western Europe to the newly arrived Sikh immigrants in North America was hostile and unwelcome. A high level of prejudice was evident in public policies and in the attitudes of white Americans. In 1907 there was an outbreak of anti-Asian riots in British Columbia, and in 1908 riots directed against Asian immigrants of Indian,

Chinese and Japanese origin broke out in California. In fact, the history of Asian immigration to the United States contradicts the global image of America being a melting pot for all cultures. The descendants of the earlier settlers in North America, particularly those who shared a common Nordic or Teutonic ancestry, promoted the notion of ethnic purity in order to protect their interests from oriental incursions. Nevertheless, the mistreatment of expatriates abroad became a major issue with significant international ramifications.

What impelled the Sikh peasants to seek a livelihood in overseas countries? In 1907, there was widespread agrarian unrest in Punjab. The immediate cause of the rural dissent in Punjab was the promulgation of the British land rights legislation, which was the final blow to an already disaffected Sikh peasantry. It was the first time that the rural population, pensioned government officials and retired army men, the section of the population known for its staunch loyalty to the government, joined together and conducted a series of anti-government campaigns. Remarkably, Sikh immigration into Canada and the United States was at a peak between 1907 and 1910. Thus, the economic and social conditions in Punjab encouraged immigration so that alternative means of livelihood could be found.

The Ghadr uprising

The vast majority of Indian immigrants to North America were Sikhs. Not surprisingly, Sikh organizations were instituted to coordinate the activities of the immigrants. The Khalsa Diwan Society was founded in 1907 in Vancouver, and initially its activities centred around religious and educational concerns. However, issues such as growing racial discrimination and anti-immigration laws soon began to dominate its proceedings. A large number of Sikh immigrants were ex-soldiers who were loyal to the British Raj.[30] Attempts to redress their grievances, such as racial discrimination and laws preventing wives and families from joining their husbands, through petitions to British administrators proved unsuccessful. Thus attempts by Sikh immigrants to seek protection and justice from the British government were seldom rewarded.

Another dimension was added to the activities of the Indian immigrants in North America through the founding of a revolutionary organization, the Hindustani Workers of the Pacific Coast, in San Francisco. In November 1913, it published the first issue of a weekly paper called the *Ghadr*, or 'revolution', and thereafter the organization came to be known as the Ghadr party. The primary objective of the Ghadr party was to liberate India by overthrowing the colonial regime. Thus, the overseas Sikh population were pioneers for espousing the nationalist cause for India's freedom from British colonialism. The Ghadr uprising sought to address the political situation in India and is significant in India's struggle for independence.[31]

The Komagata Maru incident brought world attention to the plight of

Sikh immigrants and perpetuated the seeds of revolutionary nationalism. In May 1914, *SS Komagata Maru*, a Japanese passenger ship carrying 346 prospective Sikh immigrants, attempted to circumvent Canadian immigration regulations, which stipulated that prospective immigrants must travel directly from their home country to Canada. This provision was clearly directed at stopping further Indian immigration because there were no ships sailing directly from India to Canada. Despite vigorous public campaigns in Canada as well as in India, and appeals to the Canadian government and the Viceroy of India, the Canadian government did not allow the vessel to land. Sir Richard MacBride, the prime minister of British Columbia, stated, 'To admit Orientals in large numbers would mean in the end the extinction of the white peoples and we have always in mind the necessity of keeping this a white man's country' (K. Singh 1991: 179). The plight of the passengers many of whom had put all their possessions at stake on this venture elicited considerable sympathy from the people of Punjab and provided a forum for the dissemination of Ghadr propaganda. As the ship approached the port city of Calcutta in India in September 1914, a strong police contingent ordered the Sikh passengers to immediately board a train to Punjab. The Sikhs refused to obey and in the ensuing fracas eighteen passengers were killed, twenty-five wounded and more than 200 were interned (K. Singh 1991: 181). A campaign was mounted to whip up support in India. The experience of Sikh immigrants in North America had a significant impact on events in Punjab. Accounts of harsh treatment and fierce racial discrimination accorded to the overseas Sikhs elicited considerable sympathy in Punjab. The British government was accused of not protecting the interests of its subjects abroad from the hostile policies and actions of the Canadian and American authorities.

Although the Ghadr cause was aborted, it had significant international ramifications and political significance in the decline of colonialism. Mark Juergensmeyer (1979) distinguishes two phases of the Ghadr movement. In its first phase, between 1913 and 1918, ties to the homeland were cast in the nationalist political rhetoric. In the second phase, between 1916 and 1919, the Ghadr ideology blossomed into a socialist ideology, focusing on issues of economic exploitation and class differentiation.[32] The Russian revolution had a great influence on Ghadr ideologues and many visited Russia to generate links with international communism. The question then arises, why did the immigrant Sikh community identify itself with the nationalist struggle for India's freedom? Further, why was a socialist rebellion resurrected to overthrow the colonial regime in India? A brief summary of some of the issues is offered below. Clearly, the Ghadr uprising received widespread support from the immigrant Sikh community in North America. This segment of the population was predominantly employed in low-status menial jobs on plantations, in mines, as labourers building railroads and other transportation infrastructures. In an attempt to relate the Ghadr uprising against British colonialism in India to the oppression experienced by the Sikh immigrant community in North America, Mark Juergensmeyer notes, 'a militant nationalist movement is created abroad by expatriates, for whom the movement is also an outlet for their economic and social frustration, and a vehicle for their ethnic identities' (Juergensmeyer 1979: 189). Mark Juergensmeyer further notes that Ghadr nationalism instilled a sense of nationalist Indian pride in the immigrant community to stand up to the hostile environment in North America. Certainly, the violent prejudices that the first-generation immigrant Sikh community experienced in North America contributed in raising their political consciousness. Thus, the Ghadr uprising was an endeavour to protect themselves and deal effectively with the authorities in North America by assuming control of their country of origin.

From Ghadr to Khalistan

How do we explain the transformation from Indian nationalism to Sikh nationalism among the Sikh diaspora in North America? An attempt to answer the above question is bedevilled by two issues. The first concerns the use of the term 'diaspora' for the expatriate Sikh community. If we adopt Walker Connor's influential definition[33] of diaspora as 'that segment of a people living outside the homeland', and ethnic 'homeland' designating the emotional dimension and attachment to the home of the forebears (imagined or real), then is it appropriate to talk of a Sikh diaspora before the conception of a Sikh homeland? Although a feeble demand for a Sikh state was made for the first time in the 1940s, the expression of Punjab as a homeland for the Sikhs only became an issue in the 1960s. Further, the movement for a separate Sikh state gained momentum only in the 1980s. Even so, the Sikh diaspora began to promote the formation of a sovereign Sikh national state of Khalistan only after the cataclysmic events of 1984.

Various explanations have been offered to explain the support for Khalistan by the Sikh diaspora. Some explanations emphasize the psychological aspects of the migrants' experience, the alienation and anomie generated by the experience of living in a strange country, which are believed to heighten the religious and national identity of a migrant community, promoting the desire to form a homeland state.[34] But is the diasporan Sikh community lonelier and more insecure than the non-separatist migrant groups? Why did this sense of alienation provide support for India's quest for freedom from colonialism? Why was it only after 1984 that it shifted into support for the formation of an independent Sikh state?

In a recent article, Verne A. Dusenbery has argued that

> one of the appeals of Khalistan to diasporan Sikhs may be the creation of a publicly recognized "country of origin", from which Sikhs may legitimately make claim to their own political voice and to the prerequisites of public support for cultural diversity (e.g., funding made

available under multiculturalism programs or protection under local human rights codes) in their countries of residence.

(Van der Veer 1995: 33)

If the Sikh diaspora has pressed claims for a Sikh national state in order to gain a measure of power and credibility in the country of immigration, then why have they done so only since 1984? Verne A. Dusenbery's account is based on the impact of the multi-culturalism policies of the Canadian government (1971) on the Sikh diaspora. But then how do we account for the widespread support for the Khalistan movement by the Sikhs based in America and in Europe? Moreover, Dusenbery does not empirically validate his claim that it is the second- and the third-generation North American Sikhs who support the movement for Sikh sovereignty.

The overseas Sikh community has historically maintained strong ties with Punjab through kinship and culture.[35] Traditional intellectuals (*gianis, dhadhis*), holy men (*bhais, sants, babas*) and religious musicians regularly tour *gurudwaras* worldwide to provide spiritual enhancement. They continue to be the bearers of Sikh tradition with their ability to interpret and expound on *gurbani* (the holy word of the Sikh gurus). Moreover, popular and classical performers are invited by the Sikh migrants to perform shows on a regular basis. London has become the hub of popular Punjabi folk music in recent years. In fact, it is the music connection that to some extent culturally binds the second- and third-generation overseas Sikh youths to Punjab.[36] Further, rural Punjab has been the source of spouses for the Sikh migrant group, as spouses from Punjab are believed to be of higher moral character and are therefore pure. Moreover, the development of air travel, efficient telephone services and satellite television transmitting instant regional news has facilitated the intense communication Sikh emigrants have with their homeland.

Apart from the growth of cultural and social ties, the Sikh emigrants have a flourishing economic network with their ethnic homeland. A study conducted by Helweg (1986) indicates that for Punjab until 1978 the highest proportion of expatriate money came from Great Britain (Sheffer 1986: 119). The reason was obvious enough, a large Punjabi population resided in the UK. Remittances to needy parents and relatives are of increasing importance. Further, remittances for conspicuous consumption are significant for altering a family's position in the social hierarchy. The recent policy of economic liberalization has thrown the Indian economy open to foreign investors. The Punjab government is inviting and giving incentives to the overseas Punjabi community in order to encourage investments. However, these economic policies are too recent to allow for proper evaluation.

This excursion into the nature of ties that bind the Sikh migrant group to its ethnic homeland is sufficient, I hope, to indicate how the nature of the ties between the migrant group and the country of its forebears is critical in determining the response of the diaspora community to the political and social events in its ethnic homeland. These links are particularly significant for migrant groups who constitute a minority in the country of emigration. In the case of the Sikhs, it is evident that the strong family and village ties, together with cultural and economic ties, bind the expatriate Sikhs to their homeland. These ties are critical in determining the response of the Sikh emigrants to the policies of the Indian government and the treatment meted out to the Sikhs in India. It is in this context that the overseas Sikh community shifted its support to the Sikh movement for a sovereign state after the attack on the Sikh holy shrine in 1984.

Conclusion

In the first section of this chapter I have examined how the Punjabi *suba* movement consolidated the process of religion-based linguistic differentiation. I noted that modern institutions facilitated both intercommunal collaboration and communal political competition. Further, the Punjabi *suba* movement demonstrates that the response of the central government to regional demands is critical in determining the course of a regional movement. On the one hand, the Indian government perceived the demand for Punjabi *suba* as a threat to the principles of secular India. On the other hand, the Akali Dal sought to protect the Sikh language and religion in a Hindu-dominated society and accused the central government of pursuing a political strategy of assimilating the language and culture of a minority group. More importantly, the concept of Punjab as a homeland for the Sikhs has been woven into Sikh self-definition since the beginnings of the Punjabi *suba* movement.

In the second section of this chapter, we have attempted to delineate the factors that turned a peaceful, farmers' movement, concerned with specific socio-economic issues, into a violent guerrilla movement advocating national independence. The first stirrings of Sikh discontent began with the moderate demands of well-to-do peasants, which became progressively more radical. Attention has been focused on two factors that contributed to this radicalization. First, the enormous impact of the policies and activities of the central government on Sikh communal perception. Second, the tendency of Sikh peasantry to turn to religious notions emanating from the Sikh faith in legitimizing their economic, political and social grievances. Clearly, the demands of the Akali Dal have been shaped by a desire to safeguard and promote an independent Sikh entity. It is critical to note that the vigorous Akali campaign has never construed the Anandpur Sahib Resolution as a demand for an independent Sikh state. The political objective of the Akali Dal has been to strive for the creation of a *desh-kaal*, literally meaning country and era for the Sikhs within the Indian union. The traditional Akali leadership, drawn from the dominant social and economic strata, is too strongly amalgamated with the prevailing political and economic structure to ever support the demand for a sovereign Sikh state.

Further, Sikh political campaigns have historically been staged around

Sikh shrines. Religious shrines are material embodiments of the deeply held systems of life and thought of a community. The distinctive imagery of sacred shrines binds the community of believers through a shared cosmological understanding. The *gurudwara* agitation (1920–5) established a pattern of peaceful resistance that has been resurrected by the Akali Dal from time to time. The Akali campaigns have often been based on the holding of ostensibly religious *diwans*, or 'assemblies', often in the precincts of Sikh *gurudwaras*. The campaigns have been conducted in a shroud of powerful religious and historical symbolism. Each Akali *jatha* would first of all go through a holy rite and invoke the blessings of the *sangat*, or 'religious congregation', and the Adi Granth before setting off. Such rites express a sense of collective identity and the repetitive and stylized form of these rituals nurtures a sense of order and security among its adherents. That is why the assault on Darbar Sahib, the bastion of Sikhism, in June 1984 became a powerful symbol of official repression and provoked a sense of alienation and deep anguish among the Sikhs and led to the radicalization of the Sikh diaspora.

Thus, the growing Sikh unrest in Punjab was due to the intransigence of the central government, which would not grant the seemingly legitimate demands of the Akali Dal. In the early phase, the existence of Akali Dal as a powerful ethno-regional party served to institutionalize potential conflict emanating from the ethno-region of Punjab. But the failure to seek an equitable solution to the moderate demands of the Akali Dal and the ruthless use of the repressive apparatus of the state against the Sikh minority were partly responsible for the beginnings of Sikh armed struggle. Thus, the Sikh insurrection became more radical because of the growing acrimony between the Akali Dal and the central government.

The exploited Sikh peasantry constituted the vanguard of the struggle for Sikh national independence. The growing discontent on the part of the peasantry was rooted in the prevailing material conditions of their existence. Nonetheless, it was official repression that impelled the aggrieved peasantry into an ethno-regional armed struggle. Once the Sikh peasants had been stirred up, a violent overhaul of society was under way. However, by themselves peasant insurrections have a historic record of failure. More importantly, the participation of the rural Sikh population and the Sikh professional class was critical in determining the outcome of the guerrilla movement. The particular stage of industrial development in the province precluded a fusion between the professionals and the peasantry. The lack of tacit support for guerrilla resistance by a broad cross-section of the rural and the urban Sikh population led to the virtual disintegration of the movement. Another factor that contributed to the failure of the movement was the lack of proper organizational structure to coordinate the activities of the guerrilla cadres. Thus, whether or not a peasant-led ethno-nationalist struggle becomes politically effective depends on its finding allies in other strata of the population. This in turn depends on the stage of economic development of the country and specific historical circumstances within which an ethno-regional movement emerges.

5 The agrarian crisis and the rise of armed resistance

The socio-economic impact of the green revolution

I have discussed the transition of the Sikh congregation into an ethnic community (in Chapter 3) and then into a nation demanding a state of its own (in Chapter 4). I now turn to the latest phase of the Sikh nationalist movement and its demand for Khalistan. This involves an understanding of how two aspects of social change in the latter half of the twentieth century have come together. The first of these is the green revolution and its radicalization of a section of the Sikh peasantry who spearheaded the ethno-nationalist movement. The second concerns the rise and impact of the vernacular press. In this chapter I deal with the green revolution and the social composition of the Sikh nationalist movement; in the next chapter I consider the revolution in communication, which spread the ideals of religion to wider sections of the population.

So far, the explanation for the emergence of Sikh ethno-nationalism in the late 1970s and its development up to the present time has focused on the socio-economic impact of green revolution strategy as an agent of change on the Sikh peasantry. The central task of this chapter is to bring into focus the nexus between the dislocation and alienation experienced by a section of the Sikh peasantry as a consequence of the green revolution and the subsequent demand for a sovereign Sikh state.

To comprehend fully the complex processes of social change initiated or accelerated by the technologies and policies associated with the green revolution strategy, we must first understand the agricultural system that is being changed, then discern the process of change and finally ask where the change is leading. The main focus of the chapter is on what happens to the social structure of the rural society as the processes of technological change proceed. The chapter is divided into three sections. The first section comprises three parts: the first part examines the origins of the green revolution and is followed by an exploration of the consequences of the green revolution on agrarian social structure. The third part describes the subsequent emergence of Sikh activists and establishes their socio-economic background. The second section looks at the situations that favour a peasant-led ethno-regional struggle as a consequence of the transition to commercial agriculture. Finally, the process of overseas Sikh emigration from rural Punjab is explored.

On green revolution

This section will address four questions that lie at the heart of the debate about how agricultural change in India affects the agrarian social structure and vice versa. These are:

1 What is the green revolution?
2 Was the new technology designed for the best endowed region and for the most affluent section of the society?
3 How has the green revolution transformed Punjab into 'the granary of India'?
4 Did the green revolution result in complete depeasantization?[1]

What is green revolution?

The term 'green revolution' came into use in the late 1960s and refers to the introduction of higher yielding varieties (HYVs) of wheat and rice in 'developing' countries. Andrew Pearse (1974), the director of a major United Nations research project into agricultural change, has identified three distinct ways in which the phrase 'green revolution' is used.

1 The green revolution as a breakthrough in plant breeding: the term 'green revolution' is understood, particularly by agricultural scientists, as a scientific breakthrough for creating new varieties of cereals, particularly rice and wheat. It was believed that the use of the 'new seeds' would lead to a revolutionary increase in agricultural productivity.
2 Green revolution as a technology: the high-yielding potential of the new varieties of grain could be realized only through the application of chemical fertilizer and controlled irrigation. Agronomists and agricultural economists used the term for the new technology that required agricultural mechanization, such as tractors and grain-processing machinery.
3 Green revolution as a development strategy: the phrase green revolution implies not only the technology but also the strategy used to carry it out.[2] Breakthroughs in agricultural technology could represent social and political solutions to the agrarian problem in the developing countries. Through the transformation of productive technology, production may be intensified and yields raised, especially in countries where agricultural land is limited. This further implied that the green revolution could potentially provide a technical solution to a social problem, because profound social upheaval of land reform could be prevented by the use of new technology (Hadjor 1993: 134). As John Harriss points out, 'this peaceful rational solution to the agrarian question through new technology was counterposed to the threat of a 'red revolution', which could now be averted. The expression was deliberately coined to contrast

with the phrase 'red revolution', and the notion that 'developing' countries were to undergo far-reaching changes as a result of an agricultural revolution, rather than because of radical political transformation. The strategic, geopolitical interests of the United States in changing rural social and economic conditions in Asia and Latin America, with a view to the containment of communist expansion, were clear' (Harriss 1987: 229–30). Thus the green revolution was readily regarded by development experts as the panacea they had been searching for.

In 1953, John D. Rockefeller III founded the Agricultural Development Council in America to impart the knowledge and the skills needed to transfer and implement the American model of agricultural expansion to agricultural scientists from other countries, especially Asia. Three groups of international agencies were involved in organizing, funding and transferring the American model of agriculture to India: the private American Foundations, the American government and the World Bank.

Is the green revolution a 'scale neutral' or 'resource neutral' technology?

To achieve high yields the new varieties required high fertilizer inputs, principally chemical fertilizers, and a vast water supply. Thus, the successful use of the HYVs required the adoption of what came to be called a 'package' of inputs (new seeds, fertilizers and agro-chemicals) and cultivation practices (controlled irrigation and more systematic planting). The use of the HYV package brought with it an increased demand for capital, and market structures had to be developed to handle both increased input and output. There is widespread evidence that although the new technology may theoretically be 'scale neutral' it was certainly not 'resource neutral', for the reasons outlined above. (Harriss 1987, Byres 1982, Rao 1975)

That the green revolution is heavily dependent on the capital-intensive products of agribusiness and, therefore, that it can only benefit the larger, more prosperous farmers is an influential idea (Frankel 1971, Byres 1972, Patnaik 1976, Shiva 1991). More specifically, in Punjab there is evidence that the introduction of the green revolution led to a significant increase in both food production and landlessness (Hadjor 1993, Dasgupta 1977a). Likewise, Khushwant Singh concludes,

> As farming got more mechanised, landowners began to dispense with farm hands: what had been for generations a familial patron–client association turned into an adversarial one. Rich landlords became richer, the marginal became poor; and the landless unwanted on land.
>
> (K. Singh 1991: 323)

Considerable effort has been expended to illustrate how the green revolution aggravates socio-economic polarization, and adversely affects the lives of the already impoverished peasantry. This conception of capitalist development as entailing the differentiation of rural producers and 'depeasantization' has been enormously influential despite contemporary and subsequent criticism. I shall examine the reasoning behind this and the evidence for it, and explain by reference to material from micro-level studies about trends in agrarian change in Punjab how and why the actual changes have been more complicated and contradictory. It would be misleading to make generalizations about Punjab as a whole for there is much regional and cultural diversity; therefore, I have highlighted cases where there are inter-regional contradictions within Punjab.[3]

The green revolution in Punjab

The following section describes the transformation of Punjab into the 'granary of India' through the green revolution strategy. This is established through a survey of statistical data about the expansion of the following features: (1) fertilizer consumption; (2) irrigation; (3) electricity consumption; (4) yields of rice and wheat; and (5) a comparison with other states of per capita income.

As mentioned earlier, in order to flower, the 'new seeds' required high fertilizer inputs, and irrigation occupied a key position in the package. Therefore, the 'new strategy' could apply only to those parts of India where irrigation had spread or to which it might spread. Only 17 per cent of India's arable acreage had been irrigated by the mid-1960s. Punjab has a history of irrigation and the green revolution merely expanded and intensified the existing irrigation system. In 1962, the Punjab Agricultural University (PAU) was established at Ludhiana and became the epicentre of the green revolution in Punjab. It was here that the visiting Norwegian-American agro-scientist Norman Borlaug[4] and his team of Indian scientists evolved new strains of Mexican dwarf wheat and gave the seed to the farming community.

In Punjab the technological innovations demanded large amounts of chemical fertilizers and controlled irrigation. From 1965–6 to 1982–3, fertilizer consumption increased almost fifteen times, and by 1991–2 Punjab province accounted for 10 per cent of the total fertilizer consumption in India (Department of Agriculture) (Table 5.1). Consumption of the electricity used for agriculture increased by more than six times (see Table 5.4), and the area irrigated by wells and tubewells more than doubled. By 1990–1, the area irrigated was 93 per cent of the net sown area (Tables 5.2 and 5.3).

Similarly, there was a tremendous increase in the use of agricultural implements and machinery. Between 1966 and 1981, the number of tractors increased elevenfold and that of tubewells by about thirteenfold. In 1991–2, there were nearly 275,000 tractors and 781,000 tubewells in Punjab (Statistical Abstract of Punjab). According to one source, 'Punjab has 10 per cent of India's television sets and 17 per cent of its tractors' (Jeffrey 1986: 27).

The increase in the numbers of tubewells and tractors along with new HYV seeds led to a swift growth of agricultural production in Punjab. Since

Table 5.1 Consumption of chemical fertilizers in Punjab

Year	Fertilizers *(thousands of nutrient tonnes)*
1960–61	5
1970–71	213
1975–76	295
1980–81	295
1985–86	1098
1987–88	1112
1988–89	1117
1989–90	1145
1990–91	1221
1991–92	1262

Source: Statistical Abstract of Punjab, 1992

Table 5.2 Net irrigated area in Punjab

Year	Government canals	Private canals	Tubewells and canals	Other sources	Total	Percentage of net area irrigated to net area sown
1960–61	1,173	7	829	11	2,020	54
1970–71	1,286	6	1,591	5	2,888	71
1975–76	1,366	4	1,742	7	3,119	75
1980–81	1,430	–	1,939	13	3,382	81
1985–86	1,412	–	2,274	4	3,690	88
1987–88	1,409	6	2,307	2	3,724	89
1988–89	1,452	6	2,309	9	3,776	90
1989–90	1,460	7	2,436	16	3,919	93
1990–91	1,567	9	2,233	7	3,816	90
1991–92	1,510	9	2,423	4	3,946	93

Source: Statistical Abstract of Punjab, 1992.

Table 5.3 Irrigated area in Punjab (1991–2)

	Hectares *(in thousands)*
Canals	1,559
Tubewells	2,339
Total	3,910
Percentage irrigated area	93

Source: Agriculture in Punjab 1991–92, Department of Agriculture, Chandigarh, Punjab

Table 5.4 Consumption of electric power in agriculture as a percentage of total consumption

1970–1	1975–6	1980–1	1985–6	1987–8	1988–9	1989–90	1990–1	1991–2
38.00	43.16	43.66	39.74	47.15	43.88	45.41	42.87	43.81

Source: Statistical Abstract of Punjab, 1992

Table 5.5 The production of wheat and rice in Punjab and India (percentage)

Year	Punjab		India	
	Rice	Wheat	Rice	Wheat
1960–61	48.49	41.44	88.3	60.9
1965–66	61.82	45.58	78.1	57.6
1969–70	103.04	15.12	–	–
1971–72	194.37	133.65	–	–
1973–74	240.88	123.25	–	–
1975–76	305.75	137.69	124.7	159.9
1977–78	527.62	158.01	134.7	176.0
1979–80	644.89	187.20	107.9	175.0

Source: Punjab Di Arthikta, 1983, Azad, Nirmal., Punjabi University Publication Bureau, Patiala, Punjab

Table 5.6 Contribution to central pool (percentage)

Year	Rice	Wheat
1970–71	16	74
1975–76	19	58
1980–81	45	75
1985–86	43	59
1986–87	47	62
1987–88	49	56
1988–89	41	73
1989–90	46	63
1990–91	43	61
1991–92	52	72

Source: Agriculture in Punjab 1991–92, Department of Agriculture, Chandigarh, Punjab

the introduction of the new technology Punjab has earned the name of 'food basket of the country' and 'granary of India'; it has been contributing 40–50 per cent of rice and 60–70 per cent of wheat to India's central pool for the last two decades (Tables 5.4, 5.5 and 5.6). Of the world's output Punjab State produces 1 per cent of the rice, 2 per cent of the wheat and 2 per cent of the cotton (Department of Agriculture)

In terms of per capita income, Punjab has improved from fourth position in 1960–1 to first place in 1964–5. Since then Punjab has not only maintained its lead over other states in India but over the years the province has increased its margin in per capita income over other states in India. In 1985–6 Punjab had a per capita income that was double that of the all-India average and more than three times that of Bihar, the lowest per capita income state in the country (Gill 1990: 116–7). According to another source, 'the income of the "average Punjabi" was 65 per cent greater than that of the "average Indian"' (Jeffrey 1986: 27). The increase in production was high, particularly in wheat and rice. From 1965–6 to 1982–3 wheat production rose by 4.8-fold and that of rice by around 14-fold.

From the above data it is evident that Punjab took the lead over other states in the use of almost all components of new agricultural technology and is an area of prosperity in an otherwise backward country. Thus, any discussion on Sikh ethno-nationalism must take note of this significant factor.

Agricultural change and agrarian social structure

Technology and the small peasant farmer

In this section some of the factors that have contributed to the emergence of the green revolution strategy in Punjab and the impact and repercussions on the prevailing agrarian social structure will be examined. Fifteen years of green revolution has enabled the formation of a social base for the Sikh ethno-nationalist movement through radicalization of a section of the Sikh peasantry. I am in agreement with Andrew Pearse (1980), who maintains that, on the one hand, the introduction of genetic-chemical technology is bound to cause major structural changes in society and, on the other hand, that variations in agrarian structure directly affect the mode of technology-induced economic and social transformation. The following discussion considers the consequences of the interaction between the two. I first examine how the existing farm size or the pattern of land holding affected the profitability arising from technological innovation. I then go on to discuss the implications of the new technology for local labour and the subsequent migration and occupational shifts it entailed.

PATTERN OF LAND HOLDINGS

In a landed society, the pattern of land ownership provides a guide to the concentration of power. Punjab is a highly stratified society, characterized by caste and class divisions. It is important to note that one is dealing with the caste hierarchy among Sikhs, which is rather different from the classical Hindu fourfold caste hierarchy in terms of *varnas* – Brahmins, Kshatriyas, Vaishyas and Sudras, in that order of hierarchy with the fifth category of Untouchable.[5] Moreover, this classical fourfold hierarchy is generally recognized by anthropologists to be a gross oversimplification, which fails to capture the complex reality of rural India.

Little information is available on the social characteristics of the big farmers or the small and marginal farmers of Punjab. Daniel Thorner (1976) does introduce a discussion about a new class of gentleman farmer emerging from ex-army officers, retired civil servants and other white-collar jobs, and claims that this phenomenon is unique to India.[6]

Pearse (1980) also discusses the emergence of the new class of entrepreneurial cultivator as a consequence of the incorporation of the new technology. He cites Joshi (1971), who observes that the profitability of the new technology has caused many people to choose to become cultivators who otherwise would not have done so. They consist of 'moneyed men from the business and professional classes, retired members of the bureaucracy and the army, and influential and affluent politicians' (Pearse 1980: 165). Although it is probable that most of them come from land-owning families.

There is no space to go into the historical details describing the existence of an inegalitarian social structure as reflected in the pattern of possession of the land holdings. I shall confine myself to the situation developing after the introduction of the green revolution strategy (Table 5.7).

Agricultural census data reveal that between 1971 and 1981 operational holdings declined by 358,255. The number of holdings declined from 1,375,382 in 1971 to 1,027,127 in 1981. This is a reduction of 25.3 per cent. This includes marginal and small-holdings, which declined respectively by 61.9 per cent and 23.3 per cent (Gill 1989).[7] Dasgupta's study concludes that in Punjab 'the distribution of operated land has shifted in favour of the richer farmers under the new technology' (Dasgupta 1977b: 162–4).

A word of caution is needed. On the basis of the above evidence, it is tempting to draw an oversimplified picture of the green revolution strategy that resulted in rural polarization and depeasantization. Such a view obscures the complex processes at work, as explained below.

John Harriss correctly notes that a simple survey of the indices of farm size may be misleading for an analysis of the process of social differentiation. He further explains that there is a good deal of evidence to posit that the shift in the distribution of the operated area in favour of rich peasants has not come about through the complete dispossession of poor peasants, but rather as a result of the reversion of land formerly tenanted by poor peasants and of 'reverse tenancy' under which small cultivators rent out land to bigger

Table 5.7 Classification of land holdings (in thousands of hectares)

Size class (ha)	Number	Area (000 ha)
< 1	296	164
1–2	204	328
2–4	289	842
4–10	261	1622
≥ 10	67	1077
Total	1117	4033

Source: Agriculture in Punjab 1991–92 , Department of Agriculture, Chandigarh, Punjab

owners (Harriss 1987). Further, there may be a significant range of variation in the rates of expansion. One preliminary micro-level study indicates that farms of 20–5 acres expanded by 4 per cent, whereas those of 100–50 acres increased by about 40 per cent (Rudra *et al.* 1969: A143–74). It is interesting to note that the above discussion assumes an inverse relationship between farm size and profitability. It is this assumption that I now query.

FARM SIZE AND PROFITABILITY

Discussions about farm size have generated debates and often polarized positions are found. Pearse makes the point that 'most of the debates on farm size embrace a conceptual framework discovered for a capitalist economic structure rather than livelihood support systems in pre-capitalist modes of production' (Pearse 1980: 106).

It is widely argued that as technological innovation demands large amounts of capital only the rich end of the peasant spectrum could appropriate the new technology effectively. In other words, 'the mechanical innovations were biased to scale, the larger the holding (up to a point) the greater their effectiveness' (Byres 1982: 30). He further concludes,

> ...rich peasants (and landlords) could afford to purchase the new inputs – both biochemical and mechanical – because of greater command of resources and because they captured, to a large degree, the institutional credit (supplied by both cooperatives and by commercial banks) that was made available at 'reasonable' rates of interest.
>
> (Byres 1982: 40)

This critical sense in which the 'ideal' impact of the green revolution has been described is challenged and breaks down in the face of the evidence given below. This will be illustrated by a study conducted on the change in incomes and their distribution, which reveals that most rural people have gained financially from the expansion of agricultural output.

I shall now discuss Bhalla and Chadha's incisive study, covering the years

1961 and 1977, on the impact of the green revolution on income distribution among farming households in Punjab, with a special regard to the relative position of farmers with marginal-holdings (up to 2.5 acres) and those with small-holdings (between 2.5 and 5.0 acres) in the production, income and consumption nexus. Undoubtedly, the benefits accruing from the new technology are distributed more or less in proportion to the initial land-holding position. However, despite the limited land base of the small and marginal farmers of Punjab, they have been able to record almost as much total crop output and farm business income per acre as their bigger counterparts. Bhalla and Chadha's (1983: 160) study concludes that they have been able to achieve this by recording a much higher cropping intensity by rational year-round utilization of family labour. However, in the central Punjab plains the traditional inverse relationship between farm size and productivity does not hold.

The study highlights another interesting and significant aspect. The modernization of agriculture in Punjab has created many ancillary non-cultivation activities that provide supplementary employment and income to and small farmers: the most important ones are dairy farming, hiring out of farm assets and household enterprises. It is from these activities that the farmers are able to obtain higher per capita incomes. They estimate that

> ...non-farm income constitutes about one-fifth of total household income for cultivating household in general. For marginal farmers it is about 65 per cent of total household income. In terms of per capita terms also, the marginal farmers earn the highest from non-farm activities, compared with all other categories.

> (Bhalla and Chadha 1982: 872)

Thus, supplementary earnings are significant for reducing the income inequalities that occur because of disparate land distribution. Thus, it can be seen that the agricultural expansion did not necessarily lead to depeasantization. On the other hand, it would also be preposterous to claim the contrary, as observed by Bhalla and Chadha, and other scholars. Bhalla and Chadha stated that it is surprising to note that the farmers with marginal-holdings and the small-holdings still incur substantial deficits. Their study reveals that despite the enormous advances in agricultural technology 'about one-third of the marginal farmers (tilling less than 2.5 acres of land) are living below the poverty line'. Further, 'about 24 per cent of small farmers (tilling between 2.5 to 5.0 acres of land) are also living below the poverty line' (Bhalla and Chadha 1982: 876). A similar conclusion is reached in Singh's study: that 24 per cent of small farmers and 31 per cent of marginal farmers live below the poverty line in the green revolution state of Punjab (G. Singh 1984). Bardhan concludes that even in the 'throbbing heartland of the Green Revolution', the proportion of people living at subsistence level has increased (Bardhan 1973: 245–54).

Of course, it would be misleading to interpret these data as implying that each of the marginal and small farmers is running a deficit. Besides, there are bound to be some inter-regional variations for the provinces as a whole, although studies on such variations are not available.

The evidence discussed so far raises the question, why are the small and marginal peasants accruing deficits despite substantial gains in agricultural as well as non-agricultural activities? The germ of the conflict (and I am alluding to the ethno-nationalist movement among the Sikhs), it seems to me, lies in this very contradiction in 'the process of partial depeasantization'. In this context, it will be helpful to survey the studies about the savings and investment undertaken by various households.

I return once again to Bhalla and Chadha's remarkable evidence that demonstrates that farmers with marginal- small-holdings continue to make a fair amount of investment, which compares very favourably with the bigger farmers. Since this is happening despite their deficit in current income account, they conclude that investment expenditure is financed presumably through borrowing.

In this connection, another noteworthy development is that although the big farmers are recording substantial savings in the remainder of Punjab only a fraction of these savings are used in capital formation in agriculture. Having reached a plateau in farm investment, the rich farmers tend to increase their consumer spending and improve their standard of living through the purchase of jeeps, cars and television sets; they also spend heavily on social ceremonies. The availability of these surpluses enhances the economic and political power of the upper-middle and large farmers in the Punjab countryside.[8]

At best, these results give a qualitative picture of the investment that has been made by farming households, and it would be misleading to make a general statement. But it is plausible to conclude, as Pearse comments, that 'although the economies of scale enjoyed by big users of the new technology are not so great yet the big user accrues greater economic advantages from it than the small cultivator does'.[9]

I now turn to the impact of technological innovation on the local workforce in order to illustrate the vigorous displacement it entailed.

Agrarian change and local labour

Agricultural labourers who have no rights to land constitute one-third of the rural population and 20 per cent of the total population of Punjab (D. S. Singh 1982: 59). Farmers with land holdings of five acres or less constitute 48.5 per cent of the farming households in Punjab (Shiva 1991).[10] Intensive use of new technology has greatly increased the demand for agricultural labour. The use of HYVs of wheat and rice requires high doses of chemical fertilizers, insecticides, weed killers and pesticides; they also require well-irrigated soil. This has generated a high seasonal demand for labour in agricultural operations.

Between 1965–66 and 1972–73 estimated labour requirements in agriculture increased by 78.65 per cent. Further, there has been an increase of 55.31 per cent between 1970–71 to 1980–81. It is estimated that labour requirements on account of wheat–paddy crops increased by 37.18 per cent between 1971–72 and 1981–82. Against this increase in aggregate demand there is an increase in the labour force in agriculture (excluding migratory labour) of 24.8 per cent between 1971 and 1981

(Gill 1990: 118).

S. S. Gill (1990) has identified four possible reasons for this growth in agricultural labour. First, the complete elimination of pure tenants. Pure tenant holdings constituted 13.01 per cent of total holdings in 1970–1 and were reduced to 1.56 per cent in 1980–1. He maintains that some of them have joined agricultural labourers. Second, the development process has led to a decline in traditional occupations; therefore, workers employed as barbers, potters, shoemakers, weavers and water carriers have been made redundant; their traditional skills have been rendered useless by mechanization. A study has suggested that in parts of Punjab 'this class...stands almost on the verge of extinction' (H. K. M. Singh 1979: 594). S. S. Gill has noted that a large number of them have become agricultural labourers and that they mostly belong to the lower castes. Third, it is important to note that if there has been an increase in the use of hired labour, there has also been a decline in the use of family labour. The share component of family labour in wheat farming declined from 49.54 per cent in 1971–2 to 41.36 per cent in 1981–2, and that of hired labour increased from 50.36 per cent to 58.64 per cent during this period. Fourth, migratory workers from other states, e.g. East Uttar Pradesh, Bihar, Orissa, have joined the ranks of agricultural labourers in Punjab. This factor has vital implications for the local agricultural workers. The migratory workers from other states are overwhelmingly Hindu, and this has important political implications, as we will be shown in the second section of this chapter.

'Empirical evidence shows that wages of agricultural labourers are lower in those districts (Patiala and Ludhiana) with high concentration of migrants than those districts (Amritsar and Faridkot) with low concentration of migrants' (Gill 1990: 123). This perhaps has allowed the farmers to break the monopoly of local labourers and their demand for higher wages. It is also important to note that whereas the migrant labourer is paid individual wages the local labourers demand family wages.

Another study covering the years from 1961 to 1977 reveals that 'in many years the rise in money wages lagged behind price changes, leading to reduced real wage rates for most operations between 1965 and 1968, and again in 1974, 1975 and 1977' (Bhalla 1979: A57–68). Perhaps this suggests one of the reasons why even in the 'prime' green revolution area of Punjab and Haryana the proportion of people below the minimum level of living has increased.

From this it is fairly evident that the relationship between agricultural growth, employment and poverty is not as straightforward as often claimed in conventional theories about the labour market. It is also clear that the rural labour market in Punjab has been characterized by the deliberate exclusion of local labour and is inclined towards establishing control over local labourers.

How far has the green revolution as part of the foregoing process contributed to rural proletarianization?[11]

On the basis of the evidence available, it would be misleading to claim that the green revolution resulted in the complete dispossession of the poor peasantry in Punjab. Unfortunately, no systematic data are available about the consequences of recurrent losses incurred by small and marginal farmers. However, one should not underestimate the tenacity with which peasants will attempt to hold on to their land. Moreover, there is no evidence to support any sale of land by the small or marginal farmers in Punjab as a result of hardship.

Two other studies have examined the effect agricultural expansion had on the tenants, although they came to different conclusions. It is worth noting that both studies considered different regions of Punjab. The study carried out in the Ferozepur district of Punjab (Kahlon and Singh 1973) between 1967–8 and 1971–7 showed that the average value of land in the sample studied rose by 75 per cent. In spite of increased investment in machinery, land still accounted for 84 per cent of the total value of assets. The figures from Ferozepur demonstrate that the increased demand and higher price of land favoured its concentration in the hands of large landowners. The owners of small farms, who constituted the majority of farmers, could no longer invest in the purchase and improvement of land, whereas the owners of larger farms invested profusely in land once the possibilities for new technology became apparent.

Francine Frankel (1971) has described the situation of tenants in the district of Ludhiana, Punjab, in some detail. He maintains that as the potential profits from direct cultivation look increasingly attractive, the demand for land rises. Proprietors of large properties who still lease land out are charging rents that are 50–70 per cent higher than before the introduction of the new varieties of wheat and rice; however, shared tenancies are common.

> In many instances, landowners may ask for 70 per cent of the crop as their share, arguing that with the new methods the tenant still receives a larger absolute portion from 30 per cent of a higher output than 50 per cent of a lower out-turn. But since the small owner-cum-tenant cultivators cannot afford to invest in optimum cultivation practices, they find the new rentals uneconomic and generally are forced to give up...
>
> (Frankel 1971: 125)

Another alternative mentioned by Frankel can best be described as 'share-labourer', in which a large owner provides land and inputs to a cultivator with or without resources, to whom he allows 20 per cent of the harvest in return for his cultivatorship and labour (Pearse, 1980: 125). This process has been characterized as 'partial proletarianization' by Byres, who concludes that

> The 'new technology' has produced conditions in which, by a variety of means, the poor peasantry are, increasingly, being pushed out of *self-employment* into *wage labour*. The poor peasant must, to a growing extent, sell his labour power in order to survive.
>
> (Byres 1982: 41)

Byres (1982) considers the new share cropping as a form of partial proletarianization. He argues that in the 'share-labourer' method, the landlord buys and supplies the new agricultural inputs and receives a far higher share in return. However, 'the share cropper retains possession of some of the means of production and continues to have semblance of a stake in the land (and bears more risk than a wage labourer)' (Byres 1982: 41).

OCCUPATIONAL SHIFTS

In 1971, 63.62 per cent of the workforce in Punjab were employed in agricultural and allied activities. They included cultivators, agricultural labourers and workers. Their combined share declined to 61.55 per cent in 1981. However, among these categories cultivators suffered a decline in share from 42.56 per cent to 37.39 per cent between 1971 and 1981. This indicates that 5.17 per cent of the potential cultivators changed occupations. In absolute terms the shift of potential cultivators to other occupations amounted to 273,451. The available evidence does not suggest that cultivators have joined agricultural labourers on a significant scale.[12]

It is interesting to note that the small farmers prefer paid employment outside agriculture rather than paid employment inside agriculture, even though such opportunities are available in the countryside. The reason behind this rather peculiar behaviour is attributed to the 'socio-cultural milieu in rural Punjab' (Bhalla and Chadha 1982: 833).

Some of the micro-level studies reveal that a section of these cultivators have migrated to other places where they could purchase more land at a cheaper price or they have joined non-agricultural occupations.[13]

Two significant observations regarding occupational shifts can be made. First, traditional occupations of self-employment such as cultivation and household industry are declining, and their combined share of the workforce declined from 45.63 per cent in 1971 to 39.99 per cent in 1981.[14] In contrast, occupations that depend on hired labour have increased their share of the workforce, as described in the previous section. The phenomenon of employing paid workers is true for agricultural and for non-agricultural occupations. Since most of the non-agricultural employment is concentrated in towns and cities, an increase in the percentage share of non-agricultural employment has implications in the state for rural-to-urban migration.

MIGRATION

According to Gill's estimate,

> ...until 1971 Punjab was a net migrant state but the decade of 1971–82 reversed this process. During the decade of 1971–81 there was net gain in share of urban population by 4 per cent compared to 1961–71, migration of population in urban areas during 1971–81 was seven times.
>
> (Gill 1990: 116–7)

He further notes that in the busy season, migrant labour accounts for 50 per cent of the local agricultural labourers in the state.

MACRODETERMINANTS OF OUT-MIGRATION FROM THE STATE

One of the points to establish is that despite the high level of development in the rural areas of Punjab, there has been significantly high out-migration of the rural young male population to different parts of the country and to other nations. It is surprising indeed that migration from rural areas occurs despite the existence of income-earning opportunities in agriculture and high levels of urban unemployment.

The study conducted by Oberai and Singh (1980) reveals that

> ...occupationwise, the three significant categories of employed out-migrants are cultivators (60.4 per cent), agricultural labourers (11.4 per cent), and production process workers (10.3 per cent)....A remarkable category of out-migrants is the sales workers, all of whom migrated to the urban areas. They are *banians* who normally engage in money-lending as well as trade. Their shift to towns provides an essential link with the rapid growth of agriculture, at the same time as it widens the scope of their activities.
>
> (Oberoi and Singh 1980: A-5)

Another study identifies some of the factors that conduce to rural and urban migration. 'Male literacy level, proportion of male workers in non-agricultural sector and the level of development of infrastructure facilities, particularly emerge as the more stronger push factors in out-migration of people from the rural areas' (Goyal 1990: 75).

Therefore, it would be misleading to conclude that rural development helps in containing out-migration of people as it opens up more employment avenues and opportunities in the rural areas. This may well be true in the initial stages of rural development, but after reaching a high level of development (in the context of the overall socio-economic development of the region) the aspirations of people also grow, and the effectiveness of development as a migration-controlling factor becomes limited.

Before proceeding further, it will be useful to recapitulate the main propositions put forward thus far. The examination of the impact of the introduction of new technology on the prevailing agrarian social structure of Punjab has shown that new agricultural technology was unfavourable to the lower strata of the population in three significant ways. First, the introduction of capital-intensive modern agricultural technology resulted in a shift in the distribution of operated land in favour of the rich farmers. Second, the green revolution increased the demand for agricultural labour in Punjab, thereby encouraging the migration of cheap labour from other states. This had an adverse affect on the local workforce. Third, the green revolution resulted in drastic occupational shifts and out-migration, primarily from the lower strata of the population. This induced a crisis among the small and marginal farmers in Punjab, propelling them into an armed ethno-nationalist struggle against the Indian state. I shall look at the socio-economic background of the activists.

Profile of the Sikh activists – children of the green revolution?

This section describes the evidence from three micro-level studies about the socio-economic background of the activists in the ethno-nationalist movement in Punjab.

Singh's micro-level study contradicted the commonly held notion that the activists belonged to the deprived economic group; on the contrary, it revealed that the family occupation of the majority of young people is agriculture and that they belong to relatively better off land-owning families.[15] Singh examined three features for establishing the socio-economic background of the activists. First, most of the youths were between 21 and 30 years old. Second, caste affiliation revealed that the Jat caste was dominant among activists. Third, the education level revealed that 50 per cent were below matriculation standard, of which 25 per cent were illiterate (matriculation is equivalent to the senior secondary school examinations).

Similar conclusions were reached by S. S. Gill (1990), who attempted to establish the socio-economic background of forty activists: twenty each from the Kapurthala and Ropar districts of Punjab. His data were collected in January 1991 and are reproduced with his permission(Tables 5.8–5.11).[16]

The following conclusions can be drawn from the data: first, the majority of the activists (72.5 per cent) were below 25 years old. Second, the majority of youths (75 per cent) belonged to the dominant Jat caste.[17] Third, the educational background of 62.5 per cent of the activists is below matriculation standard. Lastly, only 20 per cent belonged to the most deprived section of the rural population, i.e. the landless, and the majority of them were drawn from cultivators of small- and marginal-holdings.

Table 5.8 Age composition of the activists

Age (in years)	Number	Percentage
≤ 25	29	72.5
26–30	9	22.5
≥ 30	2	5.0
Total	40	100.0

Table 5.9 Education level of the activists

Education	Number	Percentage
Illiterate	3	7.5
Matriculation and below	25	62.5
Graduates and above	12	30.0
Total	40	100.0

Table 5.10 Family land holdings (ownership) of the activists

Size of landholdings (acres)	Number	Percentage
Landless	8	20
< 5	11	27.5
5–10	14	35.0
>104	7	17.5
Total	40	100.0

Table 5.11 Caste background of the activists

Caste	Number	Percentage
Jat sikh	30	75
Kamboj	3	7.5
Saini	2	5.0
Arkhan(carpenter)	1	2.5
Nai (barber)	1	2.5
Rai sikh	1	2.5
Harijan	2	5.0
Total	40	100.0

Source: The data in Tables 5.8 to 5.11 were collected by S. S. Gill in January 1991 and are reproduced with his permission.

I now turn to my own data which were collected in January 1992.[18] During the 1990s, the veteran journalist S. S. Bal conducted extensive interviews with the activists and their families. After interviewing him, I appropriated the data on the socio-economic background of the activists. I followed Gill's mode of analysis for Tables 5.12–5.15: this makes comparison of the two sets of data easier.

After comparing the three studies, it can be concluded that the activists belonged to the second-generation, semi-educated, high caste, low class, small and marginal farmers.

Peasant insurrection and the rise of armed resistance

So far I have focused on the effect the transition to commercial agriculture had on the prevailing social structure of the province. It has been demonstrated that, first, the green revolution strategy led to partial depeasantization of farmers with small- and marginal-holdings; second, most of the activists engaged in the Sikh ethno-regional movement belonged to this partially depeasantized section of the population. I now attempt to connect the above two strands by posing the following questions: What are the potential sources of a predominantly peasant-led armed ethno-nationalist struggle? What accounts for this form of political behaviour? More specifically, I will indicate the situations that favour a peasant rebellion as a response to the challenge of commercial agriculture.

I will not attempt to explain the religious content or appeal of the ethno-nationalist movement, since that has already been discussed in Chapter 3. The main concern of this chapter has been to explain the timing and to establish the social composition of the ethno-regional movement among the Sikhs. In this section I shall examine how changes in the social base explain the timing of an ethno-regional movement.

The pattern of modernization

One way of understanding the conditions that gave rise to the spectre of an agrarian uprising is to trace the characteristic pattern of modernization. Traditional economic explanations postulate a revolutionary outbreak when there is widespread decline in the peasants' material situation under the impact of agricultural modernization. In Punjab, there was a conspicuous improvement in the economic and social situation of a large sector of the rural population under the green revolution strategy. Even though new technology facilitated the 'take-off' for cultivators with land and some capital, there is evidence that a substantial section of the population derived some benefit from the introduction of new technology. Thus, as a general explanation, the material approach is too simplistic. The question then arises: Why did the Sikh peasants rebel in a bloody revolt despite a significant improvement in their material conditions? Another common explanation

Table 5.12 Age composition of the activists

Age (years)	Number	Percentage
≤ 25	18	51.43
26–29	7	20.00
≥ 30	10	28.57
Total	35	100

Table 5.13 Education level of the activists

Education	Number	Percentage
Illiterate	3	8.57
Matric and below	24	68.57
Graduate and postgraduate	8	22.86
Total	35	100

Table 5.14 Family land holdings (ownership) of the activists

Size of land holdings (acres)	Number	Percentage
Landless	None	0
< 5	14	40.00
5–10	10	28.57
> 10	15	42.86
Total	35	100

Table 5.15 Caste background of the activists

Caste	Number	Percentage
Jat Sikh	31	88.57
Kamboj	1	2.86
Saini	2	5.71
Tarkhan (carpenter)	1	5.71
Total	35	100

emphasizes the psychological aspects of improvement in the economic situation of the peasantry to explain potential revolutionary upsurges. The hypothesis of rising aspirations cannot explain why peasants in other Indian states, such as Haryana, did not rise in a peasant rebellion, although the green revolution wrought similar changes in their material situation. Thus material conditions by themselves are not the decisive factor for determining the outbreak of a rural uprising.

Agricultural innovation and external dependence

Some of the structural features that may have made the Sikh peasants more receptive to an ethno-nationalist armed struggle will now be looked at. First the wider implications of the commercial transformation in agriculture will be examined and then these issues will be related to the specific situation in Punjab. Commercial agriculture requires capital-intensive new technology, greater expenditure on industrially produced products and the sale of an increased proportion of its harvest. The transformation from self-provisioning to market-oriented agriculture is frequently discriminatory since the cultivator has to change too many distinct aspects of his technology all at once, and has to attempt a radical leap forward in which there is discontinuity between the existing and the new. This obligatory and brusque change into capital-intensive commercial farming is aggravated by the concentration of capital and technical services in already favoured areas. The result is that the large cultivators have increased political power because they have qualitatively more profitable agriculture and greater competitive strength in the market. The customary privileges enjoyed by the big farmers allow them to enhance their business position and accrue the maximum possible share of government-granted facilities.

When new technology replaces or is added to the older agricultural systems on a large scale, products must be purchased from the industrial sector, e.g. chemical fertilizers and machinery. The seeds, usually propagated by scientific research centres, have to be obtained from urban distributors. Further, the local cultivator has to depend upon technical services and institutional credit supplied by rural development programmes. Table 5.16 shows that short-term agricultural credit rose from Rs 568.9 million in 1975 to Rs 5529.3 million in 1992.

What then are the implications for the rural community of increased external dependence? The dependence of the locality upon the urban-technical network is that

> ...it biases the distribution of advantage in favour of those who have the experience and social attributes necessary for confronting the city and the bureaucracy, the printed instructions, and the political caucuses; and puts relative handicap on those whose assets include traditional knowledge of the local idiosyncrasies of soil and climate, and whose energies are absorbed by the labours of husbandry rather than in manipulating the rural–urban nexus.
>
> (Pearse 1980: 159)

Thus, peasants may find themselves competing for credit or irrigation facilities with farmers who have city houses and political connections. Moreover, earlier in this chapter it was noted that the upper-middle and large farmers in the Punjab countryside used the profits from cultivation to

Table 5.16 Short-term agricultural loans (rupees in millions)

Year	Cash	Kind	Total
1975–76	63.8	505.1	568.9
1980–81	752.8	1452.1	2204.9
1985–86	1143.3	2015.9	3249.2
1986–87	1179.3	1885.4	3064.7
1987–88	1399.8	1731.8	3131.6
1988–89	1859.9	1755.3	3615.2
1989–90	2491.1	2545.3	5036.4
1990–91	1820.8	1810.4	3631.2
1991–92	2829.4	2699.9	5529.3

Source: Agriculture in Punjab 1991–92, Department of Agriculture, Chandigarh, Punjab

enhance their economic and political power by increasing consumer spending on automobiles and household items and also heavy expenditure on social activities.

Further, external dependence implies that the atomized and fragmented local cultivator, the individual productive unit, will become a part of a larger system of production and exchange. This tends to withdraw much of the decision-making autonomy from the former, and subjects it to national and international networks. So far, transformation to a market-oriented agriculture has increased external dependence. Thus, the green revolution has made farmers heavily dependent on conditions over which they have no control. If the general conditions of the small peasants discussed so far indicate that the intrusion of the market into the agrarian economy led to the establishment of a strong central authority, the creation of a powerful centralized authority intensified the burden on the peasantry through administrative bureaucracy and expensive policies. Significantly, although the rapid economic leap entailed changes at all levels of society, the intrusion of external market relationships was far from positing a threat to the entire peasant mode of life, religion or the prevailing social order.

Thus, the trend towards the economic modernization of agriculture has strained the existing relationship between the peasant community and the upper level of society. These observations prompt the question: What prevented a rebellion against the landed upper classes or a communist-led peasant revolution? To discuss this question adequately would require examination of what makes Indian society immune to revolutionary tendencies. Space precludes adequate treatment of this vast and fascinating theme. Nonetheless, a skeletal treatment of some of the issues is offered below. This is followed by a discussion exploring the network of social relationships in Punjab which I believe have a significant bearing on political tendencies.

At the beginning of this research I tried to find explanations in cultural terms for the alleged absence of revolutionary change in Indian society. First of all it is argued that the institution of caste enforces hierarchical submission and provides immunity from any thorough and violent overhaul of Indian society. Not only do such explanations deny the role of the human agency by viewing society as an unhistorical, immutable entity, but the striking evidence in Indian history of numerous insurrections challenging Brahmanical hegemony, Sikhism being one of the most vital of such movements, flies in the face of such arguments. However, the second dimension of cultural explanations is more convincing. Barrington Moore's (1966) classic account of change from an agrarian to an industrial society in the major countries of the world examines the historical conditions that gave rise to alliances or conflicts between the landed classes and the peasantry, and the political consequences of these social formations. Moore's well-documented account attributes the lack of a revolution in India to the diversity and amorphousness of Indian society, which impedes any effective political action. In other words, fragmentation along caste and regional lines provides an effective barrier to widespread insurrection. Moore argues that 'petty' hostilities based on religion, caste or language neutralize each other; thus local disputes cannot fuse into one revolutionary uprising. As Moore notes, 'Revolutions come with panhuman ideals, not trivial regional ones' (Moore 1981: 385). Moore's proposition will now be tested in the concrete case of rural upheaval among Sikhs in Punjab.

Undoubtedly, the intrusion of commercial agriculture had aroused the rebellious feelings in a substantial section of the Sikh peasantry by the late 1970s, and political upheaval seemed most likely. But any potential antagonism against the landed upper classes and the peasant community was dampened by the fact that the Sikh peasantry shared a religion, notably Sikhism, and belonged to the same caste, notably Jats, as the landed upper classes. The network of social relationships promoted cohesion between the Sikh peasantry and the landed section of the population. This study of the Sikh case highlights the complex, often contradictory, role of the caste system in promoting social cohesion, but this view does not contradict the reluctance to accept arguments that stress the ideological role of the caste institution in preventing any form of change in Indian society.

The caste system induces the choice of occupations, so that the Sikhs are generally associated with working the land and the urban Punjabi Hindus are linked with petty mercantile professions. Since these castes also occupy leading positions in their respective religious categories, they are able to invoke the solidarity of their religious group.[19] This has significant political implications. In Punjab, religious divisions between the Hindus and the Sikhs overlap the cleavage between the urban and the rural sectors of the population to a large extent. Sikhs are predominantly associated with agricultural activities, whereas Hindus are mostly associated with mercantile professions. Consequently, the Sikh landed and upper classes and the poorer Sikh peasants experienced the same problems over the supply of power to pumpsets, the supply of credit and the prices of products. Therefore, any potential antagonism against the upper Sikh classes was dampened because of related rural requirement for high food prices and the urban desire for cheap food products. No wonder that the first stirrings of Sikh unrest began with a series of peaceful mass demonstrations led by the Akali Dal to present a set of 'legitimate' grievances to the central government. However, it is critical to note that at this stage it was a moderate movement concerned specifically with the demands of farmers and demands for greater state autonomy. In the initial phase the uprising was led by the traditional Akali leaders, who had close ties to the peasants. The bloody repression of the movement by the central government resulted in its progressive radicalization. This aspect has been discussed in considerable detail in Chapter 4.

In Chapter 2 the religious component in political behaviour in India has been discussed with regard to the nature of Indian cosmological self-understandings and the central place of religion in Indian society. Nonetheless, it is appropriate to re-emphasize the religious undercurrents that impinged on the Sikh peasantry and were significant in determining the political behaviour of the Sikh peasantry. The trade union experience of a leader of a powerful guerrilla organization is illuminating. Commenting on the plight of mill workers he complains,

> There was no treatment if one got injured; there were no schools for our children. The worker is producing and the officer is sitting in his chair! The worker's son is not at school; the officer's child is at boarding school! He has accommodation; we, the workers, have none! So I sought to work within the Akali Dal to bring about some changes to this situation in the light of Sikh principles.
>
> (Pettigrew 1995: 145)

After his disappointment with the trade union he observes,

> They said there was no God. I had joined them for three years in the '70s but their talk of revolution was without any basis. They talked only of Lenin. Their inspiration came from him, but they never talked anything about Sikhism. We want our independence on the basis of what Guru Gobind Singh told us, not Lenin.
>
> (Pettigrew 1995: 144–5)

Likewise, the guerrilla activists reiterated the centrality of social and economic justice in Sikh religious tradition and the fiercely egalitarian Sikh tradition to point out that the current phase of Sikh resistance was a transposition of the historic Sikh challenge to the divinely ordained Brahmanical hierarchical structure of power and wealth.[20] The repressive social forces were now believed to be represented by the central government.

To sum up, the powerful institutional and social links between the different levels of the Sikh population prevented a peasant rebellion against the established Sikh landed classes. Religion, caste and the shared experience of changing methods in agriculture bound the peasants to the landed élite. Moreover, a common web of customary relationships engaged them in face-to-face interaction. These factors are significant in explaining the remarkable curtailment of a revolutionary outbreak among the Sikh peasantry despite the political forces unleashed by the economic modernization of agricultural. However, these explanations do not account for the efflorescence of the ethno-regional movement, nor do they explain why the central government became the target of attack and discontent.

So far only the Sikh community has been highlighted. However, the mounting evidence accumulated in Chapter 4 suggests that one cannot understand the rise of ethno-regional struggle without reference to the actions of the central government that in a large measure provoked it. Here a conspectus of Donald L. Horowitz's (1985) explanation regarding secessionist movements of an advanced group in a backward region is instructive. According to Horowitz, the conditions under which an ethno-nationalist movement emerges is determined by 'domestic politics, by the relations of groups and regions within the state'. He further classifies the Sikhs as an advanced group in a backward region and argues that advanced groups are late seceders and that they just seek assurances of non-discrimination. He observes that advanced groups 'attempt secession only when all hope of salvaging their position in the country is dashed' (Horowitz 1985: 244). Since India attained independence in 1947, the Sikhs have felt increasingly discriminated and their opportunities restricted. But the central government ruthlessly used the powerful repressive apparatus of the state to quell the seemingly legitimate demands of the Akali Dal. Undoubtedly, the central government policies that violently repressed the Sikhs had a considerable bearing on Sikh communal perceptions, as has been explained in Chapter 4. Nonetheless, these preliminary formulations will be discussed further in Chapter 6 along with the spread of literacy and the effect of the mass media in conjuring a particular form of identity consciousness.

In this chapter the timing of the Sikh ethno-nationalist struggle in the late 1970s with reference to the introduction of new agricultural technology in the late 1960s has been explained. It has been shown that after 15 years of 'green revolution' the Sikh peasantry became more radical, and this enabled the formation of a social base for the Sikh ethno-nationalist movement. Further, the timing of Sikh ethno-nationalism has been explained in conjunction with the revolution in communication that also occurred in the late 1970s.

6 Transformation in social communication and religious controversy

Dialogues in vernacular languages

It is often argued that widely available and influential media such as the press and electronic media produce inclusive and exclusive forms of nationalist identities that recharge nationalism with varying degrees of symbolic significance. As has been shown in Chapter 3, the historic process of equating linguistic and religious identity was facilitated by print capitalism in the nineteenth century in British Punjab. This last chapter looks at the contribution of popular mass media, such as the vernacular press, cassettes and television, in the generation and maintenance of modes of nationalist discourse. The vast expansion in the number of people reading newspapers, listening to radiocassettes and watching television confirms that the media were central to the process of identity formation in Punjab. This bears out the contention that transformation in social communication is vital for facilitating nationalism. Although the press has been long-established in Punjab and although there is a significant literate population, there is a paucity of literature on this subject. The available research on media studies in India focuses mainly on television and on the English-language press; the role of the vernacular press in the socio-political sphere has been virtually overlooked.

Messages of popular appeal can be transmitted equally by radio, television and the press. All India Radio (AIR), the national service, was set up in 1936, and since 1947 it has been under the tight control of the central government. The state governments or independent companies have no right to run their own stations. Only AIR produces religious broadcasts, which are carefully monitored to prevent accusations that particular religious groups are favoured. In recent years, Akali Dal leaders have demanded that Sikh religious sermons be given wider coverage. Virtually the same holds true for the television medium, or *doordarshan* as it is popularly referred in India. The serialization of the *Ramayana*, the great Hindu epic poem, in seventy-eight episodes, which was broadcast on national television between January 1987 and July 1988, had remarkable repercussions. According to one estimate, the televised tale attracted a huge audience of some 80–100 million (Lutgendorf 1990: 136). The success of the dramatization of Hindu religious tales facilitated the campaign of the Hindu radical right regarding the Ayodhya controversy. Not only did the telecast enhance popular knowledge about Ayodhya as the birthplace of Lord Rama, but it cemented the vast, unrelated nation of Hindu viewers. Moreover, the projection of mainstream Hindu culture, with emphasis on the Hindu character of the Indian nation, through the medium of television exacerbated apprehension among religious minorities. Therefore, in India, radio and television are not effective media for communicating minority nationalist discourse. I will concentrate instead on the vernacular press.

The first section of this chapter examines the growth of literacy in Punjab and its impact on the religious and social spheres. The second section traces the history of the press in Punjab. The third section examines the circulation figures and the readership profile of the three major newspapers in Punjab. The fourth section considers the role of cassette culture in socio-political movements in India, and focuses on the contribution of cassettes to the meteoric rise of a charismatic religious figure in Punjab during the late 1970s.

Mass literacy

In 1961, 27 per cent of the total population of Punjab – and 24 per cent of India's – could read and write (Table 6.1).

> By 1974, 78 per cent of primary-age children in Punjab were attending school, the second highest in India, exceeded only by southern Kerala (96 per cent) – India's most literate state. Reflecting this demand, the number of primary school teachers rose from 23000 in 1966–7, as the period of green revolution began, to 34000 in 1970–1....By 1974, virtually the entire rural population had a primary school within two kilometres. The number of college students increased from 35000 in 1964–65 to 100000 in 1968–9 and 110 000 in the mid-1970s....By 1981, literacy in Punjab had risen to 41 per cent....By 1992, 49 per cent of the population in Punjab was literate.
>
> (Jeffrey: 1986: 81–3)

The rise of mass literacy in Punjab is not to be viewed in the context of urbanization and induztrialisation or as the requirement of a modern state. The processes of most significance in Punjab was the modernization of agriculture as a consequence of the green revolution and, more broadly, the consequences of nation-building in a huge, culturally diverse country such as India. In Western Europe education became a requirement and necessity of the modern state. As Gellner (1983, 1994) points out, it became necessary to have a culturally homogeneous population that was given a uniform education system by the state. Besides, education enables the formation of a civil society, forms the basis for the establishment of democracy, and allows the citizens to become fully participating members of that society. By contrast, education is received and valued in a very different cultural context in India. Leaf (1972)

Table 6.1   Percentage of literacy in total
population

Rural	6,253,432	44.06
Urban	3,699,533	61.64
Total	9,952,965	49.29

Source: Statistical Abstract of Punjab, 1992

observes the increasing importance of schools in local religious and political affairs. For farming families, education provides an opportunity for agricultural research and learning skills concerning technical agricultural knowledge. Non-agricultural income supplements income from the land. From the cultural viewpoint, education raises the value of a potential bride or bridegroom (Leaf 1984: 254–5)

The increase in literacy in Punjab went hand in hand with the expansion of the road network to every village and the increase in transport. In the mid-1960s, when the green revolution started, almost half of Punjab's villages were not connected by sealed roads. Roads became a necessity in order to fulfil the new possibilities of agriculture.

> In the entire span of the Third Five Year Plan (1961–6), the state had built only 2280 kilometres of road, but in the single year of 1969–70, it added 1,920 kilometres....By 1970, Punjab had 10,000 kilometres of sealed road by 1975, 25,000; and by the end of the decade, 95 per cent of its villages were linked by sealed roads.
>
> (Jeffrey 1986: 79)

The expansion of road networks produced a demand for all kinds of motor vehicles. Robin Jeffrey (1986) suggested that road networks broaden horizons and enhance the expectations of people. Rising literacy, in conjunction with expanding road networks, allows easier dissemination of print capitalism. Thus in Punjab, an expanding vernacular print market was sustained by mass readership. This helps to explain the role of young, literate Sikhs in the secessionist movements.

The press in Punjab

History of the press in Punjab

> We do not fully comprehend the scope of the expression 'our vernacular languages'. The vernacular of Punjab – which is that? Is it the Persian, the Urdu, the Hindi or the Punjabi? Or is it all put together? Not even the learned orientalists ever took it into their hands to solve this great preliminary question....They proceeded to build the superstructure without laying the foundations.
>
> Editorial in *The Tribune*, 9 April, 1881

A discussion of the role of the newspapers in Punjab cannot preclude the dilemma posed by the above question. In the absence of an unbroken history of a particular language as a medium of high cultural and political communication, the role of newspapers in defining religious and linguistic identities poses peculiar problems.

The history of early Indian-language journalism in Punjab can be traced back to the 1860s. Two newspapers in the Gurmukhi script were established before 1880. Until 1880, the Indian-language press was an offshoot of Hindi journalism. The two newspapers published in Gurmukhi, *The Sukavya Samodhini* and *The Kavi Chandrodaya*, were closer to Sanskritized Hindi than to Punjabi. It was only after the emergence of the Singh Sabha movement in 1873 that there was an urgent need for a medium to advocate the aims of the movement. This suggests that the vernacular press arose partly in response to the reform movements of the 1880s among the Hindus, the Muslims and the Sikhs in Punjab, which in turn were a consequence of colonialism.[1]

Barnes (1940) examined the founding of the press in India and showed how the Indian press developed along similar lines to the British press.

> There was to be the same spirit of enquiry regarding the administration of government and hitherto accepted social customs, as well as a parallel demand on the part of an ever increasing body of opinion for a share in the control of public affairs.
>
> (Barnes 1940: 25)

The English-language press was influenced by Western discourses of liberalism and was initially a vehicle for the colonial authorities.

Growth of the vernacular press

Circulation figures

The press in Punjab is multilingual. Of the three major newspapers in Punjab, the English daily, *The Tribune*, is the oldest. The two vernacular newspaper groups, the Ajit and the Hind Samachar, first published their newspapers in Urdu, which was the official language of Punjab before the partition of India in 1947.

The numbers and circulation of newspapers published in other Indian languages has risen since 1947. The Hind Samachar group first published its Hindi newspaper in 1965, and published its Punjabi newspaper in 1978. The Ajit group published its Punjabi newspaper in 1955. The Tribune group launched its Hindi and Punjabi publications in 1978. The *Hind Samachar* has the largest circulation in North India and in Punjab as a Hindi daily, the *Ajit* has the largest circulation as a Punjabi daily and *The Tribune* is the most widely read newspaper in English in Punjab, as shown in Tables 6.2 and 6.3.

Table 6.2 Circulation figures of the four major newspapers in Punjab in 1991

Name of the newspaper	Language of publication	Circulation
Hind Samachar group		
Punjab Kesari	Hindi	155,239
Hind Samach	Urdu	24,207
Jag Bani	Punjabi	45,101
Total copies per day		224,547
Ajit group	Punjabi	
Total copies per day		161,811
Tribune group		
The Tribune	English	74,541
Dainik Tribune	Hindi	8,407
Punjabi Tribune	Punjabi	55,681
Total copies per day		138,629
Express group		
Indian Express	English	18,830
Janasatta	Hindi	7,238
Total copies per day		26,068

Source: Audit Bureau of Circulation (ABC), July–December, 1991

Note
Express group figures for July–December 1991 are not available; the figures in the above table
have been taken from a previous period.

The Hind Samachar group

The historical background and the circulation figures of the three major
newspapers in Punjab will now be examined. The first newspaper group is
the Hind Samachar group. The Urdu daily, *Hind Samachar*, was established in
1948, a year after India gained independence. The newspaper was founded
by Lala Jagat Narain, who was also its founder editor. Lala Jagat Narain was
a staunch Congressman and had participated in India's struggle for
independence. He was active in the Arya Samaj movement.[2]

As a Hindi daily, the *Punjab Kesari* was established in 1965 with an 'initial
print order of 1,500 copies'. By 1975–7, the circulation had risen to nearly
100,000 copies per day. The circulation of the *Punjab Kesari* has grown by 12,500
per cent over a period of 16 years. The *Punjab Kesari*, the Hindi daily published
in Jalandhar, has the second largest circulation in the country.[3] The *Punjab
Kesari*, with an average circulation per publishing day of 342,744, is second to
Anand Bazar Patrika, a Bengali daily with an average circulation per publishing
day of 412,400. According to the 1991 Readership Survey Report conducted
by the Operations Research Group (ORG), the *Punjab Kesari* is the largest
newspaper in North India with a readership of 4,839,000 and with a total of
10.30 per cent of the readership of all newspapers. The present circulation of
187,000 copies is the highest among all the publications issued in Punjab,

Table 6.3 History of the Punjab press

	Hind Samachar group	Ajit group	Tribune group
Year of establishment	1948	1944	1881
Language of initial publication	Urdu	Urdu	English
Other newspaper publications and language of publication	*Punjab Kesari* (Hindi) *Jag Bani* (Punjabi)	*Daily Ajit* (Punjabi)	*Dainik Tribune* (Hindi) *Punjabi Tribune* (Punjabi)
Year of first publication	1965, 1978	1955	1978
Founder editor	Lala Jagat Narain	Sadhu Singh	Sardar Dyal Singh Majithia
Religion and caste of founder editor	Hindu Khatri	Sikh Khatri	Sikh Jat aristocrat
General orientation	Arya Samaji	Roots in the Singh Sabha movement	Western education, liberal outlook

Haryana, Jammu and Kashmir, Himachal Pradesh and Chandigarh. Between 1948 and 1980 the *Hind Samachar* had registered a growth in circulation of more than 2,262 per cent.[4]

The Ajit group

The second newspaper group is the Ajit group. Of all newspapers in Gurmukhi published in Punjab, the daily *Ajit* has the largest circulation. It began publication in 1944, and until 1957 it was published in Urdu. The *Ajit* launched its Punjabi publication in 1955. Dr Sadhu Singh Hamdard was its founder publisher and editor. He was born in 1918 in Paddi Matwali village, Jalandhar district. He worked for the Shiromani Gurudwara Parbandhak Committee (SGPC) and was active in the Quit India Movement (1942) against the British. He was succeeded by his son, Barjinder Singh.

Two main reasons are given for the establishment of the *Ajit*; first, the newspapers in Punjab were targeting the English-speaking population, who belonged to the upper level of society; second, the aim of the newspaper was to cater to the needs of the emerging affluent Punjab peasantry, partly as a consequence of the green revolution.[5] The growth of Gurmukhi newspaper circulation has implications for the Sikhs, Gurmukhi being the script of their sacred literature. The circulation of daily newspapers in the Gurmukhi script increased from 34,000 in 1967, when the new Punjabi-language state was formed, to 218,000 by 1979, soon after Mrs Gandhi's imposition of a state of emergency, during which the press was closely censored. These figures represent an increase of 541 per cent in the period after the formation of the new Punjab and the beginning of the green revolution (Jeffrey 1986: 84).

The Tribune group

The third newspaper group is the Tribune group. The English daily *The Tribune* was the earliest newspaper to be established in Punjab. Its readership belongs to the upper class of the Punjabi population. It is the most widely read English daily in Punjab and is the only trust-managed English daily in India.

It was founded by the Jat Sikh aristocrat Sardar Dyal Singh Majithia and was first published on 2 February 1881. Sardar Dyal Singh Majithia was widely regarded as the connecting link between the aristocracy in Punjab and the rising intelligentsia. He was born in 1849, the year that Punjab was annexed, into an orthodox aristocratic Sikh family that hailed originally from Majithia in the district of Amritsar. His father, Sardar Lehna Singh, was a prominent official of Maharaja Ranjit Singh and in 1832 he was appointed Governor of the hill territories in the Maharajah's kingdom. On the death of his father, Dyal Singh inherited one of the wealthiest estates in the province. His childhood was spent at his ancestral village, Majithia, where he was educated by private tutors and an English governess. In 1874, he decided to visit England to complete his education, to the dismay of the elders in Amritsar's landed aristocracy. He was deeply influenced by the liberalism sweeping England and spent considerable time with prominent people discussing the causes of his country's backwardness. The young Sardar developed an admiration for the Western system of education. This influence was largely responsible for his philanthropic activities later in his life and also for his persistent advocacy, through his speeches and his writings, of the English language as the medium of education.

He returned to India in 1876 and decided to settle in Lahore. He became deeply involved in religious and public affairs and became a patron of several educational institutions. He was the sole proprietor of *The Tribune*, which he started as an English daily in February 1881, and he remained so until his death in 1898. 'No one rendered greater service to the cause of liberal education and progressive thinking in North India in the closing decades of the last century than Dyal Singh Majithia' (Ananda 1986: 42). He advocated the spread of modern education among all classes of people and was a champion of social reform.

The Tribune was established to achieve specific educational aims. In the early years *The Tribune* campaigned for liberal education with special emphasis on the learning of Western literature and science. It supported English as the medium of learning. 'The paper asserted that all hopes of regeneration of the country, of intellectual, material and moral prosperity, and future glory and independence, depended entirely on the spread of English education' (Ananda 1986: 19).

S. Dyal Singh's immediate reason for establishing the newspaper was to counteract a move to establish a university in which the predominant position was to be given to the classical oriental languages, Persian, Sanskrit and Arabic, with English being relegated to the status of a secondary language. Dyal Singh challenged the plan and led the campaign for establishing English as the medium of educational instruction. An influential section of the Indian intelligentsia regarded the English language and the scientific ethos of the West as being necessary to thrust India into a new era. Another reason given for this was the dearth of textbooks in the vernacular languages; the few available textbooks had not been translated properly. In the first year of its publication, *The Tribune* contained twenty articles about education that strongly opposed the Orientalists for insisting on the adoption of the Indian vernaculars to the exclusion of English.

The need for a periodical that would advocate native interests and act as an exponent of enlightened nationalist opinion in the region was keenly felt, and Dyal Singh came forward to fill the gap and provide an organ that mirrored the impulses that stirred the minds of progressive people, including young people.

The Tribune campaigned for a united India, which was in contrast to the British view of men such as John Strachey (1888), who espoused that there is and never was an Indian nation and that people of different Indian regions do not feel that they belong to one nation. An editorial in *The Tribune* declared,

> We do not believe in the theory that India is an assemblage of countries and that her people are an assemblage of countries and that her people are an assemblage of nations. The vast continent from the Himalayas to Cape Comorin, and from the Brahmaputra to the Indus, forms one great country, and Bengalis, Punjabis and Marhattas, the Rajputs of Mewar, the Nairs of Travancore and the Gurkhas of Nepal, the Hindus, the Sikhs and the Mohammedans, all constitute members of one great nation, bound together by affinities of language and similarities of manner and customs, and by a community of intellectual, social and political interest...
>
> Editorial in *The Tribune*, 19 March 1881

Dyal Singh Majithia bequeathed most of his property to three trusts: one for establishing a library, one for a college and the third for maintaining *The Tribune* press and newspaper, which he had established in 1881.

Hindi and Punjabi Tribune

The Tribune Trust decided to extend the paper's operations to editions in Hindi and Punjabi in the early 1970s. 'The basic aim of the promoters was...to tap the large reservoir of readership in the Indian languages whose requirements were not being adequately met. The creation of new readership was also deemed essential' (Ananda 1986: 175). The need for these newspapers to be established because the medium of instruction in schools and colleges, and in certain universities in Punjab and Haryana, had changed.

The *Dainik Tribune* and the *Punjabi Tribune* were first published on 15 August 1978, 97 years after the founding of the parent paper. The circulation figures for *The Tribune* are more than five times that of the *Dainik Tribune* and more than twice the combined sale of the two other papers (Ananada 1986: 184). The combined average daily circulation of these papers increased from around 70,000 in 1979 to over 77,000 in 1983.

Readership profile of newspapers published in Punjab, Haryana and Himachal Pradesh

The readership profile of newspapers will now be considered in order to show that the growth of readership is an indicator of religious consciousness (Tables 6.4–6.10). The data in the tables are secondary; therefore, it is not possible to explain why specific socio-economic and occupational categories are used. The data are used not to establish definite correlations but to provide a general picture of possible readership profiles.

The *Punjab Kesari* has the highest percentage of readership among the top three Hindi dailies (Table 6.4). A total of 78.14 per cent and 77.89 per cent of the *Punjab Kesari* and *The Tribune* readers respectively are urban, and 58.56 per cent of the *Ajit* readers are urban (Table 6.5). Therefore, the *Punjab Kesari* and *The Tribune* have largely an urban readership compared with the *Ajit*.

Approximately 52 per cent of *The Tribune* readers are graduates. By contrast, 60.25 per cent of the *Punjab Kesari* readers are below matriculation level and approximately 63 per cent of the *Ajit* readership is under matriculation level (Table 6.6).[6] These results are supplemented by another survey (Table 6.7), which reveals that 38.4 per cent of the *Punjab Kesari* readers are below matriculation level and 31.3 per cent are matriculates. This indicates that the level of education of *The Tribune* readers is higher than that of readers of the two vernacular newspapers.

A comparison of the monthly income of the readers of the three newspapers indicates that approximately 47 per cent of the *Punjab Kesari* readers earn on average less than Rs 1501. Another survey had similar results (Table 6.9), which suggests that 42.8 per cent of the *Punjab Kesari* readers have a monthly income between Rs 501 and Rs 1000. A total of 40.51 per cent of the readers of the *Ajit* have a monthly income between Rs 1501 and Rs 2500, and 25 per cent earn between Rs 751 and Rs 1500 (Table 6.8). A total of 64.91 per cent of *The Tribune* readers have a monthly income of more than Rs 1501 (Table 6.8). These figures above indicate that readers of *The Tribune* belong to a higher socio-economic class than readers of the two vernacular newspapers, the *Punjab Kesari* and the *Ajit*.

The *Punjab Kesari* is most popular among traders and industrialists (19.69 per cent compared with 0.09 per cent and 10.41 per cent for the *Ajit* and *The Tribune* respectively), whereas the *Ajit* is most popular in the farming community (16.55 per cent compared with 0.05 per cent for the *Punjab Kesari*

Table 6.4   Total readership (in thousands) of individual newspapers in the states of Punjab, Haryana and Himachal–Pradesh

	PK	HS	JB	Ajit	TRI	DT
Total readership	2946	126	864	515	778	277

Source: National readership survey (NRS) conducted by the Operational Research Group (ORG) in 1989

Note
PK, *Punjab Kesari*; HS, *Hind Samachar*; JB, *Jag Bani*; TRI, *The Tribune*; DT, *Dainik Tribune*

Table 6.5 Readers of newspapers in urban and rural areas (in thousands)

	PK	HS	JB	Ajit	TRI	DT
Urban	2302	104	308	506	606	173
Rural	644	22	207	359	172	105

Source: National readership survey (NRS) conducted by the Operational Research Group (ORG) in 1989

Table 6.6 Education levels of readers (in thousands)

	PK	HS	JB	AJIT	TRI	DT
Below SSC	1775	94	361	550	174	159
SSC and above	584	–	98	147	195	63
Graduates and postgraduates	564	17	54	166	408	54

Source: National readership survey (NRS) conducted by the Operational Research Group (ORG) in 1989

Note
SSC is equivalent to matriculation

Table 6.7 Figures for the *Punjab Kesari* newspaper

Education	Percentage of total readers
Below SSC	38.4
SSC	31.3
Post SSC	30.3

Source: NRS-II and Audit Bureau of Circulation (ABC)

Table 6.8 Household income of newspaper readers (in thousands)

Rupees	PK	HS	JB	Ajit	TRI	DT
< 750	187	2	11	44	11	22
751–1500	764	26	90	216	111	82
1501–2500	1002	21	170	350	250	82
2501–4000	633	46	110	208	255	65
4001	359	32	33	45	152	27

Source: National readership survey (NRS) conducted by the Operational Research Group (ORG) in 1989

Table 6.9 Figures for the *Punjab Kesari* newspaper

Family income (rupees)	Percentage of total readers
< 250	3.1
251–500	23.6
501–1000	42.8
> 1000	30.5

Source: NRS-II and ABC

Table 6.10 Occupational breakdown of newspaper readers (in thousands)

	PK	HS	JB	Ajit	TRI	DT
Professionals/ executives	62	4	1	26	49	7
Clerks/salesmen industrialists/	446	16	56	122	230	59
Traders	580	48	68	81	81	47
Workers	219	6	42	96	12	10
Students	627	–	121	165	226	83
Housewife/ non-working	808	45	131	213	137	39
Agriculturist	137	4	92	143	31	28
Agricultural labour	2	–	–	1	–	–
Artisan	6	–	–	–	–	–
Others	59	2	5	18	13	5

Source: National readership survey (NRS) conducted by the Operational Research Group (ORG) in 1989

and 0.04 per cent for *The Tribune*). The majority of *The Tribune* readers are clerks and professional people (29.56 per cent compared with 15.14 per cent for the *Punjab Kesari* and 14.12 per cent for the *Ajit*). The data on readership profiles of newspapers published in Punjab, Haryana and Himachal Pradesh support the view that readers of *The Tribune* are relatively better educated and belong to a higher socio-economic level than the readers of the *Punjab Kesari* and the *Ajit*. In India English continues to be the hegemonic language of the national élite. English is the main language spoken in the higher echelons of the nationwide Indian bureaucracy. The widespread use of English binds the diversified urban middle class and connotes a class distinction. According to Brass, the English-language newspapers account for some 19 per cent of the total newspapers in India (Brass 1990: 145).

The data indicate that the majority of the *Punjab Kesari* readers are traders and industrialists, that the *Ajit* readers are mainly farmers, and that *The Tribune* readers are mostly clerks and professional people. Although it is misleading to form an opinion based on these data, it is worth noting that in Punjab the Hindus are most commonly associated with the trading profession and that the Sikhs constitute the bulk of the peasantry. This implies that the *Punjab Kesari* is popular with the urban Punjabi Hindus and that the *Ajit* is read mostly by the rural Sikhs.

This conclusion relating a specific occupation profile, notably petty traders, to a distinct religious group, notably the Hindus of Punjab, is supported by other noted scholars. In a seminal article Richard Fox (1984) has examined the historical link between a distinct class of Hindus in Punjab and a reformist Hindu identity. He notes,

> The peculiar complexion of the Punjab – that is, its caste hierarchy, land tenures, ecology, and religious composition as they had developed before the British and as the British developed them and adapted them and adapted *to* them – explains why a lower-middle economic class having a specific caste and religious composition arose and why its consciousness could be carried by a reformist Hindu identity.
>
> (Fox 1984: 485)

Fox argues that British colonialism in nineteenth century Punjab harnessed agricultural production to the world system without radically transforming rural productivity or capital investment. This led to an expansion of indigenous mercantile interests. Merchants and moneylenders combined to form the growing urban lower middle class, who received their share from the colonial appropriation of rural surplus.

> The importance of Punjabi merchants and moneylenders was in part a result of the much greater commercialization of local agriculture in comparison to other areas of India; and it also developed because the Punjabi high-caste families – mainly Khatri – who became Western-

educated professionals and civil servants were drawn from Bengali Brahmin and Kayasth caste categories.

(Fox 1984: 467)[7]

By the 1870s, the urban lower middle class existed as a distinct economic stratum within the colonial political economy, but they had evolved no ideology, formal institutions or collective social action by which to safeguard and promote their vested interests. During the 1870s the British introduced canal irrigation in Western Punjab, which contributed to this region becoming the chief producer of crops for export. Further, the Land Alienation Act of 1900 divided the population of Punjab into agricultural and non-agricultural castes, and the latter were not allowed to purchase land from the former. This was viewed as a conscious attempt to restrain the expansion of the Hindu petit bourgeoisie. The ideology of the Arya Samaj provided the traditional merchant castes,[8] who traditionally made up the lower class Punjabi Hindus, with a new, corporate identity.[9]

This digression into history has been important for highlighting the propensity among Punjabi Hindus to identify with the mainstream Hindu culture and Hindi language rather than with a region or with the Punjabi language. It must be remembered that the Arya Samaj was an active proponent of this orientation and Hindu opposition to Punjabi was stronger than Hindu opposition to Urdu. The vital role of the vernacular press in Punjab in articulating and maintaining religious dichotomies will now be examined.

A comparison of newspaper editorials

Editorials from the three major newspapers in Punjab, *The Tribune,* the *Punjab Kesari* and the *Ajit* will be compared. This section examines the role played by journalists in maintaining and consolidating religious identities. Selected editorials from the three major newspapers will be compared and contrasted. Since the editorials are written in three different languages – English, Hindi and Punjabi – I have translated the editorials into English. The biases and interpretations are mine. These data are further supplemented by interviews with the newspaper editors.[10] Editorials have been selected on the basis of the following considerations: first, editorials that cover significant events in Punjab since the late 1970s; second, editorials that bring out the religious and political positions, often dichotomous, of individual newspapers. The responses of the *Punjab Kesari* and the *Ajit* with regard to religious and political issues are now examined.

Editorials about the Akali Dal agitation

Between 1981 and 1984, the Akali Dal launched a series of mass agitations to present a set of demands to the central government.[11]

The Tribune

Highway Protests (4 April 1983)

Another unfortunate chapter in the current Akali agitation in Punjab opens today with a programme to obstruct road traffic. Mercifully, according to the agitation leaders, the Akali plan does not include interference with railway communications....It is obvious that neither the Prime Minister's acceptance of the Akali religious demands nor the subsequent appointment of the Sarkaria Commission three weeks ago has made much difference...both Mr Gurcharan Singh Tohra and Mr Parkash Singh Badal rightly took credit for having successfully pressurized the centre to agree to review centre-state relations....The 'rasta roko'[12] programme is intended to give a new and concentrated dimension to the Akali confrontation with the centre.

Negotiations between the Akalis and the Prime Minister (28 November 1981)

The Prime Minister has assured to examine the constitutional aspects of the All India Gurudwara Act[13] which is to be drafted and implemented, as requested by the Akali leaders. It is surprising that if Hindus and Muslims can manage their temples and mosques by themselves, why should the government be responsible for holding the *gurudwara* elections? If India is a secular (*dharam-nirpeksh*)[14] country, why are certain privileges given to a religious community and not to other religious communities? This way, the government can be accused of *bias* towards a particular community. Therefore, the Durgyana temple committee has appealed for the same privileges.

As regards the demand to convert Amritsar into a holy city, there can be no misunderstandings. Why was this issue not raised when the Akali brothers were in power? This demand would otherwise have been easily implemented in 1977. Why was this matter not regarded as discriminatory against the Sikhs before and has only come to their notice now?

As far as the Anandpur Sahib Resolution[15] is concerned, its disturbing section consists of the claim that Punjab is a region where the Sikhs are prosperous (*bol-bala*) and apart from five departments the rest will be managed only by Punjab. Besides, there are so many versions of Anandpur Sahib Resolution, no decision can be made in this regard until it is decided which one is authentic. Until then, how can the government make any decision even if it wants to?

Now that the Prime Minister has sincerely assured the Akalis that she will consider their demands sympathetically, it remains to be seen how sincere the Akali brothers are to their promise to denounce extremism and not to allow culprits to take shelter in the *gurudwara*s.

Hind Samachar

What we feared has happened (6 April 1983)

> The government has conceded the religious demands of the Akali leaders. The Akalis do not appreciate the acceptance of their <u>religious demands by the central government</u> and dismiss them as fraudulent. What is the purpose of starting a huge highway protest? This can lead to the extremists having an upper hand over the Akalis and the already sensitive situation in the state is bound to deteriorate.

Ajit

An appeal to all sections involved with the agitation (15 April 1983)

> Since the day the agitation was announced all the opposition parties have condemned it. According to Mr Badal, the <u>agitation does not concern a particular community</u> but the <u>demands are relevant to all communities</u>. Since the agitation has now been launched we want that participation should be wholehearted. Utmost caution must be exercised in controlling the irresponsible elements and the Akalis should <u>refrain from giving provocative speeches</u> or statements which the <u>rival press</u>, the central government or the opposition parties can take advantage of.
>
> In this regard Mr Badal has issued a statement that the agitation has been launched for the acceptance of the following demands: the transfer of Chandigarh and other Punjabi-speaking areas to Punjab; Punjab be given its just share of river waters; a federal structure be implemented; the Punjabi language be given the status of a second language in the neighbouring states of Haryana, Himachal Pradesh and Delhi and elsewhere where there is a significant Punjabi-speaking population; the protection of Punjabi peasants in Haryana and the Terai region of Uttar Pradesh; freedom for the innocent people arrested in Punjab. Besides these, some Sikh demands have also been mentioned.

The response of the three newspapers to the Akali Dal demands is varied. First of all, the newspapers have emphasized different aspects of Akali Dal demands. *The Tribune* maintains that the Akali Dal demands concern the review of relations between the central government and the Punjab state. The *Punjab Kesari* is alarmed at the religious and parochial nature of the demands. An argument against the acceptance of each religious demand is put forth in its editorial. But the *Ajit* emphasizes the regional nature of the demands, with focus on composite Punjabi culture and territory. We can discern a contrast between the *Punjab Kesari* and the *Ajit* in their understanding of the Akali Dal demands. The *Punjab Kesari* pronounces the Akali Dal demands to be religious and separatist. It launches a scathing attack on the demands and tactics of the Akali Dal. The Hind Samachar group squarely blames the Akali leadership for aggravating the conflict in Punjab in their quest for personal power. The editorial in the *Punjab Kesari* demands, 'why does the Akali Dal raise separatist demands only when it is out of power?' By contrast, the *Ajit* endorses and supports what it regards to be the Akali Dal campaign for greater regional autonomy for Punjab.

Second, the newspapers vary in their response to the central government's handling of the Akali Dal demands. *The Tribune* lauds the Akali leadership for successfully pressurizing the central government to review centre-state relations. The *Punjab Kesari* remains critical of the conciliatory attitude of the central government to what it believes are the separatist and religious demands of the Akali Dal. It fears that this would intensify separatist tendencies among the Sikhs. The editor of *Hind Samachar* maintains, 'Whom should the centre hold talks with? Failure of the accords to be implemented is because of in-fighting among the Akalis.'[16] The attitude of the *Ajit* towards the central government is confrontational. The Ajit group[17] is critical of what it regards to be gross mishandling of the situation in Punjab by the central government. It does not support an independent Sikh state but favours restructuring of centre-state relations in India so that the states get more autonomy. It opposes interference by the central government in the religious affairs of the Sikhs. It regards the Sikhs to be a *'quam'*.[18] Moreover, the *Punjab Kesari* reports acts of terror and vandalism by the guerrilla cadres and lauds the police repression. The *Ajit* reports excesses by the central government and the police – falsifying encounters, harassment of women by the police and the unleashing of terror by the police in the villages of Punjab. Reports like these alienate the population, who see an alien government bent on destroying their number as well as their identity.

Third, the newspapers seem to share different political alignments. The Hind Samachar group represents the urban Hindu community in Punjab. Hindus in Punjab have historically supported a more radical form of Hinduism. The Punjabi Hindus identify with Hindus outside Punjab and seek protection from the central government. In recent years, antagonism towards the centre for disregarding the interests of the majority Hindu community in favour of the minorities has arisen. The Bhartiya Janata Party (BJP), a radical Hindu party, aims to redress this imbalance. As Vijay Chopra, editor of the Hind Samachar group, said to me, 'The Congress party before and after partition wanted to please the minorities. The government has the responsibility not to displease the majority community.' At the time of the interview, December 1992, the Hindu fundamentalists with the support of the BJP had demolished the ancient mosque in Ayodhya. Vijay Chopra supported this action, 'The BJP is not a fundamentalist party and Hindus are not fundamentalists. The government by giving preference to the minorities did not concede their just demands and that needed to be taken care of. We have proof that it was a temple and sacrilege to construct a mosque during the Muslim invasions. Nobody seems to raise their voice to protest against the demolition of temples in Kashmir.' He claimed that the government had exploited the issue and justice had been denied.

The discussion above, and an examination of the editorials of the three newspapers indicates that the Hind Samachar group supports the Bhartiya Janata Party (BJP), whereas the *Ajit* favours the Akali Dal and opposes the Congress-led central government.

On the 9 September 1981, Lala Jagat Narain was assassinated and on the 12 May 1981 Ramesh Chander, son of Lala Jagat Narain, was assassinated. Editorials on the assassination of Lala Jagat Narain, founder editor of the Hind Samachar group, are reproduced below.

The Tribune

Foul, Senseless Murder (11 September 1981)

> In murdering Lala Jagat Narain, a veteran journalist and an eminent citizen of Punjab, the assassins have provided further evidence of a growing intolerance in this country of published comment which some people find unpalatable...Lala Jagat Narain was known for his forthright opinions on certain issues, one of which was the danger to communal peace arising from political and religious extremism....The murder itself is a warning to the two principal communities in Punjab that every immoderate act begins with immoderate thinking. It is necessary that the leaders of the two communities start thinking coolly about the possible consequences of this episode and to take steps to prevent madness from spreading any further. It is also the duty of the state government to ensure that its patience is not misunderstood to mean the lack of ability to put down crime, whether it is committed for personal gain or in the mistaken belief of service to religion or political ideology.

Tears and Anger (14 May 1984)

> Tears and anger are invariably joined when killing results from cruel political revenge....The timing of the crime may, however, be significant, Romesh Chander was gunned down within 24 hours of the release of Akali leaders detained for burning or defacing Article 25[19] of the constitution....In view of earlier attempts by some to prevent a negotiated settlement between the centre and the Akali Dal, the murder of Romesh Chander[20] was most probably intended to forestall the possibility of conciliatory talks to end the current stalemate in Punjab.
>
> A fact which has lately won increased appreciation is the demographic realities of Punjab in so far as these affect the ballot box. Neither the Sikhs nor the Hindus can form a government of their own on the basis of their strength as separate communities. This has been all along evident even after the redistribution of Punjab in 1966.[21] The situation today reflects a much sharper division. Thus the moral is plain: the two communities must come to an understanding which is based on political

realities and work on that basis to prepare for the next poll. If this means a future coalition, then so be it. After all, the Congress (I) has not acquired the divine right to rule in every state of the country. It must learn to share power where it must, or do without power as in Andhra Pradesh, Tamil Nadu, Karnataka, West Bengal and Jammu and Kashmir.

Punjab Kesari

The Lion that passed away (14 September 1981)
Let this sacrifice not go worthless (16 September 1981)

Lalaji sacrificed his life for the sake of Hindu–Sikh unity and for the country's unity. He opposed the formation of Khalistan. He did not believe that Sikhs were a separate nation (*qaum*), because he saw Hindus and Sikhs as children of the same mother–father and the same Guru. This is why he could not bear to even think of any separation between Hindus and Sikhs. He fought the separatist tendency among the Sikh community tenaciously with the power of his pen.

At this solemn hour, it would be inappropriate to condemn the Punjabi dailies, the Ajit and the Akali Patrika, but they seem bent on inflicting pain to Lalaji's departed soul. We want to make it absolutely clear that we have no association with such irresponsible elements. We will not allow the situation in Punjab to deteriorate or to cause rift in Hindu-Sikh unity at any cost.

This could possibly lead to disturbances. Under no circumstances should anybody indulge in actions which could aggravate the Hindu–Sikh harmony....The stern attitude of the authorities by not allowing any relaxation in the curfew despite persistent requests hindered the funeral procession.

Ajit

The sad assassination of Lala Jagat Narain: well-known journalist, freedom fighter and social reformer (11 September 1981)

We had major differences of opinion with Lalaji which we expressed strongly, never allowing 'jati' to come in the way. These have dissipated after his sad demise. I favoured Punjab, Punjabi and Punjabiat; he regarded this as my narrow mindedness. The statements seemingly attributed to me, published in the *Hind Samachar*, are incorrect and misleading....It has been reported that incited crowds stoned cars belonging to members of one community.

Response to Lala Jagat Narain's assassination

All the newspapers unequivocally condemned the assassination of Lala Jagat Narain, founder editor of the Hind Samachar group of newspapers. The response of the newspapers reflects the significant difference among them with regard to religious identity and the conflict ensuing from it. *The Tribune* blames the assassination on growing religious intolerance and those elements who do not favour peaceful settlement of the Punjab problem within the Indian constitution; the newspaper attributes the present turmoil to conflict over political power between the two principal religious communities in Punjab. The two vernacular newspapers, the *Punjab Kesari* and the *Ajit*, are actively involved in the process of defining religious identities for the Hindus and the Sikhs respectively. The editorials in both the newspapers pronounce their differences on the matter of religious identity. Who is a Sikh? Who is a Punjabi? Is religious and regional identity synonymous? The rivalry between the two newspapers stems from the answers they provide to these questions, as will be shown.

The *Punjab Kesari* blames the murder on those who oppose the newspapers' approach to religious identity. It affirms Lala Jagat Narain's endorsement not to recognize the Sikhs as a separate and distinct religious community. The repetitive emphasis on Hindu–Sikh unity[22] alludes to the Sikhs being part of the Hindu mainstream. 'Eleven years of conflict have not damaged the Hindu–Sikh fabric. Even today Hindus and Sikhs inter-marry, they do business with each other, they share sorrows and joys.'[23] In its tribute to Lala Jagat Narain, the *Ajit* indicates the potent ideological differences between the two newspapers. The *Ajit* claims to advocate Punjabi identity, which it feels Lala Jagat Narain regarded as its narrow-mindedness. The standpoint of the *Ajit* is to uphold the regional Punjabi identity, whereas the position of the *Punjab Kesari* is to oppose the recognition of Sikhs as a separate religious group.

The turmoil in Punjab is viewed in a remarkably different way by the editor of *The Tribune*. As mentioned earlier, *The Tribune* is managed by a trust and the editor in the 1990s was a relative outsider to Punjab: he comes from South India. He explains the expansion of the vernacular press because of the tendency of the vernacular press to emphasize the divisions between religious communities. His views on Punjab reflect an intellectually objective and secular outlook.

The turbulent events of the 1970s produced scathing attacks and counterattacks in the Jalandhar vernacular press.[24] In the 1970s an acrimonious newspaper war broke out between two of the oldest vernacular newspapers in Punjab. In response, the state government frequently imposed censorship on the dailies. The matter took a serious turn when two editors of one of the newspapers were assassinated. Thus it can be seen that the vernacular press has played a critical role in heightening religious identification in recent years by reinforcing the linguistic basis of religious identity. Consequently, a composite Punjabi identity, shared by all religious communities, has failed to emerge in Punjab. This also underlines the widespread support that the Sikh movement for Khalistan elicited from the Sikh peasantry.

Cassette tapes as a means of communicating

The rise of Bhindranwale as a cult figure

Jarnail Singh Bhindranwale was born into a peasant family in the village of Rode, near the town of Moga, in 1947. Jarnail Singh was enrolled at the Damdami Taksal at an early age by his father.[25] The bright young pupil memorized passages from the Sikh scriptures and became the favourite disciple of Sant Kartar Singh, the head of the Taksal. Sant Kartar Singh was fatally injured in a car accident, but before his death he appointed Jarnail Singh as his successor in preference to his son Amrik Singh. Amrik Singh later became a close associate of Bhindranwale, and on completion of his university education he went on to become President of the All India Sikh Students Federation (AISSF).

Bhindranwale toured the villages of Punjab exhorting the Sikhs to return to the puritanical ways of the Khalsa and enjoined them to bear the Khalsa symbols. He was actively engaged in proselytizing activities. An essential feature of his preaching was that religious values should be central to life. Bhindranwale's remarkable ability to quote religious texts when delivering sermons enabled him to establish a rapport with his audience. He urged his congregations to undercut the spread of consumerism in family life and abstain from the degenerative consumption of drugs and alcohol, the two main vices afflicting rural society in Punjab. Bhindranwale's crusade for social reform denounced customs, such as the giving of dowries, and endorsed a simple lifestyle. Bhindranwale rapidly acquired a considerable following among the unlettered Sikh peasantry, women and young Sikhs.[26] Women and children had suffered at the hands of drunken and violent men.[27] As an Indian feminist and environmentalist comments, 'The Sants following grew as he successfully regenerated the good life of purity, dedication and hard work....These basic values of life...had been the first casualty of commercial capitalism' (Shiva 1991: 185–186). People soon began to seek his intervention in addressing social grievances and he began to hold court to settle disputes. This reflected the widespread disenchantment among the masses with bureaucratic procedures, which were expensive, time-consuming and often did not ensure justice. Bhindranwale's verdicts were widely respected. This 'robinhood image gave Bhindranwale enormous popularity.'[28] Until his death, Bhindranwale maintained that he was a man of religion and not a politician.

In 1992, 49 per cent of the total population of Punjab was illiterate. It is a plausible argument that during the period under consideration there was scope for another medium to exploit the areas where the press could not reach the relevant audience. This gap was filled by radiocassettes, which were relatively inexpensive and could be bought by the people in the villages. The humble audiocassette has grown at an astounding rate to make India one of the largest producers of cassettes in the world. According to an estimate by the Indian phonographic industry,

> India's legitimate and pirate sales together (180 million music cassettes) push it way ahead of China (125 million), UK (83 million) and Japan (59.2 million) to an amazing number two position – right after the giant United States (446.2 million) market.
>
> (*India Today*, 15 January 1991: 90)

According to one rough estimate, devotional music, folk songs and regional music make up 40 per cent of the market, with the lion's share going to film music (*India Today*, 15 January 1991: 93).

In *Cassette Culture*, Peter Manuel (1993) examines how the portable cassette player – a new mass medium – has revolutionized popular culture in India. Manuel shows how the cassette revolution has revitalized local subcultures and community values throughout the subcontinent. He argues that inexpensive cassettes can mobilize regional and sectarian movements. Moreover, the campaign of the Hindu radical right has been facilitated by the effective use of video- and audiocassettes. When Uma Bharati, a leader of the BJP, gave a fiery speech about the controversial Ayodhya issue, the speech was recorded and the audiocassette of this speech is reported to have sold 1,500,000 copies in Uttar Pradesh (*India Today*, 15 January 1991: 90). The importance of the cassettes in the socio-political sphere will become salient in the following section.

Paul Brass, a distinguished political scientist and a keen observer of the secessionist movement in Punjab, observed that Bhindranwale was not a new phenomenon in Punjab, which has witnessed several local and regional revivalist movements among Hindus, Sikhs and Muslims in the past century. He remarked, 'If there is anything new in this, it is not the doctrine or the message, but the use of contemporary methods of transmission, notably the distribution of taped messages, to the faithful' (Brass 1991: 190). Similar observations were made by Robin Jeffrey (1986: 92), who observed that Bhindranwale expanded his following by putting his message on cassette tapes and through the use of loudspeakers, printed pamphlets and posters.

One of the political implications of such a movement among the Sikhs, Brass points out, is to

> create solidarity and uniformity among practising Sikhs, to turn non-Keshadhari Sikhs, low caste Sikhs, and students attracted by secular ideologies into practising Sikhs and to wean both these categories of practising and non-Keshadhari Sikhs from competing practices and ideologies, religious and political, which might dilute their identity as Keshadhari Sikhs or prevent them from embracing it fully.
>
> (Brass 1991: 190)[29]

Bhindranwale's message preaching that Sikhs remain united and strong enough to maintain their distinct religious identity was particularly appealing to the expatriate Sikh community in England, Canada and America, the socially marginal sections of the Sikh community, and Sikhs from lower castes and women. Bhindranwale and his associates moved actively throughout Punjab, exhorting Sikhs to return to the puritanical ways of the Khalsa and baptizing and preaching the basic tenets of Sikhism to the masses. They became the focal point of Sikhism, propagating the norms and beliefs of Sikhism.

In order to understand Bhidranwale's message and his role in consolidating *Khalsa*[30] identity, Juergensmeyer's examination of his rambling and folksy sermons, which had a captivating style, will be discussed. It is usual for religious leaders to denounce the evil effects of the processes of modernity, and Bhindranwale was not unusual in this. In his sermons, Bhindranwale urged the congregations to weed out the germ of consumerism and abstain from drugs and alcohol by making religious values central to life. He said,

> ...one who takes the vows of faith and helps others take it; who reads the scriptures and helps others do the same; who avoids liquor and drugs and helps others do likewise; who urges unity and co-operation; who preaches community, and be attached to your Lord's throne and home.
>
> (Juergensmeyer 1988: 69)

Bhindranwale was not an outspoken supporter of Khalistan, although he often emphasized the separate identity of the Sikhs. 'We are not in favour of Khalistan nor are we against it', Bhindranwale declared, adding that the Sikhs would opt for a separate state only if they were discriminated against and were not respected in India.[31] Bhindranwale frequently used the term *qaum* to designate the religious and national characteristics of the Sikhs. Incidentally, this term was used by the Muslims in their claim for the separate national state of Pakistan. Bhindranwale endorsed the idea of a separate Sikh state only if the Sikhs were discriminated or their distinct Sikh identity was in any way threatened. 'When they say the Sikhs are not separate we'll demand separate identity – even if it demands sacrifice' (Juergensmeyer 1988: 76). Bhindranwale deplored the status of Sikhs in India, 'Sikhs are living like slaves in independent India. Today every Sikh considers himself as a second rate citizen. A baptized Sikh is looked down upon. His handsome look, dress and his observance of Sikh tenets is ridiculed. How can Sikhs tolerate this?'[32] His rhetoric appealed to the separatists, who required legitimization for their political demands.

One of Bhindranwale's main concerns in his speeches was condemning factionalism and internal disunity among the Sikhs. This is reflected in one of his speeches,

> Our misfortune is disunity....We try to throw mud at each other. Why

don't we give up thinking of mud and in close embrace with each other work with determination to attain our goals.[33]

(Juergensmeyer 1988: 79)

He attacked the traditional Akali leadership for making compromises with the Central government for personal gain. In one speech, he quoted a great martyr in Sikh history as having said, 'even if I have to give my head, may I never lose my love for the Sikh Faith' (Juergensmeyer 1988: 78). The particular period of Sikh history that Bhindranwale looked back to was the time of the Gurus. Bhindranwale's remarkable ability as a preacher and his ability to quote religious texts and evoke the relevance of historical events in the present time contributed to his immense popularity.

This section has revealed how the revolution in cassette culture coincided with the emergence of Bhindranwale as a charismatic religious figure. By recording his message on radiocassettes, Bhindranwale was able to convey a specific definition of a Sikh. This led to the dissemination and consolidation of a puritanical Sikh identity to a large section of the population for the very first time. The movement that consequently emerged among the Sikhs, spearheaded by Bhindranwale and his associates, was characterized by religious revivalism on the one hand and a demand for a separate Sikh state on the other hand.

Conclusion

The three major newspapers in Punjab are published in three different languages. The English-language newspaper, *The Tribune*, is read by the English-educated, affluent and largely professional section of the population, both Hindus and Sikhs. The critical and significant divide is between the two vernacular newspapers, the *Punjab Kesari* and the *Ajit*. Not only are they published in separate languages, the *Punjab Kesari* in Hindi and the *Ajit* in Punjabi, they are also associated with particular religious groups, the Hindus and the Sikhs. The historic rivalry between the two newspapers became fierce in the late 1970s. This is the period when the movement for a separate Sikh state first arose in Punjab, and it is the period of this study. The editorials in the newspapers of the Hind Samachar group, whose roots are in the Arya Samaj movement, a religious reform movement among Hindus in North India in the 1870s, upheld the view that the Sikhs were part of mainstream Hinduism and therefore were not a separate religious community. This was not a new contention; various Arya Samaj leaders had insisted that the Sikhs were part of the Hindu community, and a campaign to bring them back into the fold of Hinduism was subsequently launched. The Singh Sabha movement, a religious reform movement in the 1870s among the Sikhs, repudiated the claims made by the Arya Samaj leaders and aimed at defining and asserting a separate Sikh identity. The Punjabi press, although sympathetic to the Sikhs, emphasized the existence of a Punjabi identity whereas the Punjabi Hindus repudiated this. Although the reform movements of the 1870s, among both the Hindus and the Sikhs, had already laid the institutional framework for providing a sense of unique identity to the Punjabi Hindus and the Sikhs, it is this rhetoric that marks the confrontation between the two newspapers. In other words, the vernacular press continues to play a critical role in reinforcing the linguistic basis of religious identity in Punjab.

Since the 1880s, the territorial boundaries of Punjab have altered twice: in 1947, when the partition of India took place, and once again in 1966. This resulted in a sharp division between the two religious communities in Punjab: Punjabi became associated with the Sikhs and Hindi with the Hindus in Punjab.[34] What was so novel about the situation that emerged in 1970s was that never before had such a large section of the population become available and responsive to the message and appeal of the press. By the 1970s, the vernacular press and cassettes had become the foremost means of transmitting religious messages of mass appeal. Now religious controversies were permanently recorded and were intensified. In the process, conflicts became more serious, ideas spread and identities were defined as never before. As Robin Jeffrey argues 'words on paper harden identities and reflect an attempt of increasingly literate societies to explain their relationships to the state with whom they have to deal and to the wider world that increasingly affects their lives' (Jeffrey 1986: 86). Further, the appeal of cassette culture is an appropriation of earlier forms of oral traditions. It is through the spoken word, which is dramatic, that people develop a sharper sense of their identity, of who they are; the spoken word also informs and influences mass opinion.

Conclusion

In the conclusion, I wish to bring together different strands and highlight the implications of this research. An adequate theory about nationalism in India cannot be derived from the European experience. We need to pay attention to the cultural and historical specificities of non-Western state formation. The historical preconditions that ushered nationalism into India differed sharply from those in Western Europe and the United States. India has not witnessed a bourgeois revolution, nor has there been an industrial or a peasant revolution in India. Yet there has been the development of the formal structure of parliamentary democracy in India.

An examination of the historical and social development of Sikh tradition reveals that despite the evolution of a distinct set of Sikh symbols and a doctrinal discourse, the establishment of the powerful Sikh empire under Maharajah Ranjit Singh, the establishment of an institutional framework that provided the arena and base for Sikh separatism and a separate language and territory, it is only recently that the Sikhs have demanded a separate state. This leads us to take issue with the view that once an objectively distinct, self-aware ethnic community is formed, then there is bound to be a natural movement for political autonomy. Clearly, the demand for a sovereign Sikh state was not the final manifestation of the historical evolution of Sikh identity. Rather this study explicates the vital factors that in conjunction explain the emergence of the Sikh separatist movement.

This study has a number of implications. First, it stresses the social base of an ethno-nationalist struggle as vital in determining the outcome of an ethno-nationalist movement. The investigation of the Sikh ethno-nationalist struggle has revealed that the transition to commercial agriculture induced widespread dislocation and alienation and resulted in a section of the Sikh peasantry becoming politically mobilized. Consequently, it was primarily a body of young, semiliterate men with rural backgrounds who became the motivatinfg force for the struggle for Sikh national state. The classic theories of nationalism are based on a ubiquitous premise that discounts the possibility of ethno-nationalist struggles without a bourgeois or a peasant revolution. The late-industrializing societies of the Indian subcontinent have had neither a bourgeois revolution nor a peasant revolution, yet there has been a widespread proliferation of ethno-nationalist movements in these societies. These observations impel us to reconsider the theories of nationalism in the light of two possibilities. First, to account for the possibility of ethno-nationalism without a bourgeois or a peasant revolution, and, second, to explain those ethno-nationalist struggles that are induced by agricultural change and are spearheaded neither by the bourgeoisie nor by the intelligentsia but by a section of the disaffected peasantry.

Second, there is the striking coincidence of the late twentieth century ethno-nationalist struggles in the Indian subcontinent with the spread of literacy and a revolution in communication. Although there is a considerable amount of literature on nationalism that stresses the role of social communications in facilitating nationalism, this study highlights the need to qualify these theories of nationalism in two vital respects. The first is the significance of a vernacular press and oral forms of communication, such as cassettes, in explaining the timing of strong ethno-nationalism. This study of the Sikh ethno-nationalist struggle reveals that the expansion of the vernacular press energized the existing religious communities to produce written communications. Further, we noted that cassette culture was vital in promoting the meteoric rise of the charismatic Sikh religious preacher, Sant Jarnail Singh Bhindranwale. Never before in the history of the Indian subcontinent has such a large section of the public become available and responsive to the message and appeal of the press. The striking feature of this revolution in communication is its mass appeal in the regeneration of popular and vernacular culture and in the revitalization of religious identities, especially to vast sections of the peasantry, for the very first time. It is appropriate to note that it is the peasantry – the socially marginalized sections of the population – who have been embroiled in these ethno-nationalist struggles. This stresses the significance of a vernacular press and cassettes in explaining the timing of ethno-nationalist struggles in the Indian subcontinent. Second, contrary to what the classic theories of nationalism have led us to believe, the transformation in communication has resulted in the revitalization of religion and the emergence of sharper group boundaries in the Indian subcontinent. Religious nationalism in India, with all its ambiguities and dialectical transformations, has a history of its own, which cannot be reduced to the master narrative of European modernity (Van der Veer 1994: 202).

This leads us to another striking inference of this study. Religion remains the dominant social bond that defines the characteristics of the nation within the societies of the Indian subcontinent, despite the development of modern institutions such as democracy. At the ideological level, these societies have yet to experience a revolutionary break with the past, and this highlights the importance of religious ideals and reforms for the self-sacrificing passion of ethno-nationalism. The religious context is invoked in order to legitimize these armed ethno-nationalist struggles for the establishment of a more just and equitable social order. The religious crusaders came into violent conflict not only with those whose vision of a Utopian social order is derived from other sources but also with the central authorities. Further, the violent and hostile response of the post-colonial state to regional demands and the ruthless use of the repressive apparatus of the state to suppress separatist movements provokes armed guerrilla resistance against a powerful, authoritarian state.[1]

The general implications of this study can be summed up as follows: dramatic shifts in the prevailing material conditions of existence generate mass discontent in society and unleash political forces. However, in many late-industrializing societies there is a tendency to turn to religious notions emanating from religious faith in legitimizing economic, political and social grievances. This is because these societies have not experienced a revolutionary break with the past and religion continues to be the dominant world-view. This explains the nature and efflorescence of ethno-revivalist movements in many post-colonial states.

South Asia today is in the throes of profound structural changes in economy, state and society. India embarked on a transition from a closed and controlled economy to a free-market economy in the early 1990s. The era of liberalization marks a transition from *raj*, which protected the interests of the public sector enterprise and the rich farmer by insulating them from the pressures of a competitive free-market economy and providing them huge subsidies, to a more open and competitive market system. For the 700 million people directly dependent on farming in India (*The Guardian Weekend*, 19 June 1999), the liberalization process also heralds a change from publicly controlled green revolution towards privately led genetic revolution. By turning over a few favoured regions to commercial agriculture, the green revolution strategy in the 1970s transformed India from the world's largest importer of food grain to a self-sufficient country. This study of the Sikh separatist movement in Punjab – the heartland of the green revolution – has highlighted the huge social costs of this publicly controlled transition to industrially based agriculture. In the next 40 years, India will have to feed up to 400 million more people, most of whom are likely to be desperately poor (*The Guardian Weekend*, 19 June 1999). It is too early to suggest that the onset of a privately led genetic revolution will be the solution to this challenge to India's political stability. What is clear is that if the liberalization process is not accompanied by access or distributive reforms, it is likely to generate more angry young men who may increasingly mount armed rebellions in order to establish a more equitable social order, as both the customary and the modern institutional structures fail to accommodate them. Furthermore, as the revolution in communications becomes increasingly diversified and widespread, and literacy levels increase, there is every likelihood that reactionary, ethno-nationalist outbreaks will flourish in the future.

Further, the success of an ethno-nationalist struggle will depend to a great extent on whether it can find allies within different strata of the population. In the Sikh case, it was noted that powerful institutional links bind the traditional Sikh leadership and the Sikh bourgeois to the existing political

Notes

Introduction

1 Sikh religion has evolved by a succession of ten gurus. The first Sikh guru was Guru Nanak (1469–1539) and the last Sikh guru was Guru Gobind Singh (1666–1708).

2 Operation Bluestar was the codename for the Indian army assault on the Golden Temple in Amritsar in June 1984.

1 The trouble with classic theories of nationalism

1 The *kes-dhari* Sikhs are those who maintain *kes*, or 'the unshorn hair of the Khalsa', but have not received baptism. The majority of Sikhs in Punjab are *kes-dhari* Sikhs. Those Sikhs who have taken *amrit*, or 'received the baptism of the Khalsa', are called *amrit-dhari* Sikhs. Only a small proportion of the Sikh population is *amrit-dhari*.

2 In Chapters 4 and 5, the historic and social developments that gave rise to this distinct Sikh self-identification will be discussed. This study challenges Richard Fox's (1985) view that the British view of the Sikhs as a 'martial race' created a distinct Sikh identity. Also, the view espoused by Harjot Oberoi (1994) that the Sikh commercial class of town dwellers was an indispensable element in the growth of Sikh communal consciousness and that it was, in fact, the vigorous Sikh bourgeoisie who created a new episteme, a standard discourse of modern Sikhism.

3 The Akali Dal and the SGPC, or the Shiromani Gurudwara Prabahandak Committee, are the foremost Sikh institutions. The SGPC is the guardian of most Sikh religious institutions, and the Akali Dal is a major political party in Punjab. The formation of these historic institutions of the Sikhs will be examined in Chapter 3.

4 Although Ernest Gellner's theory of nationalism (1964) is widely influential in explaining the origins of nationalism in Europe, it is tangential to the argument of the book.

5 Here, print capitalism is emblematic of a process when a book becomes a commodity. It is circulated and exchanged like any other commodity in a market.

6 According to the anthropologist Louis Dumont, India's jajmani system is a hierarchical and cosmic system of relations of production and exchange, whereby the lower castes provide ritual and non-ritual services to the high-caste *jajmans* in exchange for specified products of the land. This highly controversial concept is regarded by many scholars as a European myth to describe a non-European society. See Simon Commander, 'The Jajmani System in North India: An Examination of Its Logic and Status across Two Centuries', in *Modern Asian Studies*,

1983, Vol. 17, pp. 283–311, London: Cambridge University Press, and Christopher J. Fuller, 'Misconceiving the Grain Heap: A Critique of the Concept of the Indian Jajmani System', in J. Parry and M. Bloch (eds) *Money and Morality of Exchange*, Cambridge: Cambridge University Press, 1989, pp. 33–63.

7 See, for example, I. Habib, 'Structure of Agrarian Society in Mughal India', in B. N. Ganguli (ed.) *Readings in Indian Economic History*, Bombay, Asia Publishing House, 1964. The weight of the present evidence seems to me to indicate that European thinkers either had no access to critical knowledge about the non-European world or this knowledge was suppressed for political reasons. Even so, there is a tendency to endlessly parrot the Eurocentric assumptions that informed modern discourse in the West.

8 Another classic example that illustrates how explanations of non-European societies often reflect the scholars favoured theoretical position, rather than a fair representation which takes into account the historical specificities, is the concept of Asiatic mode of production (AMP). The explanation of world history outside Europe from the perspective of Marxist historical materialism hinges on the concept of AMP. Brendan O'Leary's original work forcefully illustrates that the key components of either the AMP or oriental despotism were insufficiently present in either Hindu or late Islamic empires in India. He concludes that the AMP concept is in fact a fatal weakness of Marxist historical materialism and without this concept Marxist historical materialism is incapable of explaining history outside Europe. See B. O'Leary, *The Asiatic Mode of Production: Oriental Despotism, Historical Materialism and Indian History*, Oxford, Basil Blackwell, 1989.

9 The term 'socio-religious reform movements' refers to an attempt to mobilize mass support in a bid to recast society through modifications in social practices and customs. An ecclesiastical authority is invoked to legitimize these changes. The basis of this ecclesiastical authority is usually the sacred scripture, which is no longer considered to be properly observed and therefore requires reinterpretation. These movements pit the reformers against the self-consciously more orthodox groups. The movement develops and maintains an organizational structure over time. The foremost reform movements among the major religious communities in the Punjab during the nineteenth century were the Arya Samaj movement among the Hindus, the Ahmadiyah movement among the Muslims and the Singh Sabha movement among the Sikhs. The Arya Samaj movement and the Singh Sabha movement will be examined in greater detail in Chapter 3.

10 C. A. Bayly has emphasized that the introduction of new communication techniques and the rapid diffusion of knowledge during the colonial era owed their success to the flourishing pattern of social and political critique entrenched in pre-colonial Indian society. He notes, 'For while the Baptists, the CMS and the crypto-Christian administrators unwittingly helped to engender an Indian critical public, its rapid development owed much to patterns in debate, publicity and the diffusion of knowledge which were already in place in India. I call this area of debate and social and political critique the Indian *ecumene*. This was the community of learned administrators, jurists, Mogul public officials and community leaders who represented the views of the populace to the rulers during the late Mogul period and the rule of the successor states of the eighteenth century. The Indian state had been sensitive to the political and social discourses of its more honourable citizens. Bodies of intelligentsia and literate administrators kept up a constant dialogue through the Persian news report, the private letter, the couplet of a satirical poem and the Persian or Hindustani written tract. The place for debate was the steps of the mosque, the space outside the city temple, the *kazi's* house or the shrine of the local saint. Debate was regulated and formalized. Literary issues preoccupied the Indo-Muslim *ecumeme*

or proto-public, as they did Habermas's eighteenth century European public. In the poetic *mushaira* the emperor's or nawab's presence was honoured, but his poem might be subject to scathing criticism. Information circulated rapidly, and well beyond the ruling élite. Theological disputations and covert political debates sometimes involved large parts of the urban population in Hogarthian scuffles. Placarding against unjust officials was as common as the *pasquinade* of Baroque Rome...The way in which the north Indian critical ecumene helped determine the nature of the nationalist public of the late nineteenth century needs to be considered in detail.' C. A Bayly, 'Returning the British to South Asian History: The Limits of Colonial Hegemony', *South Asia: Journal of South Asian Studies*, December 1994, vol. 17, p. 9.

11 Edward Lake (ed.) 'Report of the Punjab Missionary Conference held at Lahore in December and January 1862–63', Ludhiana, 1862, p.351. Quoted in Harjot Oberoi, *The Construction of Religious Boundaries*, New Delhi, Oxford University Press, 1994, p. 219.

12 For an excellent illustration of this approach, see, A. Nandy, 'The Politics of Secularism and the Recovery of Religious Tolerance', in Veena Das (ed.) *Mirrors of Violence: Communities and Riots and Survivors in South Asia*, Delhi, Oxford University Press, 1990, pp. 69–93.

13 For an illustration of this approach, see G. Pandey, *The Construction of Communalism in Colonial India*, Delhi, Oxford University Press, 1990.

14 Anthony D. Smith, *The Ethnic Revival*, Cambridge: Cambridge University Press, 1981, pp. 90, 93–98, 99–104.

2 The contradictory unity of the Indian state

1 This point has been made by Romila Thapar, 'A Historical Perspective on the Story of Rama', in Sarvepalli Gopal (ed.) *Anatomy of a Confrontation: The Babri Masjid-Ram Janambhumi Issue*, New Delhi, Zed Books, 1991, pp.141–63.

2 RSS was founded in 1925 and aimed at training young men to revive traditional Hindu ethical values. It was based in Maharashtra and Madhya Pradesh and largely consisted of urban, middle-class Hindus.

3 Ashok Singhal, Vishva Hindu Parishas (VHP) chief, quoted in the weekly magazine, *Outlook*, 27 December 1995, p.16.

4 Quoted in the weekly magazine, *Outlook*, 27 December 1995, p.13.

5 This term has been coined by Rajni Kothari, eminent Indian political scientist. For further details see Rajni Kothari, 'The Congress 'System' in India', *Asian Survey*, December 1964, Vol. 4, pp. 1161–73. Paul Brass notes that it is a misnomer to regard the Congress party as a one-party dominant system. He points out, 'there has never really been a single, national party system but instead each region of the country has had its own distinctive party system in most of which the Congress was the dominant party, but itself had a distinctive social base and pattern of relationship with opposition parties in each state', P. R. Brass, *The Politics of India since Independence*, Cambridge, Cambridge University Press, 1990, p. 69. We must note that the Congress party of Mrs Gandhi became known as Congress (I) for Indira after the split in the party in 1977.

6 For evidence about the role of the Congress party in exacerbating the conflict in Punjab, see M. Tully and S. Jacob, *Amritsar: Mrs Gandhi's Last Battle*, London, Jonathan Cape, 1985, pp. 57–83. The situation in Punjab raises some fundamental questions regarding the nature of centre-state relations in India. These aspects are addressed in Chapter 4.

7 The Indian Press recorded partisan pro-Hindu instructions by senior officers to policemen at trouble spots in Bombay during well-organized attacks on Muslims

by the Hindu extremist groups. For further evidence on the support for Hindu nationalism by state institutions, which seriously puts into doubt the religious neutrality of the Indian state, see Peter van der Veer, *Religious Nationalism: Hindus and Muslims in India*, Berkeley, University of California, 1994, pp. 152–62.

8 P. Wallace, 'Centre-State Relations in India: The federal dilemma', in James R. Roach, op. cit. p. 153.

9 For an elaboration of this point, see A. T. Embree, *Utopias in Conflict*, California, University of California Press, 1990, p. 132.

10 Weiner's statistical projection for the year 2000, extrapolated from current growth rates, indicates that the dominant caste Hindu majority, those who speak the official regional language as their mother tongue, will decline to 45–52 per cent by the year 2000 compared with 51–58 per cent range in 1971. See Weiner op. cit. pp. 99–134.

11 See note 1.

3 The historical roots of Sikh communal consciousness (1469–1947)

1 *Janam-sakhi* is a hagiographic narrative telling the story of the life of Guru Nanak.

2 The ten Sikh gurus are Guru Nanak (1469–1539), Guru Angad (1504–52), Guru Amar Das (1479–1574), Guru Ram Das (1534–81), Guru Arjan (1563–1606), Guru Hargobind (1595–1644), Guru Har Rai (1630–61), Guru Hari Krishan (1656–64), Guru Tegh Bahadur (1621–75), Guru Gobind Singh (1666–1708).

3 *Khalsa* denotes the religious order or brotherhood instituted by Guru Gobind Singh in 1699.

4 Baptized Sikhs were enjoined to wear five symbols or five Ks (each beginning with the character 'k'): *kes* (unshorn hair), *kanga* (wooden comb), *kara* (steel bangle), *kirpan* (sword) and *kachha* (type of breeches).

5 Braj was a Sanskrit variant advanced by the huge spread of the Krishna cult and it received the occasional patronage of the Agra court as a preferred language for religious poetry.

6 The Arabic word *misl* stands for 'alike' and designates the spirit of equality that characterized the Sikh *misls*. These *misls* were Ahluwalia, Bhangi, Dulewalia, Kanheya, Krora Singhia, Nakkai, Nishania, Phoolkia, Ramghariya, Shahid, Singhpuria and Sukarchakia.

7 The term 'vernacular' stands for a modern Indian language, in contrast to classical or ritual languages, such as Sanskrit or Arabic, or for a modern imperial language like English. Although the use of the term 'vernacular' implies a spoken dialect rather than a literary language, the modern North Indian languages, Urdu, Hindi and Punjabi, that are examined in this study are languages of considerable range and subtlety.

8 A *swayamsevak* is an RSS volunteer.

9 For an examination of the logic and the critical techniques used by Dayananda Saraswati to discredit all claims of Christian superiority see Kenneth W. Jones (ed.) 'Swami Dayananda Saraswati's Critique of Christianity', in *Religious Controversy in British India: Dialogues in South Asian Languages*, Albany, State University of New York Press, 1992, pp. 52–74.

10 Paul Brass has provided a comparison of census records on books and periodicals published in Hindi, Urdu and Punjabi in pre-independence Punjab. He observes that the Gurmukhi press was perhaps the slowest to develop, see P. Brass, *Language, Religion and Politics in North India*, Cambridge, Cambridge University Press, 1974, p. 308.

11 Sir Charles Gough and Arthur D. Innes, *The Sikhs and the Sikh Wars*, London, 1897, pp. 43, 78, 79, 102 and 109; Lepel Griffin, *Ranjit Singh*, Oxford, 1892, pp. 17,18,34–7; Sir John J. N. Gordon, *The Sikhs*, London, 1904, pp. vi, 3, 152, 153, 175, 179, 182, 219–23, cited from the introduction by Himadari Banerjee to S. S. Thorburn, *The Punjab in Peace and War*, 2nd edn, Delhi, 1904, 3p. vi.

12 Sehajdhari, or the slow adopters, refers to those Sikhs who do not observe the unshorn hair of the Khalsa nor accept the Khalsa normative order instituted by the last Sikh guru, Guru Gobind Singh. Historically, their numbers have dwindled over the centuries.

13 Scholars refer to the Sanatan tradition as the pluralistic mode of Sikh tradition in the nineteenth century.

14 Khan Ahmad Hasan Khan, 'Lahore, 1933', in *Government of India, 1931 Census Report, Punjab*, Vol. 17, Part I, p. 290.

15 Three categories of men, members of guru lineages, holy men (*bhais, sants, babas*) and traditional intellectuals (*gianis, dhadhis*), continued to be the bearers of Sikh tradition. For a person to qualify for the title of a *bhai* or a *giani* he had to have the ability to interpret and expound on *gurbani* (the holy word of the Sikh gurus). Thus, the traditional intellectuals kept the Sikh oral tradition of exegesis alive. It was through the existence of a highly structured body of religious thought that the unlettered Sikh peasantry learnt about the tenets of Sikhism. It was not necessary for them to be able to read the contents of the Adi Granth. As long as the religious intermediaries conveyed to them its message, they could order and express their everyday life experience according to what the text prescribed. Thus, the Adi Granth was venerated by the Sikh peasantry, who acquired familiarity with its contents and message through the traditional intellectuals. This profound historical development is bound to have transformed the religious experience of the rural Sikh population in pre-colonial Punjab. Further, the traditional intellectuals were also involved in imparting secular and religious education at Khalsa schools in villages and towns. Besides, cultural mediaries like *bhais, dhadhis* (musicians who perform in pairs and sing heroic ballads in praise of the heroic deeds of historic Sikh figures) performed in fairs and festivals in villages and towns. The establishment of educational institutions in the villages and the presence of cultural mediators, who were not confined to the urban areas, points towards a new historic form of religious experience.

16 See, for example, K. W. Jones (1989), R. G. Fox (1985), G. Pandey (1990).

17 The historical processes that facilitated the survival and expansion of commercial castes in colonial India are delineated in C. A. Bayly, *Rulers, Townsmen and Bazaars*, Delhi, Oxford University Press, 1992.

18 For usage of these categories see, C. A. Bayly, *The Local Roots of Indian Politics*, Oxford, Clarendon Press, 1975, p. 236 and R. G. Fox, *The Lions of the Punjab*, Berkeley, University of California Press, 1985, pp. 125–7.

19 N. G. Barrier, 'Vernacular Publishing and Sikh Public Life in the Punjab, 1880–1910', in Jones op. cit. p. 201.

20 The Indo-Aryan languages outside this vast Hindi–Urdu zone, Bengali, Gujarati or Marathi, underwent a broadly similar process of standardization during the nineteenth century. For an examination of the linguistic and literary aspects of this process see C. Shackle and R. Snell, *Hindi and Urdu since 1800: A Common Reader*, London, SOAS, 1988.

21 The origins of Urdu might be traced back to the Muslim invasions of India and the resulting Indo-Persian linguistic synthesis came to be termed Urdu.

22 Paul Brass has provided the census figures on religion by literacy in the vernacular languages in British Punjab. For a discussion about literacy and communications see Brass, op. cit., pp. 300–9.

23 See, for example, C. R. King 'Images of Virtue and Vice: The Hindi-Urdu Controversy in Two Nineteenth-century Hindi Plays', in Jones, op. cit., pp. 123–48.
24 *Census 1891*, p. 253 and p. lxix, Abstract 61.
25 *Report on the Census of the Punjab*, by D. C. J. Ibbetson, Lahore, 1883, p. 17.
26 See also R. G. Fox, *Lions of the Punjab: Culture in the Making*, Berkeley, University of California Press, 1985, for a major argument about the distressing conditions of the rural peasantry in the 1920s that facilitated the Akali reformers to induct the aggrieved agriculturists into a movement of mass protest.
27 See G. Pandey, *The Construction of Communalism in Colonial India*, Delhi: Oxford University Press, 1990, for an exposition of this view.

4 The rise of Sikh national consciousness (1947–95)

1 Statistical projections for the year 2000 extrapolated by Myron Weiner, show that the dominant caste Hindu majority, those who speak Hindi, the official regional language as their mother tongue, will decline from 52 per cent to 45 per cent by the year 2000. For further details see, Myron Weiner, 'India's minorities: Who are they? What do they want?', in James R. Roach (ed.) *India 2000: The Next Fifteen Years*, Maryland, The Riverdale Company, 1986, pp. 99–135.
2 In post-independence Punjab, the Shiromani Akali Dal has split into rival factions from time to time. In this study, reference to the Akali Dal is to the dominant Shiromani Akali Dal. Moreover, the elevation of Sant Fateh Singh as leader of the Akali Dal was a vital signal of the displacement of non-Jat Sikh Akali leaders. The proportion of Jat Sikh legislators has increased steadily in post-independence Punjab. A study conducted by the Centre for Research in Rural and Industrial Development (CRID) shows that between 1967 and 1980 the proportion of Jat Sikh ministers in the Punjab government was some 49 per cent.
3 The prefix 'sant' refers to 'a worthy and virtuous man'. The institution of the 'sant' is widespread in Punjab. The 'sants' often reside in *deras*, or 'hospices', which are scattered all over Punjab and provide food and shelter free of cost.
4 It was at the holy city of Anandpur that the tenth Sikh master, Guru Gobind Singh, founded the Khalsa *panth*.
5 The Anandpur Sahib resolution was drafted by Kapur Singh, a former officer in the prestigious Indian Civil Service (ICS) and a product of Oxford University. He was an advisor to the Akali Dal and in 1962 he was elected to the Parliament.
6 Khushwant Singh is of the view that the Akali Dal formulated the demand for a Sikh personal law only in January 1984. Under article 25 of the Indian constitution, the Hindu marriage Act and the Hindu Succession Act were applicable to the Sikhs. The Akali Dal demanded an amendment to article 25 of the constitution on the grounds that Sikhs were a distinct religious community. See K. Singh, *History of the Sikhs*, New Delhi, Oxford University Press, Vol. 2, 1991, p. 352.
7 For evidence and detailed argument about the role of the Congress party in exploiting the political potential of Bhindranwale in a bid to disintegrate the Akali Dal see M. Tully and S. Jacob, *Amritsar: Mrs Gandhi's Last Battle*, London, Jonathan Cape, 1985, pp. 57–83. Similar arguments on the role of the Congress party in bringing Bhindranwale to the forefront of Punjab politics are presented in K. Singh, op. cit., pp. 332–341.
8 It is critical to note that Bhindranwale's outrage at the burning of his sermons must be viewed in the context of the Sikh doctrine of *guru granth* which embodies in the scripture the figure of an eternal guru.

9 Guru Nanak Nivas is a building in the precincts of the Darbar Sahib and adjacent to the SGPC offices.

10 Sant Harchand Singh Longowal (1934–85) was a Jat Sikh whose induction into politics was through the religious network. He had earlier been the guardian of the *gurudwara* at his native village Longowal and achieved a reputation for piety and social work. His links with the SGPC had brought him into the political arena and he had contested the Punjab state assembly elections in 1969 on the Akali ticket. After the arrest of the established Akali leadership during the Akali campaign against the imposition of emergency (1975–7) in India, Sant Harchand Singh Longowal emerged as the leader of the Akali Dal.

11 See K. Singh and K. Nayar, *Tragedy of Punjab*, New Delhi, Vision Books, 1984, p. 66, and Tully and Jacob, op. cit., p. 89. Major General Shahbeg Singh became a close associate of Bhindranwale and played a crucial role in the fortification of the Darbar Sahib and directed the armed resistance to the Indian army during Operation Bluestar. Major General Shahbeg Singh was a hero of the Bangladesh war in 1971, during which he had trained and led successful guerrilla operations. He was dismissed from service without a court martial on charges of corruption on the day he was due to retire. He proved his innocence later on when the civil courts dismissed the charges against him. He still felt that injustice had been done to him by the Indian government despite the distinguished service that he had given the country.

12 For a list of violent incidents see *White Paper on the Punjab Agitation*, New Delhi, 1984, pp. 110–62.

13 This account is based on an eye witness report by Brahma Chellani of Associated Press published in *The Times*, London, 14 June 1984.

14 The original workmanship on Akal Takht was done by Muslim craftsmen and many Sikhs lament the fact that the building can never be restored to its original grandeur.

15 The Indian press published a spate of allegations accusing the Pakistan government of offering training and weapons to Sikh guerrillas.

16 People's Union for Democratic Rights and People's Union for Civil Liberties *Who are the Guilty?: Report of a Joint Inquiry into the Causes and Impact of the Riots in Delhi from 31 October to 10 November*, New Delhi, 1984, pp. 1–4.

17 Ibid.

18 My main source of information on the guerrillas was Mr S. S. Bal, a journalist with the *Punjabi Tribune*. He had conducted extensive first-hand interviews with the guerrillas and their families and greatly obliged me by providing his rare data, which he had collected with considerable difficulty that involved risking his life.

19 The economic context of the armed resistance is discussed in Chapter 7. It may be appropriate to emphasize that militants construed the state repression as an extension of the economic repression that they were being subjected to. Further, an armed resistance was a means to resurrect Sikh honour, which was an extension of their personal honour.

20 This point is attested in the information that I gathered about the militants during my fieldwork. A similar observation is made by Joyce J. M. Pettigrew. The method of recruitment was based on traditional associations of kin and friendship. For information on the personal experience and circumstances that drove them into guerrilla activity. See Pettigrew (1995), pp. 137–86.

21 The split was between two main guerrilla organizations, the Khalistan Commando Force (KCF) and the Car Jhujharu Jathebande (CJJ). The Car Jhujharu Jathebande (CJJ) constituted two other guerrilla groups, The Babbar Khalsa and Khalistan Force. For details of the guerrilla organizations, see Pettigrew (1995), pp. 70–100.

22 *India Today*, 15 January 1991. The method of recruitment was based on traditional associations of kin and friendship.

23 The way in which the decentralized organizational structure of the guerrilla groups resulted in civilian casualties is described in Pettigrew (1995) pp. 89–98.

24 Evidence and description of atrocities on civilians are attested in reports presented by Amnesty International. See reports of Amnesty International, *India: Review of Human Rights Violations*, London, 1988; Amnesty International, *India: Some Recent Reports of Disappearances*, London, 1989; Amnesty International, *India: Human Rights Violations in Punjab: Use and Abuse of the Law*, London, 1991; Amnesty International, *India: Torture, Rape and Deaths in Custody*, London, 1992. Everyday forms of state repression are detailed in the work of Pettigrew (1995), pp. 10–29, pp. 68–9, pp. 110–33, based on case studies of typical happenings of harassment and torture involving the rural population.

25 The two activists in the KCF who belonged to well-placed families were Dr Sohan Singh, a former director of health services, who raised the issue of Khalistan in 1986, and Daljit Singh Bittoo, a postgraduate student at the Punjab Agricultural University (PAU) in Ludhiana, where his father was a professor.

26 Simranjit Singh Mann hails from a distinguished Jat Sikh family. His grandfather was awarded an OBE by the British, and his father, Sardar Joginder Singh, was an honorary colonel in the British army and was awarded an MBE. His father was also a member of the Legislative Council of the United Punjab. He has associations with the erstwhile Sikh aristocracy through his wife, whose sister is married to the Maharaja of Patiala.

27 It is appropriate to note that the SGPC and the Akali Dal have not preserved the bulk of their historical records.

28 The President of Shiromani Akali Dal maintains extensive correspondence and contact with various organizations of the United Nations and other international human rights organizations.

29 For further details see John De Witt, *Indian Workers Associations in Great Britain*, Oxford, Oxford University Press, 1969.

30 Many leaders of the KCF reside in London.

31 According to one estimate 75 per cent of the immigrants had served in the British army. See M. Juergensmeyer, 'The Ghadar Syndrome: Immigrant Sikhs and Nationalist Pride', in M. Juergensmeyer and N. G. Barrier (eds) *Sikh Studies: Comparative Perspectives on a Changing Tradition*, Berkeley Religious Studies Series, 1979, p. 178.

32 In a major study, Hugh Tinker (1974) has argued that Britain lost the Raj mainly because of the way the overseas Indian community was treated. See Hugh Tinker, *A New System of Slavery*, London, Oxford University Press, 1974, p. xv.

33 The international connections of the Ghadr Party are described by Gail Omevedt, 'Armed Struggle in India: The Ghadar Party', *Frontier*, 9 November 1974 and 16 November 1974. The links between the Ghadr Party and the Communist party in Punjab are described by Tilak Raj Chadha, 'Punjab's Red and White Communists: Scramble for Funds from America', *Thought*, 14 June 1952.

34 Walker Connor, 'The Impact of Homelands upon Diasporas', in G. Shaffer (ed.) *Modern Diasporas in International Politics*, London, Croom Helm Ltd, 1986, p. 16.

35 See, for instance, Arthur Helweg, 'Sikh Politics in India: The Emigrant Factor', in G. N. Barrier and V. A. Dusenbery (eds) *The Sikh Diaspora: Migration and the Experience Beyond Punjab*, Columbia, South Asia Books, 1989, pp. 305–336. A similar approach emphasizing the psychological and cultural aspects of the migrants experience in giving rise to the demands of independence of the homeland in the case of Britain is presented by Harry Goulbourne, *Ethnicity and Nationalism in Post-Imperial Britain*, Cambridge, Cambridge University Press, 1991, pp. 126–69.

36 Cultural associations are developed through the entertainment industry. Classical and popular performers, folk artists, film stars are invited by the Sikh diaspora. In fact, London has become an important centre for the Punjabi music industry. In recent years, Punjabi music has assumed great popularity among the second- and third-generation Punjabi immigrants.

5 The agrarian crisis and the rise of armed resistance

1 By 'depeasantization' is meant 'the separation of peasants from the land and the means of production', T. Byres, *The Green Revolution in India*, Milton Keynes, The Open University Press, 1982, p. 41.

2 Warning of the political and ideological implications of the green revolution, Francine Frankel notes, 'Agriculture, it suggests, is being peacefully transformed through the quiet workings of science and technology, reaping the economic gains of modernisation while avoiding the social costs of mass upheaval and disorder usually associated with rapid change.', see Francine Frankel, *India's Green Revolution: Economic Gains and Political Costs*, Princeton, Princeton University Press, 1971, preface.

3 Note that the Punjab province is further divided into twelve districts. The geographical area of Punjab is 5033 (thousands of hectares) and the population is 20,190,795, of which 70.28 per cent is rural and 29.72 is urban. Further, 36.93 per cent is Hindu and 60.75 per cent is Sikh, *Statistical Abstract of Punjab, 1991–92*.

4 Norman Ernest Borlaug (born 1914), microbiologist at the University of Minnesota, was awarded the Nobel Prize for Peace in 1970 for his contribution to the improvement of wheat and rice. He visited Ludhiana after having spent 14 years in Mexico at the Maize and Wheat Improvement Centre.

5 It is critical to note the relationship between caste background and the farm size ownership pattern. In the case of Punjab, all upper caste lessees and lessors are predominantly 'Jats'. According to Puri, 'Jats with 20 per cent of the Sikh population own 60 per cent of land', H. Puri, 'The Akali Agitation: An analysis of socio-economic bases of protest', *Economic and Political Weekly*, 22 January 1983, Vol. 18, p. 117.

6 Typically (the superior right-holders) found it more profitable to rent out their land than to manage them personally...this complex of legal, economic and social relations uniquely typical of Indian countryside served to produce an effect which I should like to call that of a built-in depressor', D. Thorner, *The Agrarian Prospect in India*, Bombay, Allied, 1976, p. 16. His ideas are developed by U. Patnaik, 'The Agrarian Question and Development of Capitalism in India', *Economic and Political Weekly*, 1986, Vol. 21, pp. 781–93. It is perhaps worth noting that the British inducted large numbers of Sikhs into the army. According to one source, in 1914 more than 47 per cent of the number of infantry units in the Indian army were composed of recruits from Punjab; 57 infantry units out of the total of 121 consisted of persons from Punjab in 1914, See B. Josh, *Communist Movement in Punjab*, New Delhi, Anupama Publishers, 1979, p. 18.

7 A similar conclusion is drawn by P. S. Sandhu and S. S. Grewal, 'The Changing Land Holdings Structure in Punjab', *Indian Journal of Agricultural Economics*, 1987, Vol. 42, pp. 294–300.

8 The complex agrarian relations that make it a paying proposition for landlords make a living from extracting rent rather than go in for productivity raising investment is a theme elaborated by U. Patnaik, 'The Agrarian Question and Development of Capitalism in India', *Economic and Political Weekly*, 1986, Vol. 21, pp. 781–93.

9 'By cultivator is meant the person(man or woman) who performs the role of organizing and carrying out the sequence of acts that make up agricultural production. He must ensure access to land and water for the period of the crop, he must possess a "production recipe" or body of technical knowledge about the tasks to be performed, the inputs to be used, the timing of the tasks in relation to growth rates, weather, soil types etc., and the precautions that must be taken against the numerous threats to his crop. He must make dispositions and investments in order to obtain seeds, manures, draught animals, tools, and other objects necessary to the productive process. He is responsible for seeing that the appropriate labour is available, whether it be his own or that of his family and dependants and neighbours, or that which he can contract for wages. And when the crop has been harvested, the cultivator will settle outstanding accounts with those whose goods and services have contributed to the process of production, and retain the balance. Cultivatorship is a kind of "natural entrepreneurship". At its most simple, the tasks of cultivatorship may all be performed by a single individual. In the case of most small farms they are performed by the head and members of the household, with some additional labour on an exchange basis or in return for wages in kind or cash. In larger farms, labour becomes separated from the other aspects of cultivatorship and large "business" farms present a picture of sharp and hierarchical division of function, with labour, management, entrepreneurship, and possibly land-ownership all performed by different persons' (Pearse 1980: 23–4).

10 See also S. S Gill and K. C. Singhal, 'Farmers Agitation Response to Development Crisis of Agriculture', *Economic and Political Weekly*, 1984, Vol. 19, p. 1728.

11 This is, the creation of a class which survives and reproduces itself simply by selling its labour'(Byres 1982: 41).

12 See, S. S. Gill, *Migrant Labour in Rural Punjab* (mimeo), National Commission on Rural Labour: Government of India, 1990, p. 31.

13 Paramjit Singh, *Changes in Pattern of Land Holdings in Punjab – A Case Study of Sangrur District*, Unpublished M. Phil dissertation, Punjabi University, Patiala, 1989.

14 The growth rate of household industries is a sluggish 14.64 per cent. See Gill, op. cit., pp. 33–6.

15 J. S. Singh, *The Role of Sikh Youth Activists in the Current Punjab Crisis*, Unpublished M. Phil thesis, Department of Sociology, Punjab University, Chandigarh, 1987–8.

16 I owe deep gratitude to Professor S. S. Gill for providing me with the data, which was collected by him in January 1991.

17 Details of the various castes mentioned in Table 5.10 are provided in the Introduction.

18 I am indebted to Mr S. S. Bal, sub-editor of *The Punjabi Tribune*, for providing me with relevant material on this matter.

19 In Punjab the Sikhs belonging to the Jat caste and the Hindus belonging to the Khatri caste occupy the dominant positions among the Sikh and the Hindu caste groups respectively.

20 Wassan Singh Zaffarwal, leader of the Khalistan Commando Force (KCF), quoted in J. Pettigrew (1995), pp. 144–5.

21 Wassan Singh Zaffarwal, leader of the Khalistan Commando Force (KCF), quoted in Pettigrew (1995), pp. 144–5.

22 This inference is based on my fieldwork experience in Punjab, conducted between October 1992 and April 1993, during which I interviewed several key persons involved in the guerrilla movement. See also the social profiles of guerrillas presented by Pettigrew (1995), pp. 154, 155, 159, 161, 170, 174.

6 Transformation in social communication and religious controversy

1 This theme is well illustrated in Emmett David, *Press and Politics in British Western Punjab (1836–1947)*, Delhi, Academic Publications, 1983.

2 A detailed account of the emergence and the political and social consequences of the Arya Samaj movement is provided in Chapter 3. Some aspects of the ideology and appeal of the Arya Samaj movement to the urban Hindus of Punjab are also discussed.

3 These are the 1990 figures, released by the Ministry of Information and Broadcasting, Government of India.

4 This information is given in the pamphlet published by the Hind Samachar group.

5 These reasons are given in the pamphlet on the history of *Ajit*.

6 In the Indian education system, matriculation is equivalent to the senior secondary school examinations.

7 Most historians are united in locating the social base of Hindu and Muslim communalism in the urban petit bourgeoisie or middle class. In a situation of economic stagnation, colonial patronage and increasing competition within the urban middle classes for government appointments, educational placing, and political positions in legislative councils and municipal bodies, mobilization along explicitly communal lines made sense – especially as it had real effects on the direction of colonial patronage. Organizations with explicit communal programmes such as the Rashtriya Swayamsevak Sangh (RSS), Hindu Mahasabha and Muslim League were based preponderantly on the urban petit bourgeoisie, A. Vanaik, *The Painful Transition*, London, Verso, 1990, p. 143.

8 Khatris, Aroras and Baniyas are the three major sub-castes or *jati* (or *zat*) of the merchant castes. They belong to the Vashiya caste.

9 Fox characterizes the urban Hindu Punjabi population as being lower middle class but does not explain why he uses these categories.

10 The advantage of reading these newspapers regularly over a long period of time was a great help. Please note that the statements considered significant are underlined for the purpose of drawing inferences.

11 The background to the Akali Dal demands and the political turmoil that proceeded the Akali Dal agitation has been discussed in Chapter 4.

12 *Rasta roko* is a Punjabi word meaning literally block the roads. It is an Indian type protest involving blocking of roads by the agitators.

13 Details of the All India Gurudwara Act, which resulted in the constitution of the SGPC, are discussed in Chapter 3.

14 Non-sectarian.

15 The Anandpur Sahib Resolution is a charter of demands made by the Akali Dal to the central government. It was formulated in 1973 by Kapur Singh, who was a member of the élite Indian Civil Service and a product of Oxford University. The Anandpur Sahib Resolution is regarded as the source of confrontation between the Akalis and the central government. The contents of the Anandpur Sahib Resolution have been examined in Chapter 4.

16 In his interview with me in December 1992.

17 These views are of the editor of the *Ajit*, whom I interviewed in December 1992.

18 The term implies a cultural and a religious unit as one.

19 Article 25 of the Indian constitution proclaims that Sikhs are a sect of Hinduism. It therefore does not recognize the Sikhs as a distinct religious community. In the late 1970s, the Akali leaders demanded that Article 25 be either dropped from the Indian constitution or reformulated so as to recognize the Sikhs as a separate religious community.

20 Romesh Chander was the eldest son of Lala Jagat Narain, who was the founder and editor of the Hind Samachar Group of newspapers. After the assassination of Lala Jagat Narain in September 1981, he was succeeded by his son, Romesh Chander. Romesh Chander was gunned down by unknown men on 12 May 1981.

21 In 1956, India was divided into various states on the basis of language, but Punjab was left out of this linguistic territorial division. The Akali leaders launched a fierce campaign for the formation of a state formed on the basis of a common Punjabi language. This finally led to the formation of the present Punjab in 1966.

22 It is worth noting that the term Hindu–Sikh brotherhood *(bhaichara)* features nine times in editorials on the death of Lala Jagat Narain. Another interesting term used is 'sharing of food and daughter'*(roti-beti de saanch)* between Hindus and Sikhs.

23 Vijay Chopra, in an interview with me in December 1992.

24 The Punjab press shifted from Lahore to Jalandhar city in Punjab after the partition of India in 1947.

25 Damdami Taksal is a historic seminary founded by Shaheed, or 'martyr', Baba Deep Singh, a heroic figure in Sikh history. Sikh tradition informs us that Baba Deep Singh had vowed to defend the Golden Temple from desecration by the Afghan army. In 1757, Baba Deep Singh had led an army to defend the Darbar Sahib and in the ensuing conflict with the Afghan army Baba Deep Singh was intercepted and decapitated. Tradition has it that Baba Deep Singh still managed to fight his way to the Darbar with his head in one hand and wielding his sword in the other. 'Taksal', or 'mint', describes the pure and unalloyed Sikh precepts taught and preached at the seminary. Young boys trained at the seminary are taught Sikh scriptures in the traditional mode of education. On completion of their education, they serve as traditional intellectuals, or *ragis*, or 'a group of three hymn singers'. The Taksal is engaged in a range of religious activities, including social work, missionary activity and education. At present it is involved in the reconstruction of the Akal Takht, damaged during the army invasion of the Darbar Sahib in 1984. In the late 1990s it is headed by the aged, Baba Thakur Singh. The headquarters of the Damdami Taksal are at *gurudwara* 'Gurdarshan Prakash' in the village of Mehta Chowk, some 25 miles from Amritsar. The name Mehta Chowk is often used to refer to the *gurudwara*. The Taksal is a widely respected institution of the Sikhs.

26 At a later stage, smugglers, petty criminals and Naxalites, a term used to refer to left-wing extremists in India, also infiltrated Bhindranwale's retinue.

27 Punjab has the highest per capita intake of alcohol in the country, M. Tully and S. Jacob, *Amritsar: Mrs Gandhi's Last Battle*, London, Jonathan Cape, 1985, p. 74.

28 For further evidence of this see K. Singh and K. Nayar, *Tragedy of Punjab*, New Delhi, Vision Books, 1984, p. 28, and Tully and Jacob, op. cit., p. 102–3.

29 The *kes-dhari* Sikhs are those who maintain kes, or the unshorn hair of the Khalsa, but have not received baptism.

30 The term *Khalsa* is derived from the Arabic-Persian term *khalis*, or pure. It refers to the Sikh brotherhood instituted by the tenth Sikh Guru, Guru Gobind.

31 S. Jalandhary, 1985, *Bhindranwale Sant*, cited in M. Juergensmeyer, 'The Logic of Religious Violence: The Case of the Punjab', *Contributions to Indian Sociology*, 1988, Vol. 22, p. 76.

32 Ibid, p. 70.

33 Ibid, p. 79.

34 A particular language has recently become associated with a certain religious group in Punjab. This theme is very significant in understanding the crystallization of identity formation in Punjab and has been discussed in Chapter 3.

Conclusion

1 Dennis Austin's book, *Democracy and Violence in India and Sri Lanka*, New York, The Royal Institute of International Affairs, 1995, explores the paradox of violence and democracy in India and Sri Lanka. His central argument is that in plural societies such as India democracy further accentuates divisions. The Indian subcontinent is fundamentally divided into majorities and minorities and conflict is endemic in these situations as the minorities reject the majority verdicts.

Bibliography

Akbar, M. J. (1985) *India: The Siege Within: Challenges to a Nation's Unity*, Middlesex: Penguin books.

Amnesty International (1988) *India: Review of Human Rights Violations*, London.

—— (1989) *India: Some Recent Reports of Disappearances*, London.

—— (1991) *India: Human Rights Violations in Punjab: Use and Abuse of the Law*, London.

—— (1992) *India: Torture, Rape and Deaths in Custody*, London.

Ananda, P. (1986) *A History of The Tribune*, New Delhi: Indraprastha Press.

Anderson, B. (1983) (revised 1991) *Imagined Communities: Reflections on the Origin and Spread of Nationalism*, London: Verso Editions and New Left Books.

Armstrong, J. (1982) *Nations before Nationalism*, Chapel Hill: University of North Carolina Press.

Austin, D. (1995) *Democracy and Violence in India*, New York: The Royal Institute of International Affairs.

Azad, N. (ed.) (1983) *Punjab Di Arthikta*, Patiala: Punjabi University Publication Bureau.

Ballard, R. (ed.) (1994) *Desh Pardesh: The South Asian Presence in Britain*, London: Hurst & Co.

Banaji, J. (1976) 'A summary of Kautsky's: The Agrarian Question', *Economy and Society*, 5, 1: 2–49.

Bardhan, P. K. (1973) 'On the Incidence of Poverty in Rural India of the Sixties', *Economic and Political Weekly*, February, annual no.: 245–54.

—— (1977) 'Rural Employment, Wages and Labour Markets in India. A Survey of Research: II and III, Agricultural Growth and Technological Change: Impact on Wages and Employment', *Economic and Political Weekly*, 2, 12 and 27: 1062–74.

Barnes, M. (1940) *The Indian Press*, London: Allen and Unwin.

Barrier, G. N. (1968) 'The Punjab and Communal Politics 1870–1907', *Journal of Asian Studies*, 27, 3: 523–39.

Barrier, G. N. and Dusenbery V. A., (1989) *The Sikh Diaspora: Migration and the Experience Beyond Punjab*, Columbia: South Asia Books.

Barrier, G. N. and Singh, H. (eds) (1976) *Punjab Past and Present: Essays in Honour of Dr Ganda Singh*, Patiala: Punjabi University.

Barth, F. (ed.) (1969) *Ethnic Groups and Boundaries*, Boston: Little, Brown & Co..

Bayly, C. A. (1975) *The Local Roots of Indian Politics*, Oxford, Clarendon Press.

—— (1985) 'The Pre-history of 'Communalism'? Religious Conflict in India, 1700–1860', *Modern Asian Studies*, 19, 2: 177–203.

—— (1992) *Rulers, Townsmen and Bazaars*, Delhi: Oxford University Press.

—— (1994) 'Returning the British to South Asian History: The Limits of Colonial Hegemony', South Asia: *Journal of South Asian Studies*, 17, 2: 1- 25.

Bhaduri, A., Rahman, H. Z. and Arn, A. L. (1984) 'Persistence and Polarisation: A Study in the Dynamics of Agrarian Contradiction', *Journal of Peasant Studies*, 13, 3: 82–9.

Bhalla, G. S. and Chadha, G. K. (1982) 'Green Revolution and the Small Peasant: A Study of Income Distribution in Punjab Agriculture – I and II', *Economic and Political Weekly*, 17, 20 and 21, 826–33, 870–7.

—— (1983) *Green Revolution and the Small Peasant: A Study of Income Distribution Among Punjab Cultivators*, New Delhi: Concept Pub. Co.

Bhalla, S. (1977) 'Agricultural Growth: Role of Institutional and Infrastructural Factors', *Economic and Political Weekly*, 12, 45 and 46: 1898–1905.

—— (1979) 'Real Wage Rates of Agricultural Labourers in Punjab 1961–77', *Economic and Political Weekly*, 14, 26: A57–68.

—— (1987) 'Trends in Employment in Indian Agriculture, Land and Asset Distribution', *Indian Journal of Agricultural Economics*, 42, 4: 537–60.

Bhardwaj, K. (1982) 'Regional Differentiation in India – A Note', Economic and Political Weekly, Annual numbers 17, 14, 15 and 16: 605–14.

Brass, P. R. (1974) *Language, Religion and Politics in North India*, Cambridge: Cambridge University Press.

—— (1990) *The Politics of India Since Independence, The New Cambridge History of India* Vol. IV, Part 1, Cambridge: Cambridge University Press.

—— (1991) *Ethnicity and Nationalism*, London: Sage Publications.

Breuilly, J. (1982) *Nationalism and the State*, Manchester: Manchester University Press.

Byres, T. (1972) 'The Dialectic of India's Green Revolution', *South Asian Review*, 5, 2: 99–116.

—— (1981) 'The New Technology, Class Formation and Class Action in the Indian Countryside', *Journal of Peasant Studies*, 8, 4: 405–54.

—— (1982) *The Green Revolution in India: Third World Studies, Case Study 5*, Milton Keynes: The Open University Press.

Chandan, A. (1979) 'Punjab: Victims of Green Revolution', *Economic and Political Weekly*, 14, 25: 1035.

Chatterjee, P. (1986) *Nationalist Thought and the Colonial World: A Derivative Discourse?*, London: Zed Press.

—— (1993) *The Nation and its Fragments: Colonial and Postcolonial Histories*, New Jersey: Princeton University Press.

Citizens for Democracy (1985) *Oppression in Punjab*, A Hind Mazdoor Kisan Panchayat Publication.

Cole, W. O and Sambhi, P. S. (1978) *The Sikhs: Their Religious Beliefs and Practices*, London: Routledge and Kegan Paul.

Commander, S. (1983) 'The Jajmani System in North India: An Examination of its Logic and Status Across Two Centuries', *Modern Asian Studies*, 17, 2: 283–311.

Connor, W. (1972) 'Nation-building or Nation-destroying?', *World Politics*, 24, 3: 319–55.

—— (1978) 'A Nation is a Nation, is a State, is an Ethnic Group, is a…', *Ethnic and Racial Studies*, 1, 4: 378–400.

—— (1984) 'Eco- or Ethno-nationalism?', *Ethnic and Racial Studies*, 7, 3: 342–59.

—— (1986) 'The Impact of Homelands upon Diasporas', in G. Shaffer (ed.) *Modern Diasporas in International Politics*, London: Croom Helm Ltd.

—— (1990) 'When is a Nation?', *Ethnic and Racial Studies*, 13, 1: 92–103.

Cunningham, J. D. (1849) (reprinted 1966) *A History of the Sikhs*, London: John Murray.

Dasgupta, B. (1977a) *Agrarian Change and the New Technology in India*, Geneva: United Nations Research Institute for Social Development.

—— (1977b) 'Changing Land Relations in Punjab and Implications for Land Reforms', *Economic and Political Weekly*, 24, 25: 162–4.

Davis, E. A. (1983) *Press and Politics in British Western Punjab (1836–1947)*, Delhi: Academic Publications.

Department of Agriculture *Agriculture in Punjab, 1991–92*, Chandigarh, Punjab.

Deutsch, K. W. (1963) *Nationalism and Social Communication*, 2nd edn, New York: MIT Press.

DeWitt, J. (1969) *Indian Workers Associations in Great Britain*, Oxford: Oxford University Press.

Dumont, L. (1970) *Homo Hierarchicus: The Caste System and Its Implications*, London: Weidenfeld and Nicolson.

Embree, A. T. (1990) *Utopias in Conflict: Religion and Nationalism in Modern India*, California: University of California Press.

Fox, R. G. (1984) 'Urban Class and Communal Consciousness in Colonial Punjab: The Genesis of India's Intermediate Regime', *Modern Asian Studies*, 18, 3: 459–89.

—— (1985) *The Lions of the Punjab: Culture in the Making*, Berkeley: University of California Press.

Frankel, F. R. (1971) *India's Green Revolution: Economic Gains and Political Costs*, Princeton: Princeton University Press.

Frykenberg, R. E. (1988) 'Fundamentalism and Revivalism in South Asia', in J. W. Bjorkman (ed.) *Fundamentalism, Revivalists and Violence in South Asia*, pp. 20–39, Delhi: Manohar.

Fuller, C. J. (1989) 'Misconceiving the Grain Heap: A Critique of the Concept of the Indian Jajmani System', in J. Parry and M. Bloch (eds) *Money and Morality of Exchange*, Cambridge: Cambridge University Press.

Gandhi, M. K. (1933) *Speeches and Writings of Mahatma Gandhi*, 4th edn, Madras: G. A. Natesan.

Geertz, C. (1963) *Old Societies and New States*, Free Press of Glencoe, Collier–Macmillan: New York.

Gellner, E. (1964) *Thought and Change*, London: Weidenfeld & Nicolson.

—— (1983) *Nations and Nationalism*, Oxford: Blackwell.

—— (1994) *Encounters with Nationalism*, Oxford: Blackwell.

Gill, S. S. (1980) 'Impact of Economic Development on Rural Artisans in Punjab', *The Indian Journal of Labour Economics*, 23, 3: 154–65.

Gill, S. S. and Singhal, K. C. (1984) 'Farmers Agitation Response to Development Crisis of Agriculture', *Economic and Political Weekly*, 19, 40: 1728–32.

—— (1988) 'Contradictions of Punjab Model of Growth and Search for an Alternative', *Economic and Political Weekly*, 23, 42: 2167–73.

—— (1989) 'Changing Land Relations in Punjab and Implications for Land Reforms', *Economic and Political Weekly*, 24, 25: A79–85.

—— (1990) 'Migrant Labour in Rural Punjab' (mimeo), National Commission on Rural Labour: Government of India.

Glazer, N. and Moynihan. D. (eds) (1975) *Ethnicity: Theory and Experience*, Cambridge, MA: Harvard University Press.

Gopal, S. (ed.) (1991) *Anatomy of a Confrontation: Ayodhya and the Rise of Communal Politics in India*, London: Zed books.

Goulbourme, H. (1991) *Ethnicity and Nationalism in Post-Imperial Britain*, Cambridge: Cambridge University Press.

Government of India (10 July 1984) *White Paper on the Punjab Agitation*, New Delhi.

Goyal, R. S. (1990) 'Migration and Rural Development in Punjab: A Study of Inter-relationships', *Man & Development*, 67–76.

Graham, B. D. (1990) *Hindu Nationalism and Indian Politics: The Origins and Development of the Bharatiya Jana Sangh*, Cambridge: Cambridge University Press.

Grewal, J. S. (1969) *Guru Nanak in History*, Chandigarh: Punjab University.

—— (1990) *The Sikhs of the Punjab, The New Cambridge History of India II*, Vol. 3, Cambridge: Cambridge University Press.

Griffin, K. (1979) *The Political Economy of Agrarian Change: An Essay on the Green Revolution*, 2nd edn, London: Macmillan.

Gupta, D. (1985) 'Communalising of Punjab – 1980–85', *Economic and Political Weekly*, 20, 28: 1185.

Habib, I. (1964) 'Structure of Agrarian Society in Mughal India', in B. N. Ganguli (ed.) *Readings in Indian Economic History*, Bombay: Asia Publishing House.

Hadjor, K. B. (1993) *Dictionary of Third World Terms*, London: Hardmondsworth Penguin.

Harriss, J. (1982) *Rural Development: Theories of Peasant Economy and Agrarian Change*, London: Hutchinson & Co. Ltd.

—— (1987) 'Capitalism and Peasant Production: The Green Revolution in India', in T. Shanin (ed.) *Peasants and Peasant Societies*, 2nd edn, Oxford: Blackwell.

—— (1991) 'A Review of Research on Rural Society and Agrarian Change in South Asia', *South Asia Research*, 11, 1: 16–39.

Harris, N. (1990) *National Liberation*, London: I. B. Tauris and Co. Ltd.

Harrison, S. (1960) *India, the Most Dangerous Decades*, Princeton: Princeton University Press.

Hechter, M. (1992) 'The Dynamics of Secession', *Acta Sociologica*, 35: 267.

Hechter, M. and Levi, M. (1979) 'The Comparative Analysis of Ethno-regional Movements', *Ethnic and Racial Studies*, 2, 3: 260–74.

Helweg, A. W. (1986) *Sikhs in England*, 2nd edn, Delhi: Oxford University Press.

—— (1986) 'The Indian Diaspora: Influence on International Relations', in G. Sheffer (ed.) *Modern Diasporas in International Politics*, London: Croom Helm Ltd.

—— (1987) 'India's Sikhs – Problems and Prospects', *Journal of Contemporary Asia*, 17, 2: 140–59.

Hobsbawm, E. and Ranger, T. (1983) (eds) *The Invention of Tradition*, Cambridge: Cambridge University Press.

Horowitz, D. (1985) *Ethnic Groups in Conflict*, Berkeley: University of California Press.

Hroch, M. (1985) *Social Preconditions of the National Revival in Europe*, Cambridge: Cambridge University Press.

Hutchinson, J. (1987) 'Cultural Nationalism, Élite Mobility and Nation-Building – Communitarian Politics in Modern Ireland', *British Journal of Sociology*, 38, 4: 482–501.

Jaffrelot, C. (1996) *The Hindu Nationalist Movement and Indian Politics, 1925 to the 1990s: Strategic Identity-building, Implantation and Mobilisation (with special reference to Central India)*, London: Hurst.

Jalandhary, S. (1985) *Bhindranwale Sant*, Jalandhar: Punjab Pocket Books.

Jeffrey, R. (1986) *What's Happening to India: Punjab, Ethnic Conflict, Mrs Gandhi's Death and the Test for Federalism*, London: Macmillan Press Limited.

Jones, K. W. (1968) 'Communalism in the Punjab: The Arya Samaj Contribution', *Journal of Asian Studies*, 28, 1: 39–54.

—— (1973) 'Ham Hindu Nahin: Arya-Sikh Relations, 1875–1905', *Journal of Asian Studies*, 32, 3: 457–75.

—— (1976) *Arya Dharm, Hindu Consciousness in 19th-Century Punjab*, Berkeley: University of California.

—— (1989) *Socio-religious Reform Movements in British India, The New Cambridge History of India III*, Vol. 1, Cambridge: Cambridge University Press.

—— (1992) (ed.) *Religious Controversy in British India*, Albany: State University of New York Press.

Josh, B. (1979) *Communist Movement in Punjab*, New Delhi: Anupama Publications.

Juergensmeyer, M. (1979) 'The Ghadar Syndrome: Immigrant Sikhs and Nationalist Pride', in M. Juergensmeyer and G. N. Barrier (eds) *Sikh Studies: Comparative Perspectives on a Changing Tradition*, Berkeley Religious Studies Series.

—— (1988) 'The Logic of Religious Violence: The Case of the Punjab', *Contributions to Indian Sociology*, 22, 1: 65–88.

—— (1994) *The New Cold War? Religious Nationalism Confronts the Secular State*, California: University of California Press.

Kahlon, A. S. and Singh, G. (1973) *Social and Economic Implications of Large-Scale Introduction of New Varieties of Wheat in the Punjab with Special Reference to the Ferozepur District*, a Global-2 Report, Ludhiana: Punjab Agricultural University.

Kapferer, B. (1988) *Legends of People, Myths of State: Violence, Intolerance, and Political Culture in Sri Lanka and Australia*, Washington DC: Smithsonian Institute Press.

Kapur, R. A. (1986) *Sikh Separatism: The Politics of Faith*, London: Allen and Unwin.

Kedourie, E. (1960) *Nationalism*, London: Hutchinson.

—— (1970) (reprinted 1971) (ed.) *Nationalism in Asia and Africa*, London: Weidenfeld & Nicolson.

Kohli, A. (1990) *Democracy and Discontent: India's Growing Crisis of Governability*, Cambridge: Cambridge University Press.

Kohn, H. (1945) *The Idea of Nationalism: a Study on its Origins and Background*, New York: Macmillan.

Kothari, R. (1976) *Democratic Polity and Social Change in India: Crisis and Opportunities*, Bombay: Allied Publishers.

Kundu, A. (1994) 'The Indian Armed Forces: Sikh and Non-Sikh Officers Opinion of Operation Bluestar', *Pacific Affairs*, 67, 1: 46–69.

Laeser, B. (1987) *The Green Revolution Revisited: Critique and Alternatives*, London: Allen and Unwin.

Leaf, M. J. (1972) *Information and Behaviour in a Sikh Village: Social Organisation Reconsidered*, Berkeley: UCP.

—— (1984) *Song of Hope: The Green Revolution in a Punjab Village*, New Jersey: Rutgers University Press.

Lutgendorf, P. (1990) 'Ramayan: The Video', *The Drama Review*, 4, 2, 127–76.

MacCulley, B. T. (1966) *English Education and the Origins of Indian Nationalism*, New York: Columbia University Press.

McLeod, W. H. (1989) *Who is a Sikh? The Problem of Sikh Identity*, Oxford: Clarendon Press.

—— (1989) *The Sikhs: History, Religion, and Society*, New York: Columbia University Press.

Madan, T. N. (1989) 'Religion in India', *Daedalus*, 118, 4: 115–46.

—— (1991) 'The Double-Edged Sword: Fundamentalism and the Sikh Religious Tradition', in M. E. Marty and R. S. Appleby (eds) *Fundamentalisms Observed*, Chicago: The University of Chicago Press.

Mahmood, C. K. (1989) 'Sikh Rebellion and the Hindu Concept of Order', *Asian Survey*, 29, 3: 326–40.

Mahmud Ali, S. (1993) *The Fearful State: Power, People and Internal War in South Asia*, London: Zed Books.

Manuel, P. (1993) *Cassette Culture: Popular Music and Technology in North India*, Chicago: The University of Chicago Press.

Mayall, J. (1984) 'Reflections on the New Economic Nationalism', *Review of International Studies*, 10, 4: 313–21.

—— (1985) 'Nationalism and the International Order', *Millennium*, 14, 2: 143–58.

—— (1990) *Nationalism and International Society*, Cambridge: Cambridge University Press.

Moore, B. (reprinted 1981) *Social Origins of Dictatorship and Democracy: Lord and Peasant in the Making of the Modern World*, New York: Penguin books.

Nairn, T. (1977) *The Break-up of Britain*, London: New Left Books.

Nandy, A. (1980) *At the Edge of Psychology*, Delhi: Oxford University Press.

—— (1989) 'The Political Culture of the Indian State', *Daedalus*, 118, 4, 1–26.

—— (1990) 'The Politics of Secularism and the Recovery of Religious Tolerance', in Veena Das (ed.) *Mirrors of Violence: Communities and Riots and Survivors in South Asia*, Delhi: Oxford University Press.

Narain, D. and Joshi, P. C. (1969) 'Magnitude of Agricultural Tenancy', *Economic and Political Weekly*, *Review of Agriculture*, 4, 38: A139–42.

Oberai, A. S. and Singh, M. H. K. (1980) 'Migration Flows in Punjab's Green Revolution Belt', *Economic and Political Weekly*, 15, 13, A2–12.

O'Brien, C. C. (1988) *God Land: Reflections on Religion and Nationalism*, Cambridge, MA.: Harvard University Press.

O'Connell, J. T., Israel, M. and Oxtoby, W. G. (eds) (1988) *Sikh History and Religion in the Twentieth Century*, Toronto: Centre for South Asian Studies.

O'Leary, B. (1989) *The Asiatic Mode of Production: Oriental Despotism, Historical Materialism and Indian History*, Oxford: Basil Blackwell.

Orridge, A. (1981) 'Uneven Development and Nationalism', *Political Studies*, 29, 1: 1–15.

Pandey, G. (1990) *The Construction of Communalism in Colonial North India*, Delhi: Oxford University Press.

People's Union for Democratic Rights and People's Union for Civil Liberties (1984) *Report of a Joint Inquiry into the Causes and Impact of the Riots in Delhi from 31 October to 10 November, 1984*, New Delhi.

Patnaik, U. (1976) 'Class Differentiation Within the Peasantry: An Approach to the Analysis of Indian Agriculture', *Economic and Political Weekly*, *Review of Agriculture*, 11, 39, A82–101.

—— (1986) 'The Agrarian Question and the Development of Capitalism in India', *Economic and Political Weekly*, 21, 18: 781–93.

Pearse, A. (1974) 'Green Revolution – Concepts and Terms', *Journal of Peasant Studies*, 1, 3, 386–7.

—— (1980) *Seeds of Plenty, Seeds of Want: Social and Economic Implications of the Green Revolution*, Oxford: Clarendon Press, for United Nations Research Institute for Social Development.

Pettigrew, J. J. M. (1975) *Robber Noblemen: A Study of the Political System of the Sikh Jats*, London: Routledge and Kegan Paul.

—— (1987) 'In Search of a New Kingdom of Lahore', *Pacific Affairs*, 60, 1: 1–25.

—— (1995) *The Sikhs of the Punjab: Unheard Voices of State and Guerrilla Violence*, London and New Jersey: Zed Books.

Puri, H. (22 Jan 1983) 'The Akali Agitation: An Analysis of Socio-economic Bases of Protest', *Economic and Political Weekly*, 18, 4: 113–8.

Rao, C. H. H. (1975) *Technological Change and Distribution of Grains in Indian Agriculture*, Delhi: Macmillan.

Roach, J. R. (1986) *India 2000: The Next Fifteen Years*, Maryland: the Riverdale Company Inc.

Rothstein, R. L. (1991) 'Democracy, Conflict, and Development in the Third World', *Washington Quarterly*, 14, 2: 43–63.

Rudolph, L. I. and Rudolph, S. H. (1987) *In Pursuit of Lakshmi: The Political Economy of the Indian State*, Chicago: University of Chicago Press.

Rudra, A., Majid, A. and Talib, B. D. (1969) 'Big Farmers of Punjab: Some Preliminary Findings of a Sample Survey', *Economic and Political Weekly*, 4, 39: A143–74.

Sandhu, P. S. and Grewal, S. S. (1987) 'The Changing Land Holdings Structure in Punjab', *Indian Journal of Agricultural Economics*, 42, 3: 294–300.

Sarhadi, A. S. (1970) *Punjabi Suba: The Story of the Struggle*, Delhi: U. C. Kapur.

Seal, A. (1971) *The Emergence of Indian Nationalism*, Cambridge: Cambridge University Press.

—— (1973) 'Imperialism and Nationalism in India', *Modern Asian Studies*, 7, 3: 321–46.

Sen, A. (April 1993) 'The Threats to Secular India', *Social Scientist*, 21, 3–4, 5–23.

Seton-Watson, H. (1965) *Nationalism, Old and New*, Sydney: Sydney University Press.

—— (1977) *Nations and States*, London: Methuen.

Shackle, C (1983) *An Introduction to the Sacred Language of the Sikhs*, London: SOAS.

—— (1988) *Hindi and Urdu since 1800: A Common Reader*, London: SOAS.

Shanin, T. (1987) (ed.) *Peasants and Peasant Societies*, 2nd edn, Oxford: Basil Blackwell.

Sharma, M. L. and Dak, T. M. (1989) *Green Revolution and Social Change*, Delhi: Ajanta.

Sheffer, G. (1986) *Modern Diaspora in International Politics*, London: Croom Helm.

Shiva, V. (1991) *The Violence of the Green Revolution: Third World Agriculture, Ecology and Politics*, London: Zed Press.

Singh, A. P. (1979) 'Farm Workers v. Rich Farmers: Class and Caste in a Punjab Village', *Economic and Political Weekly*, 14, 42 and 43: 1753–4.

Singh, D. S. (1982) *Agricultural Growth and Employment Shifts in Punjab*, New Delhi: Birla Institute.

Singh, G. (1984) 'Socio-Economic Basis of the Punjab Crisis', *Economic and Political Weekly*, 19, 1: 42–7.

Singh, H. (1964) *The Heritage of the Sikhs*, Bombay: Asia.

Singh, H. K. M. (1979) 'Population Pressure and Labour Absorbability in Agriculture and Related Activities: Analysis and Suggestions Based on Field Studies Conducted in Punjab', *Economic and Political Weekly*, 14, 11: 593–6.

Singh, K. (1962) (reprinted 1991) *A History of the Sikhs: 1839–1988*, Vols. 1 and 2, 2nd edn, New Delhi: Oxford University Press.

Singh, P. (1989) Changes in Pattern of Land Holdings in Punjab – A Case Study of Sangrur District, Unpublished M. Phil. dissertation, Punjabi University, Patiala.

Singh, S. (1945) *The Forgotten Panth*, Amritsar.

Singh, K. and Nayar, K. (1984) *Tragedy of Punjab: Operation Bluestar and After*, New Delhi: Vision Books.

Smith, A. D. (1979) *Nationalism in the Twentieth Century*, Oxford: Martin Robertson.

—— (1981a) *The Ethnic Revival in the Modern World*, Cambridge: Cambridge University Press.

—— (1981b) 'States and Homelands: The Social and Geopolitical Implications of National Territory', *Millennium*, 10, 3: 187–202.

—— (1983) *Theories of Nationalism*, 2nd edn, London: Duckworth.

—— (1986) *The Ethnic Origins of Nations*, Oxford: Blackwell.

—— (1991) *National Identity*, London: Penguin Books.

Smith, A. D and Hutchinson, J. (eds) (1994), *Nationalism*, Oxford: Oxford University Press.

Smith, D. E. (ed.) (1966) *South Asian Politics and Religion*, Princeton: Princeton University Press.

—— (1974) (ed.) *Religion and Political Modernisation*, New Haven: Yale University Press.

Statistical Abstract of Punjab, 1991–92, Chandigarh, India

Stone, J. (ed.) (1979) 'Internal Colonialism', *Ethnic and Racial Studies*, 2, 3: 255–9.

Tandon, P. (1961) *Punjabi Century*, London: Chatto and Windus.

Taylor, D. and Yapp, M. (eds) (1979) *Political Identity in South Asia*, London: Curzon Press, SOAS.

Thorner, D. (1976) *The Agrarian Prospect in India*, Bombay: Allied Publishers.

Tinker, H. (1974) *A New System of Slavery*, Oxford: Oxford University Press.

Tully, M. and Jacob. S. (1985) *Amritsar: Mrs Gandhi's Last Battle*, London: Jonathan Cape.

Vanaik, A. (1990) *The Painful Transition*, London: Verso.

Van Der Veer, P. (1994) *Religious Nationalism: Hindus and Muslims in India*, Berkeley: University of California Press.

—— (ed.) (1995) *Nation and Migration: The Politics of Space in the South Asian Diaspora*, Philadelphia: University of Pennsylvania Press.

Wallace, P. (1986) 'Centre-State Relations in India: The Federal Dilemma', in James R. Roach (ed.) *India 2000: The Next Fifteen Years*, Maryland: The Riverdale Company Inc. Publishers.

—— (1988) 'The Dilemma of Sikh Revivalism', in J. W. Bjorkman (ed.) *Fundamentalism, Revivalists and Violence in South Asia*, Delhi: Manohar.

Weiner, M. (1986) 'India's Minorities: Who Are They? What Do They Want?' in James R. Roach (ed.) *India 2000*: The Next Fifteen Years, Maryland: The Riverdale Company Inc. Publishers.

Westley, J. (1989) 'Agriculture and Equitable Growth, 1986', Review in IJAE, *2: 211*.

White Paper on the Punjab Agitation (1984), New Delhi, 110–62.

Index